Helping Children with ADHD

Praise for *Helping Children with ADHD: A CBT Guide for Practitioners, Parents and Teachers*

"This book is recommended to all professionals wanting to increase their skills in working with children affected by ADHD. It presents a detailed and practical scheme based on cognitive-behavioural therapy, with well-worked-out sessions and advice. Teachers and clinicians will find good ideas for promoting resilience and overcoming disability."

– **Professor Eric Taylor,** *Retired Head of the Child & Adolescent Psychiatry Department, Institute of Psychiatry, King's College London, UK*

"Finally a comprehensive resource applying research proven principles to address the myriad of co-occurring problems children with ADHD frequently experience. Drs. Young and Smith are to be commended for providing clinicians with this thorough guide filled with practical ideas and strategies for the novice and experienced clinician."

– **Sam Goldstein, Ph.D.,** *Editor in Chief, Journal of Attention Disorders, University of Utah School of Medicine*

"This is a valuable resource for parents, carers and school staff, and fills an important gap in the support available for children diagnosed with ADHD. Most important of all, it addresses the criticism often levelled at current services, in that it places the child at the heart of the treatment process, and helps them to understand how best to minimise the difficulties that they may face at home and in school, and how best to make the most of their potential. The programme will help increase skills, planning, organisation, and personal resilience, and so lead to more positive outcomes for this vulnerable population."

– **Bill Colley,** *Educational Consultant, The UK ADHD Partnership, London, UK*

"Drs. Young and Smith's CBT Guide to working therapeutically with children is a must have for any CBT therapist or children's counsellor who is involved in supporting young people with ADHD. Providing clear and effective strategies that offer the child a framework to learn how to understand and live successfully with ADHD, this guide is long overdue."

– **Dr. Tony Lloyd, CEO,** *ADHD Foundation*

Helping Children with ADHD

A CBT Guide for Practitioners, Parents and Teachers

Susan Young and Jade Smith

WILEY Blackwell

This edition first published 2017
© 2017 John Wiley & Sons Ltd

All rights reserved. No part of this publication may be reproduced, stored in a retrieval system, or transmitted, in any form or by any means, electronic, mechanical, photocopying, recording or otherwise, except as permitted by law. Advice on how to obtain permission to reuse material from this title is available at http://www.wiley.com/go/permissions.

The right of Susan Young and Jade Smith to be identified as the authors of this work has been asserted in accordance with law.

Registered Office(s)
John Wiley & Sons, Inc., 111 River Street, Hoboken, NJ 07030, USA
John Wiley & Sons Ltd, The Atrium, Southern Gate, Chichester, West Sussex, PO19 8SQ, UK

Editorial Office
The Atrium, Southern Gate, Chichester, West Sussex, PO19 8SQ, UK

For details of our global editorial offices, customer services, and more information about Wiley products visit us at www.wiley.com.

Wiley also publishes its books in a variety of electronic formats and by print-on-demand. Some content that appears in standard print versions of this book may not be available in other formats.

Limit of Liability/Disclaimer of Warranty
While the publisher and authors have used their best efforts in preparing this work, they make no representations or warranties with respect to the accuracy or completeness of the contents of this work and specifically disclaim all warranties, including without limitation any implied warranties of merchantability or fitness for a particular purpose. No warranty may be created or extended by sales representatives, written sales materials or promotional statements for this work. The fact that an organization, website, or product is referred to in this work as a citation and/or potential source of further information does not mean that the publisher and authors endorse the information or services the organization, website, or product may provide or recommendations it may make. This work is sold with the understanding that the publisher is not engaged in rendering professional services. The advice and strategies contained herein may not be suitable for your situation. You should consult with a specialist where appropriate. Further, readers should be aware that websites listed in this work may have changed or disappeared between when this work was written and when it is read. Neither the publisher nor authors shall be liable for any loss of profit or any other commercial damages, including but not limited to special, incidental, consequential, or other damages.

Library of Congress Cataloging-in-Publication Data

Names: Young, Susan, 1957– author. | Smith, Jade, 1984– author.
Title: Helping children with ADHD : a CBT guide for practitioners,
  parents and teachers / Susan Young and Jade Smith.
Description: Hoboken, NJ : John Wiley & Sons, 2017. | Includes index.
Identifiers: LCCN 2016059297 (print) | LCCN 2017005372 (ebook) |
  ISBN 9781118903209 (cloth) | ISBN 9781118903186 (pbk.) | ISBN 9781118903162 (pdf) |
  ISBN 9781118903179 (epub)
Subjects: LCSH: Attention-deficit hyperactivity disorder–Treatment–Handbooks,
  manuals, etc. | Cognitive therapy for children–Handbooks, manuals, etc.
Classification: LCC RJ506.H9 Y667 2017 (print) | LCC RJ506.H9 (ebook) |
  DDC 618.92/8589–dc23
LC record available at https://lccn.loc.gov/2016059297

Cover Design: Wiley
Cover Image: Courtesy of authors

Set in 10/12pt Warnock by SPi Global, Pondicherry, India

Contents

About the Authors *vii*
Foreword *ix*
Acknowledgements *xiii*
Preface *xv*
About the Companion Website *xix*

1 **Introduction** *1*

2 **The Young–Smith Programme** *11*

3 **Introduction to Buzz and His Family** *35*

4 **Attention** *45*

5 **Hyperactivity** *75*

6 **Impulsivity** *99*

7 **Anxiety** *121*

8 **Frustration and Anger** *147*

9 **Social Skills and Relationships** *179*

10 **Setting Goals and Planning Ahead** *205*

11 **Problem-solving** *225*

12 **Mood and Self-Esteem** *247*

   Index *269*

About the Authors

Susan Young is a Clinical Senior Lecturer in Forensic Clinical Psychology in the Centre for Mental Health, Imperial College London and Visiting Professor at Rekjavik University. She has an honorary contract as a Consultant Psychologist at Broadmoor Hospital and is Director of Forensic Research and Development for West London Mental Health Trust. Professor Young has extensive clinical experience in the assessment and treatment of youths and adults with ADHD and in the assessment and treatment of offenders with mental illness and/or mental disorder. Previously, she was employed as a Clinical Neuropsychologist at the Maudsley Hospital, where she set up and developed the neuropsychology service at the first adult ADHD service in the United Kingdom.

Professor Young participated in the British Association of Psychopharmacology Consensus Meeting (2007; 2013) to develop guidelines for the management of ADHD in children, adolescents and adults. She was a member of the National Institute for Health and Clinical Excellence (NICE) ADHD Clinical Guideline Development Group (2008; 2013), her main contributions being discussions on psychological treatment of children and adults with ADHD, transition and the provision of expert guidance on the clinical procedures and services required for the diagnosis and treatment of ADHD in adults. Professor Young is President of the UK ADHD Partnership (www.UKADHD.com) and Vice President of the UK Adult ADHD Network (www.UKAAN.org), a member of the European Network in Adult ADHD (www.eunetworkadultadhd.com) and a Trustee of the board of the ADHD Foundation (www.adhdfoundation.org.uk).

Professor Young has published over 100 articles in scientific journals and is the author of three psychological intervention programmes and three books. Her work has been translated into Icelandic, Swedish, Danish, Hebrew, Spanish, Catalan, Polish, Chinese, Japanese, French, Italian, Portugese, Dutch and Turkish.

Jade Smith is a Clinical Psychologist in paediatric and child mental health services, with significant experience in assessment and therapeutic intervention for young people with neurodevelopmental conditions and co-morbid mental health needs. Previously, she has worked in community and secure settings across the United Kingdom, including with National & Specialist Child Mental Health Services in South London & Maudsley NHS Foundation Trust and has successfully developed ADHD pathways in child services.

Dr Smith regularly adapts evidence-based therapies to increase accessibility for young people with neurodevelopmental differences and their families. She uses a range of models including cognitive-behavioural, systemic and interpersonal therapies. Alongside this, she has a number of publications, is a member of the training committee for the UK ADHD Partnership (www.UKADHD.com) and has contributed to the development of clinical assessment tools and national educational resources for child health.

Foreword

ADHD is a complicated set of problems, and people with ADHD are more complicated still. Over the years we have developed better understanding and a few ways of helping, but the development has been somewhat lopsided. This book fills a big gap, by creating a detailed plan for a new psychological intervention.

A great deal of good science has been published on the neuroscience and cognitive analyses for ADHD, and on the genetic basis. These have helped to shape professional and public understanding: ADHD does not point to inadequate parenting but to a constitutional alteration of development. The lessons drawn, however, have sometimes been over-simple. Genetic influences are clear and strong, but ADHD is not a genetic disorder in any simple sense. To begin with, the inheritance is complex. Only a very few single genetic changes are capable of causing the features of ADHD to appear and then only in rare cases. Rather, the genetic changes involved are each of weak effect. Many genes have to work together; and interact with each other to alter the response to features of the environment. Furthermore, environmental influences can be strong – as in the case of the very severe neglect previously encountered by infants in the orphanages of Romania, which seem to have a direct influence on the development of impulsiveness and inattention.

Changes in the structure and function of the brain are well established, but – like the genetic alterations – they are of many kinds and no one change can be seen as "the cause of ADHD". Rather, several different problems of function exist in different combinations in different people. Some have big difficulties in "executive function" (the self-control of thought processes). Some find it very hard to suppress a wrong response to a situation. Some have such a poor memory that they cannot completely orient themselves in time and space. Some have a different motivation – they try to avoid waiting at all costs. Some find that their mind wanders so much that they cannot keep focus on an activity. Some cannot temper their emotions and calm themselves down. Some have all these problems, and more. Indeed, coexistent problems are often responsible for the impairments in everyday life. Some become antisocial; some cannot profit well from their education in schools; some never learn good ways of getting on with other people of their own age.

The practical conclusion from all this work is that effective interventions need to take account of several kinds of problem, and treat the individual rather than the diagnosis.

The best-researched treatment uses medications, such as (but not confined to) stimulant drugs that work on the brain in similar ways to amphetamines. They can indeed make a big difference, especially for the children who are most disabled by the conditions. A mass of randomized controlled trials has led to medication being adopted into the treatment plans recommended by guidelines internationally. Nevertheless, there are real limitations to the benefit that can come from medication. It can have adverse effects, especially on eating. There is very little evidence that it is valuable for periods longer than a couple of years, at least for most children. Guidelines from NICE and the European Guidelines Group indicate that most children with ADHD can be helped reasonably well without using medication.

By contrast with the neurobiological approaches, the emotional and social aspects have received less formal study. The psychological approaches to treatment have for the most part been focused on teaching parents (and, to a lesser extent, teachers) the skills of controlling bad behaviour. This has been a success, but not matched by the creation of evaluated education for the children themselves. Even children who have been treated well can suffer impairment into adult life.

Public understanding is often lopsided too. Many educators, at least in Europe, have felt a distaste for the perceived reductionism and 'medicalization'. The result has sometimes been to divert their attention away from helping children to cope with high levels of inattention and impulsive activity. Families have often been bemused and worried by the clash of different approaches, and avid for knowledge about how they can help their children's development.

What needs to change? We need the development of interventions that can help children to overcome their individual problems as much as possible, and cope with those that cannot yet be fully helped. The interventions need to be acceptable to the wider public. They should be attractive and interesting for children so that they want to engage with them and persist with what they have learned. They should be useful to children at different levels of development. They should address the broad range of functional impairments and not just the core symptoms of impulsiveness and inattention. In short, the balance in treatment should shift towards the development of competence rather than, or as well as, the suppression of symptoms.

This book is now redressing the balance. It is of equal relevance to educating children and treating their problems. It presents a detailed and practical scheme based on cognitive-behavioural therapy, with well-worked-out sessions and advice. It treats the young child as an agent, with respect and appreciation of the full range of strengths and weaknesses that influence psychological development. It addresses the wide range of difficulties that affected children encounter. It provides a distinctive, and testable, model of how to help the individual child to cope successfully with their ADHD.

For all these reasons it is very welcome, and I wish it had been available earlier in the development of the subject. Use it!

Professor Eric Taylor

Acknowledgements

Every so often a happenstance event comes along or an unexpected opportunity opens up. This is what happened to me when I met Jade Smith and this led to me taking a new direction by writing this intervention to help children with ADHD. I have always believed that we should be providing early intervention programmes that work directly with the child as well as with those involved in their care and education and this programme, drawing on the adventures of a young boy called Buzz, does just that. It took a surprisingly long time to write and required us to maximise every ounce of creativity we possess – in fact I was feeling at one point that I was spending my whole weekend with Buzz and his family! Unfortunately some children will have problems as they grow up – these may be chronic problems that cause them to struggle in everyday life; others may be transient problems due to an unsettling period at home or in the family. They need help, support, strategies and skills and we have tried to do this, not only in a fun way, but in a way that empowers the child. Let me explain. The child becomes the 'expert' by considering what they know that would help Buzz cope with a situation and then they think of how they can apply that advice to themselves. So first and foremost I thank Jade Smith for opening this window. Thank you Bill Colley for reading through the whole draft and providing feedback from an educational perspective. I am also grateful to other colleagues I've written with, especially Jessica Bramham, Bob Ross and Gisli Gudjonsson. You are all important branches on my professional tree. Life is one long lesson and we never stop learning and in the past year I have learned the importance of a work-home balance. For too long it has been tipped on the work end. I have never been frightened of change and the future will redress the balance. I am fortunate to have a wonderful daughter, Charley, and great friends (both old and new). Thank you for being there for me, for your love, wit, laughter and debate. Special thanks to Sue Curtis, Beverley and John Iosco, Emma Woodhouse, Jill and Mike Brodie and Gisli Gudjonsson. Your enrich my life.

Susan Young

My sincerest and special thanks to all the families who have contributed to this book via their eternal openness, determination and care. I have been privileged to meet and work with some fantastic, enthusiastic and creative young people. Of course, thanks to Suzy for her never ending energy, courage to travel in new directions and generosity with her knowledge. Thanks to Emma Woodhouse, Jack Hollingdale, Bill Colley and Gisli Gudjonsson for being great advocates in the world of ADHD and sharing their enthusiasm and expertise. Also thanks to Debra Keay, Iris Rathwell and Nadia Barrett for their compassion in healthcare, value of psychology and shared experiences and opportunities. Additional thanks to Hannah Mullens for her wonderful IT skills and attention to detail. Lastly special thanks to family and friends who are ever supportive, interested, patient and available.

Jade Smith

Preface

For many years I have focused on the adolescent and adult end of the ADHD spectrum and found that entrenched and learned maladaptive behaviours often hamper therapeutic engagement and progress. I've always believed that the earlier we can intervene, the better the outcome and now there is empirical data to support that view. When I participated as a member of the guideline development group to develop the UK National Institute for Health & Clinical Excellence Guidelines on the diagnosis and management of ADHD in children young people and adults (NICE, 2008), I kept thinking to myself that what is needed is a programme that joins all the dots – one that can reach the child directly as well as one that involves parents/carers and teachers. In my view it is critical to provide a holistic and integrative approach to combat this pervasive and impairing condition if we are to nurture confident and successful young people who will have pride in their achievements and life satisfaction over the longer term. Hence, following the success of my previous two cognitive behavioural therapy (CBT) books for treating adolescents and adults with ADHD (Young & Bramham, 2007; 2012) and in light of the international acclaim they have received (including translations into Spanish, Norwegian and Polish), with the encouragement and support of my co-author Dr Jade Smith I turned my attention to develop the current progamme that caters for the needs of younger children.

The Young–Smith Programme offers a template for healthcare and allied professionals to provide CBT techniques for use with children aged 5–12 years with ADHD. It addresses the symptoms, associated comorbid conditions and problems commonly experienced by young children with ADHD and aims to meet the heterogeneous needs of this population through its modular approach. As with its predecessors for young people and adults, the programme provides practical strategies and techniques to address ADHD symptoms, problem behaviours and emotional difficulties that can be readily accessed and applied by the reader. These may be delivered consecutively or be tailored to meet the specific needs of the child through delivery in self-contained subsections in a 'pick and mix' style. Each topic follows a standardized format describing the presentation of the child in daily life, assessment methods, CBT techniques and implementation advice for parent/carers and teachers. We also provide guidance for working with parents/carers and teachers on how to successfully introduce and extend therapeutic techniques into the home and classroom. Importantly, we devote sections within each chapter on how they might deliver the Young–Smith Programme themselves, supported by the worksheet materials that can be downloaded from the Companion Website www.wiley.com/go/young/helpingadhd.

In addition we reference supplementary psychoeducational materials that can be downloaded from the Psychology Services Website (www.psychology-services.uk.com/resources). These include a newly developed semi-structured interview to assess ADHD in children, the ADHD Child Evaluation [ACE] which is available for download in several languages.

Engagement is ensured through the introduction of the activities and adventures of Buzz, a young boy who lives with his mum, his older brother and Wilma his dog. The worksheets introduce children to the core concepts and skills they will learn about in each module. These are discussed through the eyes of Buzz and the child thinks up ideas that might help Buzz with his problem, thus providing a narrative for children to generate and apply techniques that they may subsequently trial themselves when the focus of the session shifts to their own difficulties and problems. Due to the modular design of the programme, the core tasks of learning to acquire new skills and setting reward systems are included in every chapter.

Finally I am grateful to the help and support of colleagues in the development of this treatment programme. A huge thank you goes to Dr Jade Smith, my co-author and clinical psychologist, for initially suggesting and then 'encouraging' me to embark on the project and for bringing her knowledge and skills in working therapeutically with children with ADHD to the programme. Your dedication to help, support and improve the lives of young people with ADHD is inspiring. Without your enthusiasm and hard work, this programme would not have been written. Another huge thank you goes to Bill Colley, who is an awesome teacher trainer and educational consultant who spent much of his career in the independent sector before becoming the headmaster of a residential special school. Thank you for reading the draft chapters, providing such helpful and thought provoking comments, and ensuring that we achieved something that would be of help to those working in the educational sector. Many thanks to Professor Eric Taylor for his consistent support for the project and early advice and comments on the design. I am very grateful to Hannah Mullens for her eye for detail, proofing and checking and keeping us all to time and in order! Finally I'm grateful to Charley, for being the beautiful daughter that you are. Don't ever forget that you reach your dreams one step at a time.

Susan Young

References

National Institute for Health and Care Excellence. (2008). *Attention deficit hyperactivity disorder: Diagnosis and management of ADHD in children, young people and adults.* NICE clinical guidance 72. London: NICE.

Young, S. & Bramham, J. (2012). *Cognitive Behavioural Therapy for ADHD Adolescents and Adults: A Psychological Guide to Practice, Second Edition.* Chichester: John Wiley & Sons.

Young, S. & Bramham, J. (2007). *ADHD in Adults: A Psychological Guide to Practice.* Chichester: John Wiley & Sons.

About the Companion Website

This book is accompanied by a companion website:

www.wiley.com/go/young/helpingadhd

The website includes the worksheets for Therapist and Child.

1

Introduction

Attention deficit hyperactivity disorder (ADHD) is a neurodevelopmental disorder characterized by symptoms of inattention, impulsivity and hyperactivity that are inconsistent with a child's developmental level and cause impairment to their functioning.

The prevalence of ADHD is around 5 % in children and 2.5 % in adults (American Psychiatric Association, 2013). In childhood, boys are diagnosed with ADHD up to four times more than girls, whereas in adulthood, females are just as likely to be diagnosed as males (Ford, Goodman & Meltzer, 2003; Kessler et al., 2006). This may be because young boys present with greater hyperactivity than girls, with girls presenting as more inattentive, and thus boys may be more likely to be noticed and referred for assessment.

ADHD is highly heritable and it is believed to be caused by a complex mixture of genetic and environmental factors including: genes associated with the dopamine and serotonin systems in the brain (Stergiakouli & Thapar, 2010); a variety of prenatal and perinatal factors such as smoking, substance use, pre-term birth, low birth weight, birth trauma and maternal depression (Thapar, Cooper, Jefferies & Stergiakouli, 2012); and the degree of nurture and stimulation that a child receives in early life (Rutter, 2005).

Due to the cognitive and behavioural impact of ADHD, there is an association between ADHD and a variety of problems, including academic underachievement, conduct problems and interpersonal relationship difficulties (Shaw et al., 2012). Boys are at greater risk of developing behavioural and conduct difficulties than girls, and such problems may increase the rate of referral and assessment for boys. The behaviour of young people presenting with comorbid disruptive behavioural problems is especially challenging for both parents/carers and teachers, and the demands of managing these problems can often lead to stress.

Helping Children with ADHD: A CBT Guide for Practitioners, Parents and Teachers,
First Edition. Susan Young and Jade Smith.
© 2017 John Wiley & Sons Ltd. Published 2017 by John Wiley & Sons Ltd.
Companion website: www.wiley.com/go/young/helpingadhd

ADHD Across the Lifespan

As children grow and develop, their brains and behaviour are constantly adjusting and evolving; they will refine their cognitive abilities, learn to cope with challenges and learn to overcome obstacles. However, there are key transitions in an individual's life when ADHD may become more prominent. Children with ADHD are often first recognized when demands at primary school begin to move away from play and academic expectations increase. The child may present as being unable to stay seated on the carpet, listen to a story and/or complete a short task on their own without getting up and/or becoming distracted. Their behaviour is noticeably different to that of their peers.

The transition to secondary school may also be a trigger for referral due to changes in the curriculum, with a greater need to plan and organize, longer days, fewer breaks and higher expectations for sustained periods of concentration. At this time, children are expected to navigate new peer groups, manage their own time and belongings, and organize themselves at home and school whilst receiving reduced adult support and direction. In parallel, they are also coping with the changes that puberty brings and managing new feelings and body changes.

For some individuals, symptoms and impairments will persist into adulthood. Most typically this includes inattention and restlessness, whilst overt hyperactive and impulsive symptoms may reduce.

ADHD and Comorbidity

It is widely observed that coexisting conditions are the rule rather than the exception, with up to two-thirds of children with ADHD having one or more coexisting conditions. Common comorbidities include oppositional defiance and conduct disorder, anxiety and mood disorders, as well as emotional regulation difficulties (Biederman, Newcorn & Sprich, 1991; Goldman, Genel, Bezman & Slanetz, 1998; Pliszka, 1998; Elia, Ambrosini & Berrettini, 2008). Other comorbid conditions include autism spectrum disorders, tic disorders, social problems, sleep difficulties, generalized intellectual impairment and/or specific learning difficulties such as dyslexia.

Gifted children may also develop ADHD. In these cases, impairment is relative to intellectual ability, as the child doesn't reach its potential. Gifted children often develop compensatory strategies that mask their problems; however, this may become challenging with increasing academic demands and feelings of stress.

ADHD and the Family

Greater parenting stress has been associated with the families of children with ADHD, especially in the presence of oppositional behaviour and/or maternal depression (Theule, Weiner, Tannock & Jenkins, 2013). Whilst there may be many positive and fun times, it is not always easy bringing up a child with ADHD, and parents/carers need support too, especially at times when they feel weary, fatigued and emotionally drained. This highlights the need to stand back from the condition and the child, and take into account what is going on within the family. Hence, the therapist must not only focus on the needs of the child, but also on the needs of other family members and consider whether these are being met. It is important to note family dynamics and gain an understanding of how reciprocal relationships operate within the family, as the behaviour of one will influence the behaviour of another. Whilst negative cycles within the family have been reported, there is a potential positive here: change in the behaviour of one may influence change in the behaviour of another.

When taking a family perspective, it is important that siblings are not forgotten. This may reinforce what is happening in everyday life, with the needs of the child with ADHD demanding so much attention that the relatively fewer needs of the non-ADHD sibling are often deferred. Whilst siblings may be caring and supportive (Kendall, 1999), they may feel minimized or overlooked and resent or envy the attention received by their brother or sister (Mikami & Pfiffner, 2008). It is important that parents/carers maintain positive family relationships by ensuring that the needs of all siblings are met, and that rewards and sanctions are fair.

ADHD and School

Classrooms are rich and stimulating environments. For a child with ADHD they are also places with a mass of distractions; for example, teachers speaking, children chatting, outside noise from sport or lawnmowers, other classes/people coming and going, the scribble of pencils, rustling papers, bells ringing and chairs scraping. For a child with ADHD it can be an overwhelming sensation, leading them to lose focus, go off-task and miss important information. In addition, teachers have many competing demands in the classroom, hence it is important that they have a good understanding about the difficulties experienced by children with ADHD and the potential methods that can be applied to minimize problems and maximize effort. Additional demand is put on teachers when ADHD is combined with oppositional behaviours, conduct problems and/or social communication impairments (Greene et al., 2002).

This emphasizes the need for early and targeted interventions to help promote skills for children with ADHD and the people around them.

Some children will access additional support in schools to enhance learning, self-monitoring and staying on task. For children with high levels of self-doubt or low self-efficacy, such learning support can make a wealth of difference by encouraging them to take achievable steps, and by receiving recognition and reward for effort.

Promoting Resilience

All children have their own unique skills, talents, qualities and priorities. The difference between a child with ADHD and a child without ADHD is that the former needs more guidance and nurture during their journey to learn how to overcome life's hurdles and reach their potential. It is important that they focus on the positive and learn to embrace what makes them unique. Children with ADHD often have fast and creative minds, which helps them to be innovative and to develop new and exciting ideas. They may be sociable, funny, extroverted and intuitive. They may channel their energy into sports and seek out novel and interesting ways of doing things. However, they also need to learn how to cope with challenges and difficult times. They must develop skills to cope with setbacks, promote interpersonal skills, set goals and work toward their aspirations.

Resilience is a quality that draws upon a person's inner strength as well as their skill set. It is a lifelong characteristic that requires a person to have developed confidence, skills and competencies across life domains. Early intervention is important for promoting strength and resilience and reducing risk factors, such as low self-esteem, which may impact on the child's future development and wellbeing. With resilience, a person can adapt and bounce back from stressful or adverse incidents. As research adds to our knowledge about ADHD as a lifespan condition, the contribution of early interventions in building psychological resilience will become better understood. The aim is not to solely promote skill development, but to also strengthen coping and support mechanisms, which may protect children from emotional distress, behavioural problems and academic underachievement. Early intervention may prevent the development of maladaptive patterns that lead a child to become entrenched or stuck.

We are strongly influenced by those who are around us. Children are like sponges; they soak up what they see and hear. As a child grows up it will receive various (and sometimes conflicting) 'messages' from parents/carers, teachers, peers, the media and others in society. These messages may shift between generations and cultural norms, but the messages that are communicated need to be hopeful and positive if a child is to internalize a view of him-/herself that is functional and adaptive. A child who perceives themselves as a problem or burden is more likely to develop low self-esteem and lack the resilience to cope with the challenges and difficulties in life that they will inevitably face as they mature and become a young adult.

As described by Sonuga-Barke and Halperin (2010), ADHD does not have to be understood as a fixed pattern of core deficits, but rather a fluctuating interplay between individual child factors, developmental neurobiology, phenotypes and interpersonal dynamics. This means ADHD has to be seen as a condition that changes as the child develops. Hence, ADHD has a dynamic presentation across the child's trajectory, and early intervention allows this to be shaped through the creation of positive social support, positive self-beliefs, sensitive and warm parenting environments and engaging in physical activity.

Cognitive Behavioural Therapy

The Young–Smith Programme is a cognitive behavioural therapy (CBT) intervention that focuses on the relationship between cognitions (what we think), affect (how we feel), body response (how this affects our body) and behaviour (what we do) – see Figure 1.1. There is good evidence that CBT is an effective intervention for the treatment of a variety of problems experienced by children, including anxiety, depression, interpersonal problems, phobias, school refusal, conduct disorder, obsessive-compulsive disorder and the management of pain.

CBT aims to reduce psychological distress and maladaptive behaviour by altering cognitive processes. The underlying assumption is that cognitive and behavioural interventions can bring about changes in thinking, feeling and behaviour, as affect and behaviour are largely a product of cognitions. Hence, CBT aims to restructure negative and unhelpful thinking errors whilst establishing more

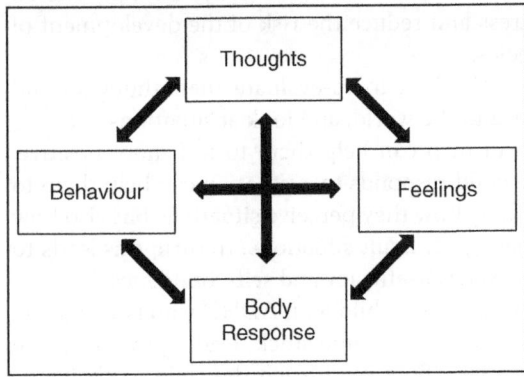

Figure 1.1 The CBT Cycle.

adaptive and flexible behaviours to promote coping. This is achieved by teaching children that the way they think about things can change how they feel and what they do. The way their body reacts provides clues to how they are feeling. For example, a child who sees a dog (even a friendly dog) and thinks, 'That dog looks scary!' will feel scared. They may recognize the feeling because their stomach is churning and they feel shaky. In response to these feelings an automatic action kicks in and the child will draw away from the dog and run to safety. Anxiety about dogs is likely to be maintained if the child does not face their fear, as this means that they do not learn to manage their thoughts, feelings and behaviours.

When working with young children, the therapist usually sets targets of treatment that focus more on the behavioural aspect of the CBT cycle because young children are less able to work at a cognitive level. However, as the child matures, more cognitive interventions can be introduced, which in turn will optimize treatment outcomes. The cognitive approach examines what a person thinks about themselves, other people and the world. CBT considers 'thinking errors' to be distorted or biased thinking which tend to be negative, overly general and/or restrictive thoughts about themselves, other people and/or the world. These 'thinking errors' interfere with the functional thinking process by altering our perception and preventing the adoption of positive coping techniques. In the Young–Smith Programme, we refer to 'thinking errors' as 'enemy thoughts'.

Furthermore, individuals may selectively dismiss relevant information that contradicts their thinking error. For example, the thought, 'All my teachers think I am rubbish' is likely to be an over-generalization displaying catastrophic or 'black and white' thinking. The child is likely to dismiss evidence to the contrary, such as receiving praise from a teacher the previous day. Over time, core beliefs may develop from these thoughts. These are stronger representations of the way the child perceives and evaluates events. Early intervention hopes to prevent the development of harmful, negative and strongly rooted core beliefs, reduce future distress and reduce the risk of the development of (negative) self-fulfilling prophecies.

CBT techniques will support children to re-evaluate their thoughts and beliefs about themselves, others and the world, and look at situations in a new and more adaptive way, which in turn can help them to feel more positive. Similarly, changing the way the child responds to a situation can help them to cope in a new way, altering not only how they perceive situations but also how they perceive their ability to manage difficult situations. In turn, this leads to more positive feelings and improved self-efficacy and self-confidence.

Figure 1.2 demonstrates an example of a child with ADHD who is struggling to write an essay in class. The child has become stuck, leading to a negative self-fulfilling prophecy. In this case, CBT would teach the child to challenge enemy thoughts/thinking errors and instead apply positive self-talk such as,

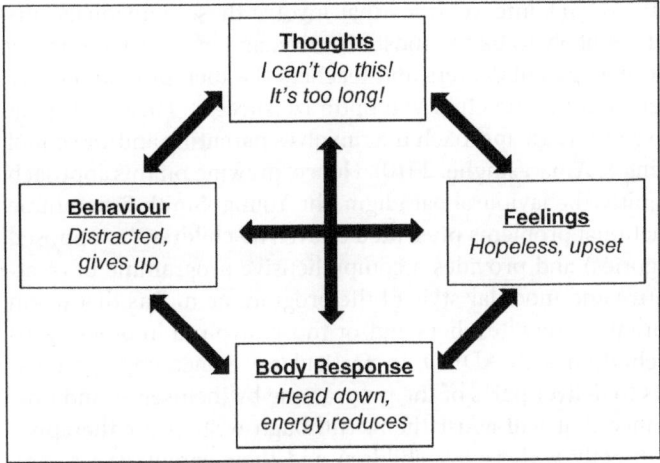

Figure 1.2 School example of a negative self-fulfilling prophecy.

'Come on, I can do this. Just five more minutes and then I'll ask for help.' This will motivate the child to try a bit harder, do a bit more, and ask for help if they continue to struggle.

The Young–Smith Programme

The Young–Smith Programme offers a template for healthcare and allied professionals and provides CBT techniques for use with school-aged children with ADHD or symptoms associated with ADHD. As the Young–Smith Programme and associated worksheets do not refer to ADHD directly, they are also suitable for use more generally with children who do not have ADHD but who are experiencing cognitive and/or behavioural problems for another reason (e.g., due to disruption within the family).

The Young–Smith Programme provides practical strategies and techniques to address problem behaviours and cognitive and emotional difficulties in children. In particular, cognitive problems are likely to hamper their engagement in standard interventions. For example, they may become restless and inattentive and need shorter sessions; they may need visual prompts to aid memory; they may need creative methods of delivery to maintain engagement; and there may need to be flexibility in the therapeutic approach, including frequent breaks and rewards. By offering a flexible approach, the Young–Smith Programme provides an adaptive model of CBT that embeds the model in the networks around the child. This will support the child in rehearsing and generalizing newly acquired skills into their daily activities.

For children with ADHD, interventions that involve those individuals surrounding the child are likely to be the most effective, and by working directly with the child and their parents/carers and teachers the therapist can ensure that scaffolding surrounding the child will optimize success. There is a great deal of evidence to support an approach that involves parenting and/or school interventions (Young & Amarasinghe, 2010). Hence, drawing on this approach and applying a cognitive behavioural paradigm, the Young–Smith Programme focuses on the functional problems presented by ADHD children (as opposed to diagnostic categories) and provides a comprehensive programme of treatment. The interactive and modular style of the programme means that it can be delivered by parents/carers, teachers and/or those involved in other agencies that support children with ADHD. In particular, we encourage parents/carers and teachers to deliver parts of the programme by themselves and provide specific guidance that will assist them. Although written for therapists who are working directly with young children and their parents/carers and teachers, the programme is novel in the inclusion of additional advice and guidance about how to deliver the programme for non-healthcare professionals. They will be aided in this endeavour by the structured approach to the programme and the inclusion of materials that can be downloaded from the companion website (www.wiley.com/go/young/helpingadhd).

Moreover, teachers and Special Educational Needs Coordinators can easily embed component modules into existing or newly formulated Individualized Educational Programmes. Short-term targets may thus be set around the completion of specific modules, or, perhaps more effectively, the application to school situations of specific strategies learnt during the module. Example targets include the pupil using a five-point scale (as discussed later in this book) to communicate their emotions at a particular time; the use of techniques introduced in one of the Buzz scenarios to avoid impulsive behaviour, avert frustration or manage conflict; or signs that the child is learning to form and manage friendships with peers.

Within the Young–Smith Programme, we intentionally avoid using the term ADHD for three reasons. Firstly, we believe that it is more meaningful for the child to focus on the functional presentations that cause them difficulties in their everyday life rather than a diagnostic category; secondly, we wish to avoid the stigma associated with a label; and thirdly, we don't want the child to feel that their problems are outside their control and due to a disorder that they can't manage. If the child believes that a problem (behaviour, events) controls them, this may, in turn, make the child feel as though they can do nothing to help control the problem, behaviour, events, and so on. This belief would be wrong because there is a lot that can be done (including strategies that children can learn themselves) to support them in controlling their behaviour and their emotions. This is well established from the evidence supporting CBT interventions in children more generally. It takes some effort and practice, but it can be achieved. At the same time, it is important that the child does not feel blamed for their condition and that the adults around them are able to distinguish between the child and the ADHD.

Nevertheless, for children diagnosed with ADHD, and if the healthcare practitioner considers it beneficial to inform them about ADHD, the authors have written psychoeducational materials that can be freely downloaded from the Psychology Services Website (www.psychology-services.uk.com/resources). Two versions of these psychoeducational materials are available, one targeted at the child, 'So I have ADHD', and another targeted at parents/carers and teachers, 'ADHD? Information for Parents, Carers and Teachers'.

References

American Psychiatric Association. (2013). *Diagnostic and Statistical Manual of Mental Disorders* (5th ed.). Washington, DC: American Psychiatric Association.

Biederman, J., Newcorn, J., & Sprich, S. (1991). Comorbidity of attention deficit hyperactivity disorder with conduct, depressive, anxiety, and other disorders. *American Journal of Psychiatry, 148*(5), 564–577.

Elia, J., Ambrosini, P., & Berrettini, W. (2008). ADHD characteristics: 1. Concurrent co-morbidity patterns in children and adolescents. *Child and Adolescent Psychiatry and Mental Health, 2*(15), 1–9.

Ford, T., Goodman, R., & Meltzer, H. (2003). The British child and adolescent mental health survey 1999: The prevalence of DSM-IV disorders. *Journal of the American Academy of Child and Adolescent Psychiatry, 42*(10), 1203–1211.

Goldman, L. S., Genel, M., Bezman, R. J., & Slanetz, P. J. (1998). Diagnosis and treatment of attention-deficit/hyperactivity disorder in children and adolescents. *Journal of the American Medical Association, 279*(14), 1100–1107.

Greene, R., Beszterczey, S., Katzenstein, T., Park, K., & Goring, J. (2002). Are students with ADHD more stressful to teach?: Patterns of teacher stress in an elementary school sample. *Journal of Emotional and Behavioral Disorders, 10*(2), 79–89.

Kendall, J. (1999). Sibling accounts of attention deficit hyperactivity disorder (ADHD). *Family Process, 38*(1), 117–136.

Kessler, R. C., Adler, L., Berkley, R., Biederman, J., Connors, C. K., Demler, O., et al. (2006). The prevalence and correlates of adult ADHD in the United States: Results from the national comorbidity survey replication. *American Journal of Psychiatry, 163*(4), 716–723.

Mikami, A.Y., & Pfiffner, L. J. (2008). Sibling relationships among children with ADHD. *Journal of Attention Disorders, 11*(4), 482–492.

Pliszka, S. R. (1998). Comorbidity of attention-deficit/hyperactivity disorder with psychiatric disorder: An overview. *Journal of Clinical Psychiatry, 59*(Suppl 7), 50–58.

Rutter, M. (2005). Environmentally mediated risks for psychopathology: Research strategies and findings. *Journal of the American Academy of Child and Adolescent Psychiatry, 44*(1), 3–18.

Shaw, M., Hodgkins, P., Caci, H., Young, S., Kahle, J., Woods, A., et al. (2012). A systematic review and analysis of long-term outcomes in attention deficit hyperactivity disorder: Effects of treatment and non-treatment. *BMC Medicine, 10*(99), 1–15.

Sonuga-Barke, E. J. S., & Halperin, J. M. (2010). Developmental phenotypes and causal pathways in attention deficit/hyperactivity disorder: Potential targets for early intervention? *Journal of Child Psychology and Psychiatry, 51*(4), 368–389.

Stergiakouli, E., & Thapar, A. (2010). Fitting the pieces together: Current research on the genetic basis of attention-deficit/hyperactivity disorder (ADHD). *Journal of Neuropsychiatric Disease and Treatment, 6*, 551–560.

Thapar, A., Cooper, M., Jefferies, R., & Stergiakouli, E. (2012). What causes attention deficit hyperactivity disorder? *Archives of Disease in Childhood, 97*, 260–265.

Theule, J., Wiener, J., Tannock, R., & Jenkins, J. M. (2013). Parenting stress in families of children with ADHD: A meta-analysis. *Journal of Emotional and Behavioral Disorders, 21*(1), 3–17.

Young, S., & Myanthi, Amarasinghe, J. (2010). Practitioner review: Non-pharmacological treatments for ADHD: A lifespan approach. *Journal of Child Psychology and Psychiatry, 51*, 116–133.

2

The Young–Smith Programme

This chapter provides general information and guidance on how to deliver the Young–Smith Programme. We strongly advise that anyone intending to deliver the programme reads this chapter as it includes an overview of the programme, including information about the content and structure of sessions, a description of the programme materials, and discusses the style of delivery for the programme. There follows advice for healthcare and allied professionals about joint working, including practical advice and strategies that may be helpful in managing a child with ADHD. The chapter concludes with advice for parents/carers and teachers who are seeking to acquire specific strategies that can be applied in the respective home or school settings to support children with ADHD and associated problems. Whilst the Young–Smith Programme is presented for delivery by therapists, we encourage parents/carers and teachers to deliver parts of the programme themselves. The interactive and modular style of the programme means that this can be achieved as each chapter, together with the worksheet materials, provides a directed and stepped structure to guide them.

Programme Content

The Young–Smith Programme consists of nine modules on topics of functional problems that most commonly present in children with ADHD (see Table 2.1). This is not an exhaustive list of topics and nor are they mutually exclusive, but we have had to be selective when considering the topics that will be most helpful to those who are delivering the programme.

The modular style of the programme allows for flexibility in its delivery, as specific modules can be selected and prioritized to meet the needs of the child. Hence, delivery of the programme follows a 'mix and match' approach. The programme uses age-appropriate methods for working with young children to

---

Helping Children with ADHD: A CBT Guide for Practitioners, Parents and Teachers,
First Edition. Susan Young and Jade Smith.
© 2017 John Wiley & Sons Ltd. Published 2017 by John Wiley & Sons Ltd.
Companion website: www.wiley.com/go/young/helpingadhd

Table 2.1 The Young–Smith Programme Modules.

Chapter 3	Introduction to Buzz and his Family
Chapter 4	Attention
Chapter 5	Hyperactivity
Chapter 6	Impulsivity
Chapter 7	Worries and anxiety
Chapter 8	Frustration, anger and challenging behaviour
Chapter 9	Social skills and relationships
Chapter 10	Setting goals and planning ahead
Chapter 11	Problem-solving
Chapter 12	Self-esteem

foster engagement, motivation and understanding through the introduction of a boy called Buzz and his family (see Chapter 3). Each module contains worksheets that describe the adventures of Buzz and introduce the child to problems or difficulties that Buzz experiences in his everyday life. These are experiences that the child may empathize with and, in discussion with the therapist, the child is encouraged to adopt a problem-solving approach to think up strategies that Buzz may use to help him with his problems. The therapist then shifts the discussion away from Buzz and his problem and towards any shared or similar experiences that the child has had (or is currently having) and considers how suggestions put forward to help Buzz may also help the child. This approach fosters a sense of therapeutic collaboration and cohesion as well as offering a stimulating, practical and visual delivery method. This method of delivery is, however, optional and can be adapted if it is considered unsuitable for children at the upper end of the target age range.

The child is then set Home Missions to test out whether these strategies are helpful; if not, a different strategy can be identified and tried out in a subsequent Home Mission. Thus, in this way, the child learns and acquires a repertoire of adaptive skills that he/she can apply to help and support him/her at difficult times.

To maximize effectiveness, it is important that parents/carers and, whenever possible, teachers are involved in the programme. Thus, within each module, the child-directed strategies are paralleled with advice for parents/carers and teachers on joint working, and on how to implement strategies at home and at school. We also 'speak' directly to parents/carers and teachers who may be seeking guidance on specific 'stand alone' strategies that can be applied at home and in school (i.e., independent of the delivery of the programme to the child).

Format of Modules

Following the first introductory module in Chapter 3, each subsequent module follows a standardized format (see Table 2.2). The module first describes the common problems and functional deficits or impairments related to the topic that are experienced by children with ADHD (i.e., what this looks like in everyday life). There follows advice about how to make an assessment of the problem; this often includes suggested questionnaires and/or measures that can be used at different times to monitor change. The CBT interventions section provides a suggested agenda for the session, advice about the review of the child's folder (which contains materials produced during and between sessions and therefore builds over time to become a resource that documents strategies that are helpful to the child), suggested worksheets and how to deliver these within the session, and advice about feedback and rewards.

There follow sections about working with parents/carers and with teachers, each containing suggested approaches, techniques and/or strategies to which they can be introduced. The 'What can we do' sections are for parents/carers or teachers who are not actively involved in the delivery of the programme but who wish to learn more about 'stand alone' strategies that they can apply in the home or school setting.

The Young–Smith Programme has been designed so that teachers and Special Educational Needs Coordinators can easily embed component modules into existing or newly formulated Individualized Educational Programmes. Short-term targets may thus be set around the completion of specific modules or, perhaps more effectively, the application of specific strategies learnt during the module to school situations. Example targets include the pupil using a five-point scale (as discussed later in this chapter) to communicate their emotions at a particular time; the use of techniques introduced in one of the Buzz scenarios to avoid impulsive behaviour, avert frustration or manage conflict; or signs that the child is learning to form and manage friendships with peers.

Table 2.2 Format of the Young–Smith Modules.

Presentation
Assessment
Cognitive behavioural therapy Interventions
Working with parents/carers
What can we do as parents/carers?
Working with teachers and schools
What can we do as teachers?

Long-term targets might be an improvement in academic performance, a reduction in sanctions or enhanced participation in school activities and higher self-esteem. Target setting tends to be most effective when framed positively and when (relative) strengths are consolidated. For example, progress could be linked to a child's improvement in performance on the football field or in completing a new level of a computer-based learning activity.

Resources

There is a companion website at www.wiley.com/go/young/helpingadhd where all the materials (e.g., Home Missions Record Form and worksheets) associated with the Young–Smith Programme can be freely accessed and downloaded. Additional resources, including a sleep guide and psychoeducational materials for children and the adults around them, can be downloaded from: www.psychology-services.uk.com/resources.

Style of Delivery

When using direct tasks with children, it is important to bear in mind their age and ability. We suggest that younger children are introduced to the 'Buzz and his Family' worksheet-based interventions (note that the first treatment session should commence with Worksheets 1–3, see Chapter 3) as these have been designed to be appropriate across a younger age range. The therapist should select and read through worksheets that describe the adventures of Buzz and, as directed, discuss the activity with the child. They should discuss the problem from Buzz's perspective and from the perspective of others, and think about ways to resolve the problem or situation through their thinking and behaviour. The therapist should then shift focus by relating the issue or topic to the child's own experience and behaviour.

For older children (*possibly* 12 years plus) or children who may not engage with the worksheets, the therapist may dispense with the Buzz Worksheets, and instead adapt the material by introducing the child directly to the topic and applying it to the child's experience using the suggested cognitive and/or behavioural strategies. A similar format is therefore followed, except the discussion focuses solely on the child's experience and behaviour. Alternatively, older children may find it easier to relate to characters in a movie or soap opera, or the subjects of documentaries about young people who are experiencing their own difficulties (e.g., 'Brat Camp'); the Buzz prompts used in the worksheets can be easily adapted to render them more age-appropriate in such cases.

We have not provided a fixed 'cut-off' chronological age for which either style should be used, as this will depend on the maturity of the child. We believe that matching the style to the child will be a relatively simple matter in most cases; however, in borderline cases where there may be uncertainty about which style is most appropriate we suggest that the therapist commences with the worksheets but be prepared to swiftly switch the focus to the child's personal experiences if these are forthcoming.

Prior to using the worksheets and conducting the intervention the therapist should ensure he/she has a full understanding of the child's language capabilities. Whilst the worksheets have been designed for a younger age group, adjustments may still be required to make the language suitable for some children. In addition, the intervention requires reflection and understanding of emotions, and some young children may not have developed a full grasp of the range of emotions possible. For these children, the worksheets may be adjusted accordingly and five-point scales of emotion (e.g., happy, angry, sad and scared) may be introduced to prompt the child to consider intensities of emotion, for example, a five-point scale ranging from very unhappy (0) to very happy (5). Some children may hold a positive illusory bias, in which they do not recognize that they have a problem and/or the associated impairments they suffer. This can lead to the child over-rating his/her abilities, disregarding strategies for improvement and disengaging from the programme; therefore any positive illusory biases should be identified, considered throughout and worked upon at the earliest possible stage.

Psychoeducation

The term ADHD does not appear in the Young–Smith Programme worksheets. This is for two reasons: Firstly, we believe that it is more meaningful for the children to focus on the functional problems that cause them difficulties in their everyday life rather than on a diagnostic category. Secondly, we wish to avoid the stigma associated with a label, because we don't want to externalize their problems with the perception that something 'out there' is the cause of it. If we do that, there is a risk that the child will believe that the problem controls him/her, which in turn means that the child believes he/she can do nothing to help himself/herself control the problem, behaviour, events and so on. This would be wrong because there is a lot that can be done (including strategies that children can learn themselves) to support the child to control his/her behaviour and emotions, as indicated from the evidence supporting CBT interventions for children. Controlling behaviour and emotions takes some effort and practice, but it can be achieved. This also means that the Young–Smith Programme and associated materials are suitable for use more generally with children who do not have ADHD but who are experiencing impaired functioning in everyday life for some other reason.

However, in some circumstances, it may be useful to provide psychoeducational information about ADHD to children. This should be in collaboration with discussion with parents/carers. To meet this need, we have developed some materials which can be downloaded from the Psychology Services Website (www.psychology-services.uk.com/resources). A child psychoeducational resource ('So I have ADHD') is available, in addition to a version for those who are closely involved in the child's care ('ADHD? Information for Parents, Carers and Teachers'). These can be used as a basis for discussion in face-to-face contact and/or provided as handouts.

Agenda

At the beginning of each session the therapist should give the child a written agenda that has been prepared prior to the session. Go through the agenda, verbally linking the themes and worksheets that will be introduced during the session.

So far as possible, the agenda should be supplemented with visual material – don't worry if you are not a great artist, it really doesn't matter! As you work through the session, use the agenda to refocus attention and tick off tasks that have been completed. This provides an opportunity to role-play behavioural techniques. Unfinished material can be carried over. The agenda should be placed in the child's folder so he/she can show it to parents/carers and, if appropriate, teachers.

For older children, you can introduce time-management techniques by generating a discussion about the duration of the session and how long tasks might take in order to identify what can realistically be achieved. The aim is to complete all set tasks on the agenda in the session; however, sometimes important issues arise during a session that need to be dealt with, and this may mean you are unable to cover everything. In this case, incomplete tasks can be carried over as a Home Mission and/or placed on the agenda for the following session. The agenda should be placed in the child's folder so the child can monitor progress and share it with parents/carers and/or teachers.

CBT Worksheets

The aim of the interventions and worksheets is to introduce children to the core concepts and skills they will be learning about in each module. The therapist will achieve this by setting an agenda, reviewing work completed between sessions in their folder, working through the worksheets (or for older children introducing the child directly to the topic and discussing their experiences and potential strategies) and setting Home Missions. These techniques are described in detail for each module topic presented in each chapter.

Just as the modules allow for flexibility in the delivery of the Young–Smith Programme, so do the contents of each module, as different worksheets can be selected to suit the child's needs. Thus, there can be some 'mixing and matching' of worksheets, with the therapist selecting worksheets that are considered helpful to either replace or supplement those that we have presented within each module. We recommend that a module is covered by a minimum of two worksheets, but children with more severe problems and/or complex needs may need more. A list of the worksheets and the skills they introduce is presented in Table 2.3.

Always commence with the Introductory Module and associated worksheets, as these are designed to introduce the child to Buzz, his family and his daily activities (see Chapter 3). The aim is to foster a therapeutic relationship and promote the child's ability to express him/herself. They introduce the child to symptoms and behaviours associated with ADHD, encourage the child to develop empathy and understanding of others' positions, introduce challenges and skills as concepts and encourage the application and transfer of knowledge and skills to the child's own life. Importantly, the child is introduced to the key concepts of rewards, praise and self-praise through positive thinking. The advantage of using the worksheets in this programme is that they avoid the difficulties that many children have, especially younger children and those with ADHD, in discussing their own behaviours directly. The discussions about Buzz should put the child at ease with regards to discussing his/her own behaviours.

The worksheets are generally presented in three parts.

1) *Stimulus Sheet* – this sheet tells a story about Buzz and highlights a problem (with the exception of the introductory module when the Stimulus Sheet introduces the child to Buzz and his family and the core strategies of positive thinking and rewards). The Stimulus Sheet is read out to the child and forms the basis of a discussion. The Stimulus Sheet is the child's to keep. All artwork on the worksheets consists of simple black outlines reminiscent of those in a children's colouring book so that the child may colour in the worksheets during a session break and/or as a Home Mission. Ask the child to bring their favourite crayons to the session for this purpose, although it is also advisable to have some on hand for the child to use.
2) *Discussion Sheet* – the therapist has a discussion sheet which contains questions relating to the story that should be posed to the child.
3) *The Task Sheet* – this includes exercises for the child to complete, such as writing out ideas that might help Buzz with the problem.

Depending on ability, either one or two worksheets can be introduced in a session. For a 50-minute session, the therapist should plan to complete two worksheets, or one for a 30-minute session. If a child takes longer than anticipated the therapist has the option of stopping after completing one worksheet. All the worksheets are available on the companion website resource page (www.wiley.com/go/young/helpingadhd).

Table 2.3 Young–Smith Programme Worksheets.

Worksheet	Chapter	Description
Worksheet 1: Buzz and his Family	Chapter 3: Introductory Module	Introduces Buzz, his family and activities that foster empathy
Worksheet 2: Buzz and Self-talk		Develops skills to self-monitor and engage in positive thinking
Worksheet 3: Buzz enters a Competition		Introduces the concepts of rewards, praise and self-praise
Worksheet 4: Spot the Difference	Chapter 4: Attention Module	An attention task to develop self-monitoring skills
Worksheet 5: Buzz gets his Cycling Badge		An attention task that introduces the concepts of focus and distraction
Worksheet 6: Buzz does his Homework		Introduces self-talk for attention
Worksheet 7: Buzz at School	Chapter 5: Hyperactivity Module	Develops knowledge of restlessness and how to cope with it
Worksheet 8: Buzz at Bedtime		Introduces sleep problems and sleep hygiene
Worksheet 9: Buzz goes to Hospital	Chapter 6: Impulsivity Module	Develops knowledge about impulsivity and compensatory strategies
Worksheet 10: Buzz at the Theme Park		Considers self-regulation and interpersonal difficulties
Worksheet 11: Buzz goes Camping	Chapter 7: Anxiety Module	Introduces the concept of anxiety as 'worries' and how to manage them
Worksheet 12: Buzz and the School Play		Develops understanding of the maintenance of anxiety, avoidance and management
Worksheet 13: Buzz reads a Book	Chapter 8: Frustration Module	Introduces stress and frustration and how to manage these
Worksheet 14: Buzz makes a Birthday Present		Identifies physiological responses and develops coping strategies
Worksheet 15: Buzz goes to the Movies	Chapter 9: Social Skills Module	Introduces conversation skills
Worksheet 16: Buzz goes to the Park		Considers the nature of friendship and conflict resolution

Table 2.3 (Continued)

Worksheet 17: Buzz goes to the Circus	Chapter 10: Planning Module	Develops skills in setting realistic goals and persevering in order to reach targets
Worksheet 18: Buzz and his Birthday Party		Learning to plan and organize using internal and external prompts
Worksheet 19: Buzz makes a Castle	Chapter 11: Problem-Solving Module	Identifies maladaptive problem-solving and consequences
Worksheet 20: Buzz and the New Boy		Develops problem-solving skills
Worksheet 21: Buzz Writes a Story	Chapter 12: Self-Esteem Module	Acknowledges positive qualities, skills and talents
Worksheet 22: Buzz has a Bad Day		Develops positive thinking styles and self-talk to counteract negative thinking

Mid-Session Break

For children of all ages, it will be important to offer breaks, rewards and frequent feedback to enhance attention, motivation and learning. This does not necessarily mean a stop/start interruption to treatment, as you could offer refreshments to the child at a convenient midpoint together with a break-time activity (e.g., younger children could colour in worksheet illustrations). The mid-session break also provides an opportunity to work towards a check-point; in other words instead of the child focusing on the whole session, the focus is only on the work to be done up to the check-point (in this case, the break) and at this point the therapist revises where they have got to on the agenda and what will be done after the break. The use of check-points can help to motivate children and help them sustain attention as they work towards a tangible goal (and associated reward, in this case a drink and/or some colouring). For children who have severe attention and/or hyperactive/impulsive impairments, the therapist will need to judge on an individual basis whether having additional check-point breaks is necessary, and tailor the session to suit (e.g., by having a check-point after the completion of each worksheet).

For children who are very restless and hyperactive, break-time activities may include physical activities such as stretches/lunges, star jumps, bunny jumps (like a press-up with hands on the floor and they jump both their legs in then out behind them) or wall pushes (a standing press up, with feet placed at a wide stance a few steps back from the wall and hands against the wall above the shoulders, with the child performing a press-up like action). The activity will depend on the space available and an assessment of risk, for example some children may become overly excited and become difficult to control. In such cases, it may be necessary to include a calming down exercise after the activity, such as deep breathing (instructing the child to breathe in for around four seconds and out for six, for example).

Feedback and Rewards

Aside from giving feedback to parents/carers and, if appropriate, teachers regarding the child's progress (and encouraging them to review the folder with the child between each session), the therapist should also provide frequent feedback to the child during the session. This is important for three reasons:

1) Praise will increase self-confidence and raise self-esteem.
2) The child will learn from constructive feedback.
3) It will motivate engagement and improve self-efficacy.

Hence, feedback aims to help the child to develop and progress in a positive and constructive way. This can be achieved by providing regular summaries of what has been discussed together with praise; for example, a summary of Worksheet 5 when Buzz gets his Cycling Badge could be:

> That's really good. So we know that Buzz wants to earn a Cycling Badge but his problem is that there are a lot of children playing in the area and they are making a lot of noise. Buzz is also very aware that his Mum and the Scout Leader are nearby and are watching him. He is feeling under pressure! You suggested that Buzz tries not to look up but keeps his eyes on the wheel. That's a great idea, as it will help to stop him being distracted. You also suggested that he keeps his mind on earning the Cycling Badge by imagining the badge in his head. That's another good idea. I think that Buzz did those things, because he got his badge!

In addition, you should ask the child to feedback his/her understanding of the topic or story as this provides an opportunity to check that they have grasped the concept and its subtleties. At the same time, this can be a paired with the provision of positive feedback. For example, following the child describing the story presented in Worksheet 1 (which introduces the child to Buzz and his family) the therapist could say:

> That's a really good summary. So we know Buzz lives with his Mum and brother and he sometimes gets into trouble at school. You said he finds it difficult to do the work sometimes; he gets really excited and has

lots of energy. You said he sometimes does things without thinking. I'm going to give you a smiley face on your worksheet for listening so carefully about Buzz.

When reviewing the folder, look at the illustrations, colouring, paintings, magazine cuttings and photographs that the child has added to the folder. Start a conversation with the child about these illustrations to find out more about their likes, dislikes and interests. This will help you to set and work towards specific goals. If the child has illustrated the folder with any pictures of concern (e.g., depicting anger or violence) then discuss the theme of the picture with them during the session, as it is possible they are trying to communicate a problem that they cannot easily discuss.

In addition, ensure that you regularly reward effort and positive behaviours by giving praise. It is important to be explicit about why the praise is being given in order that the child makes a clear association between the reward and the behaviour or skill, for example, 'Well done Annie, you got all of those right'. You should also give rewards by adding stickers, handwritten notes or smiley faces on the worksheets or other materials in the folder.

Home Missions

We know that learning new skills in CBT is more effective when these are practised outside of the session, ideally across contexts. The aims of Home Missions are to optimize skill development by bridging activity in the therapy session with everyday life, and for adults in the child's life to be working together to optimize positive reinforcement. It is important that children learn how to transfer the skills they learn in the therapy session and apply these skills in their daily activities. However, one potential barrier is that children don't like homework, so we have avoided the use of the word 'homework' in favour of the term 'Home Missions' as this sounds different and more exciting. We have also included 'fun' Home Missions, such as colouring and illustrating the folder.

Within each module, we have suggested Home Missions for each worksheet. This is not to say that all of the Home Missions have to be done; the therapist should select what is deemed to be most appropriate and what is likely to provide most help to the child. It is important not to overload the child as they may already have homework to do for school. We suggest that a standard weekly Home Mission is to colour the pictures on the worksheets from that session as this provides an opportunity for (inadvertently) reviewing the material. Children should also be encouraged to add illustrations of their own to the worksheets, perhaps relating Buzz's activities to their own. It is important that they personalize their folder in this way as it helps them apply the treatment and make it more meaningful to them.

It is essential that parents/carers (and if involved, teachers) are aware of the Home Missions set in order that they can prompt and, if necessary, assist the child to complete them. This is especially important with younger children. We have therefore developed a Home Missions Record Form (available on the companion website) on which the Home Mission can be noted at the end of

---

Home Missions Record Form

Home Missions   Date of next session: 18th April

1. Cut out a photograph or draw a picture of you and your family and stick it on the cover of your folder.
2. Decorate the Worksheet by colouring in the picture and/or add to it with pictures on the theme of the story. These could be photographs or pictures in magazines or comics.

Comments:
I hope Joe enjoys these tasks.

Feedback

Home Missions were completed by: Joe

How did the child find the Home Missions?

Joe was keen to tell us about the session and do the home mission when he got in. He drew a great picture of us all enjoyed colouring in his picture and the worksheet.

What reward was given?

M&M's and lots of praise for his great drawing and colouring. Joe took it to school and showed his teacher who rewarded him with a sticker in his home school diary.

Figure 2.1 Example of a completed Home Missions Record Form relating to Worksheet 1.

each session and placed in the folder. Home Missions Record Forms completed by the parent/carer should be reviewed with the child at the next session and praise should be given. Examples of completed Home Missions Record Forms for a boy called Joe and a girl called Annie are provided in Figures 2.1 and 2.2.

Home Missions Record Form

Home Missions   Date of next session: 18th April

1. Decorate the Worksheet by colouring in the pictures and bubbles, and/or add to them with pictures on the theme of the story. These could be photographs or pictures in magazines or comics.

2. Choose one or two friendly thoughts from the Task Sheet. Write it on a cue card and put it somewhere where you are most likely to have enemy thoughts (e.g. where you do your homework, or next to your bed at night). This will prompt you to 'kick them out'.

Comments:
Annie came up with some great positive thoughts and self-talk in the session. Try and practice them as much as possible this week

Feedback

Home Missions were completed by: __Annie (with help from mum)__

How did the child find the Home Missions?

Annie enjoyed doing the colouring. Annie chose two helpful thoughts from the sheet and put one near her shoes which she finds difficult to tie and one on her desk near her homework. I noticed she is getting less frustrated with tying her shoes.

What reward was given?

Annie was allowed to play on the computer for half an hour.

Figure 2.2 Example of a completed Home Missions Record Form relating to Worksheet 2.

Preparing for Termination of Treatment

We have not written an 'end of treatment' module because the content would depend on the modules that have been delivered and the response of the child. We suggest that a final session is arranged where the therapist looks through the folder with the child to revise the modules and worksheets. In particular, it will be important to review Task Sheets as these will contain potential strategies that might be helpful and those that have been successfully applied. It would be helpful to add a summary of all the strategies and/or notes that were helpful to both the child and Buzz at the end of the folder.

Next, the therapist should discuss with the child that there are 'good' and 'bad' days, and sometimes strategies might be more difficult to remember and apply (especially on the 'bad' days). Make a list of things that the child can do on the 'bad' days, such as revising the strategies in the folder and talking things over with someone (make a list of who). It is important that the child learns that there may be setbacks in the future and understands that this is a normal part of life rather than a failure on their part. The difference now is that they have a repertoire of things that they can do when they feel upset and/or stressed; all the child has to do is remember to look at their folder, which will prompt them.

Joint Working with Parents/Carers and Teachers

With school age children, joint working between school and home is essential to help children understand that the adults around them work in a united way and to provide optimum opportunity for learning and for skills to be embedded. When joint working occurs, it allows reinforcement of the same desirable skills and behaviours across contexts, which can improve learning. It also allows the adults around the child to notice his/her strengths and struggles in a holistic way. This can increase opportunities for helpful strategies to be created and applied. If parents, carers or teachers have limited knowledge and understanding of ADHD and its prognosis, a psychoeducational booklet 'ADHD? Information for Parents, Carers and Teachers' can be downloaded from the Psychology Services Website (www.psychology-services.uk.com/resources).

If effective cognitive and behavioural change is to be achieved, there will need to be a triangle of collaboration between the child, therapist and parent/carer. To cover all bases, a 'square' collaboration would also include teachers! Lots of parents/carers and teachers find that using a Home–School Diary is an efficient way to share this information daily. Your child may already have one, or you could simply purchase a notebook for this purpose. In addition, the Young–Smith Programme folder could also be shared with teachers provided everyone is happy with this. If this is arranged, it is important that teachers read it and add comments that relate the child's efforts to how behavioural change is occurring in the school setting, in addition to giving praise and stickers.

Parents/carers may also set up an agreement to make weekly contact with the teacher to update them on the specific strategies being tried that week, and in turn the teacher will give feedback on the child's progress. This way, through teachers also helping the child with the specific goals in school and by jointly giving the rewards and praise, the effect of the therapist's and parent/carer's work can be doubled. For example, the teacher may give points or stickers when they notice the child demonstrating the desired skills that are the current focus of treatment, such as listening well to instructions. This has additional benefits for the child, who will perform better within a consistent and clear framework.

Working With Parents/Carers

When meeting with parents/carers it is really important that they are brought on board to work constructively with the therapist to maximize the effectiveness of the programme. Too often, parenting interventions are labelled 'parent training' which, in our view, is unhelpful and disengaging as it implies that they require training to develop 'good' parenting behaviours. Parents/carers are usually very good and caring towards their child; they love their children and see the best in them. They want to do what they can to help and support them, and this programme will teach them to be their child's 'coach'. Coaching techniques are a growing industry in the world of ADHD and some are better than others. The Young–Smith Programme, with its grounding in cognitive behavioural techniques, will teach parents/carers evidence-based strategies that they can apply in supporting, or 'coaching', their child.

It is important to assess what the parent/carer already does in the management of the child. What practices work out? What practices are less helpful? Does this depend on specific circumstances or contexts? We have found it to be essential to establish whether there are inconsistencies in the approach of family members, as this is not helpful. There must be agreed goals and methods to achieve them, the latter being consistent and constructive. Behavioural management strategies are listed in the publication 'ADHD Do's, Don'ts and Rewards; A Guide for Parents and Carers' which can be downloaded from the Psychology Services Website (www.psychology-services.uk.com/resources). In particular, it will be helpful to agree house rules, expectations of behaviour and methods to motivate effort and reward achievement.

House Rules

Most families have some house rules to follow to help keep people safe and make things to run smoothly. With both the child and their family, discuss what house rules they have and help parents/carers and children to phrase the house rules in a positive way, for example 'look after each other', rather than 'no hitting'. Ask parents/carers and children to display the house rules in a visible position; explain how to direct their child's attention back to the rules when encouraging functional behaviour at home, and remind them to praise the child each time they notice them following the rules.

Talk to the child's parents/carers and ask for their help to work out the best time and place for the child to do the Home Missions. Inform them of the use of 'Do Not Disturb' and 'Remember Notices' and encourage them to try these out and see whether they help.

Expectations

Ensure that parents/carers have realistic expectations of the child when setting targets. The key here is the word 'realistic'. Are they setting a goal that is too difficult for the child and one that sets them up for failure? If it appears that expectations from adults are too high, the child is likely to lose motivation, lack effort, and fail. This means that they don't learn how much of the task they could have achieved with maximum effort. Similarly, if expectations are too low, motivation to achieve and progress may also not be maximized, which means that the child may not acquire important skills. It may be that the fault does not lie completely with the child but with the expectations that people have of the child. For parents/carers these often arise from an expectation that their child will be like them (good at sport or music, academic, sociable) and it is important for parents/carers to learn that their child is not a mirror image of themselves, but an independent person with their own talents and skills, which may differ from those of their parents.

Rewards, Praise and Motivators

A key strategy to change behaviour and improve cognitive skill is to find motivators to promote success. Children with ADHD tend to respond better to immediate rewards; indeed, immediate rewards are helpful for the child to hold on to the idea of delayed gratification for a bigger goal.

Parents/carers will need to decide how they will motivate their children, especially on mundane or repetitive tasks, in order to help them sustain attention. Rewards should be proportionate to the task. Parents/carers can create a 'Rewards Menu' with the child and select a weekly reward to work towards. Rewards do not need to cost anything; they could be having a friend round for tea or a sleepover, going to the park, having a favourite dinner or having an extra story at bedtime. If token economies (i.e., collecting points or tokens) are used to build up to larger rewards, these should be charted visually and referred to in order to help the child remember. We describe later in this chapter how parents/carers can make a Star Chart.

Praise should be given alongside any rewards for desired behaviour; children with ADHD benefit from small, frequent rewards and praise. This should be positive verbal feedback and the use of stickers, and it should be given as soon as the target behaviour or skill has been observed so that the child understands that the two things are connected. Children especially like to have stickers in their Home School Diary, as then the teacher sees it as well (and they might get more praise which reinforces the behaviour or skill!). If parents/carers find it unnatural to praise their children, the therapist should role-play this in the session, and remind the parent/carer that praise should be immediate and specific as it is important that the child associates the desired behaviour with the praise. For example, 'Well done for listening so well to me just then', 'You have been concentrating on your homework excellently. Great job!' and 'I'm really pleased that you did so well on your maths test'.

The Young–Smith Programme includes a core worksheet in the Introductory Module which introduces the child to the concept of rewards, praise and self-praise. This exercise teaches children to reflect and self-monitor their behaviour and to motivate themselves by applying positive self-statements as self-rewarding techniques.

Star Chart

Parents/carers will be supported in a behavioural management routine by introducing a Star Chart to reinforce positive behaviours. How to create and use a Star Chart is described in the publication 'ADHD Do's, Don'ts and Rewards: A Guide for Parents and Carers' which can be downloaded from the Psychology Services Website (www.psychology-services.uk.com/resources). The rationale is that you reinforce positive behaviours that you wish to occur again in the future by setting up a reward system that combines both immediate and short-term rewards (e.g., on a daily basis) with larger rewards after a delay (e.g., after a week of good behaviour). It is like imagining that you are aiming to reach the top of the stairs where there is a big reward, but to motivate you to climb the steps you will receive a smaller reward after every three steps.

Figure 2.3 provides an example of a Star Chart. The first stage is to sit down with the child and together set the behavioural targets (goals). It is very important that these are clearly defined. Next, determine a list of short-term and long-term rewards. In the example, short-term rewards are a packet of sweets, football with dad, new colouring pens, a chocolate milkshake, having friends visit and going swimming. The long-term reward is a trip to the zoo. Next, draw up a Star Chart with a column to record good behaviour and another to list the rewards the child is working towards. The Chart should be pinned up in a visible place such as the kitchen. In order to reach the rewards, the child must gain five 'stars' in a row. These could be rewarded for social acts (e.g., sharing nicely with a sibling), completing a task (e.g., tidying their bedroom) or for avoidance of troublesome behaviour (e.g., a supermarket trip without a tantrum). If the child misbehaves in some way, however, they 'crash out' and receive a cross. This cancels out the previous stars and the child must start again until they obtain five stars in a row to earn their reward.

☆✗☆☆✗☆☆☆☆☆✓	Packet of Sweets
☆☆☆☆✗☆☆☆☆☆✓	Football with Dad
☆✗☆☆✗☆☆☆☆☆✓	New colouring pens
☆✗☆☆☆☆☆✓	Chocolate milkshake
☆☆☆☆✓	Have a friend over
☆☆✗	Go swimming
	TRIP TO THE ZOO!

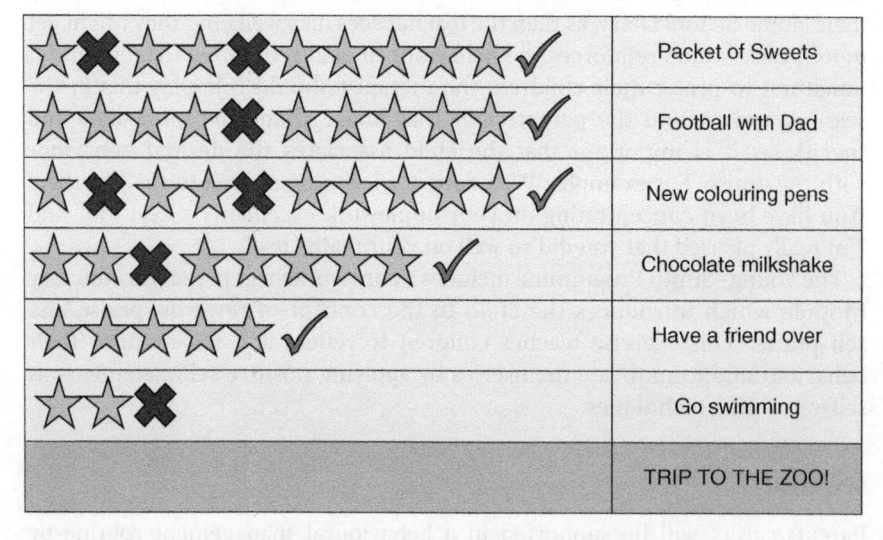

Figure 2.3 Example of a Star Chart. *Source:* From 'ADHD Do's, Don'ts and Rewards: A Guide for Parents and Carers' (www.psychology-services.uk.com/resources).

The Star Chart is organized with a short-term reward being given on a daily basis but working towards a greater reward (i.e., the child is working towards a trip to the zoo which is the long-term reward). Thus, as the child progresses towards this goal, the smaller short-term rewards are awarded along the way; this will maintain motivation. In the example, the child has earned a packet of sweets, a game of football with dad, new colouring pens, a chocolate milkshake and had friend over for tea. You can see that the child's behaviour has improved during the period, with fewer 'crash outs'. The child is getting closer to getting the trip to the zoo!

Strategy Monitoring

In order to gauge how effectively strategies are being applied outside of sessions, it is helpful to monitor how these techniques work and record the outcome (both successes and failures) in a Strategy Evaluation Record.

This is useful as it can illuminate whether there are particular circumstances when the child has difficulty (e.g., in the evening when they feel tired). The therapist can troubleshoot any issues in subsequent sessions and consider how to overcome these problems by adapting a strategy (or finding an alternative) for that context. An example of this type of record is given in Table 2.4 for a child named Joe.

When troubleshooting, the following should be considered: Is the task/check-point achievable? Is the reward balanced with the task? Has the child got used to doing the task the same way? Do the goals need changing to sustain attention and motivation? If the task is too aversive the child may simply refuse to give it any effort. If the task is too complicated, needs too much attention for the resources the child has, or the child is tired then tasks will need adapting.

Table 2.4 Strategy Evaluation Record.

Date	Task	How I helped (e.g., making check-points and goals)	How well did this work? (0 not at all/5 extremely well)	If not, how could I adapt the method?
Monday 6 March	For homework Joe had a short story to write but he complained that it would take him too long to do.	We decided he needed to do four paragraphs. At the end of each paragraph he had a five-minute break and a small piece of chocolate.	4 – It helped him stay on task and do three paragraphs but then he couldn't do any more.	It worked well and he did the other paragraph the next day.
Saturday 11 March	To make his bed.	I set him a task to strip the bed in under five minutes for a reward of ten minutes extra time on the Xbox. Then I set him the task of putting the new bed linen on in under ten minutes for a further ten minutes on the Xbox.	5 – He asked for my help with the duvet but he managed to do the whole task. He was allowed to play the Xbox for an additional 20 minutes.	This worked well but without my help the duvet would have been inside out (but I don't think he would have noticed!).

Working With Teachers

Classrooms are often the most interesting, creative and stimulating places that children will come across, and this is immensely important for their learning and development. To a child with ADHD, however, they may represent a mass of competing and overwhelming visual information. Hence, the provision of a screened-off 'quiet space' inside the classroom can help the child to relax and calm down when needed. A 'quiet space' outside the classroom is the ideal place for children to go if they need 'Time Out' if they are feeling upset, overwhelmed and/or simply because the classroom has become an overly noisy and distracting environment and they need to refresh. Teachers need to ensure, however, that the use of 'quiet space' is associated with a quiet, calming and productive area, rather than punishment and distress.

Teachers and schools will already have structures in place to support many of the interventions introduced in the Young–Smith Programme, and it is worth noting and reinforcing that, in addition to the implementation of ADHD-specific techniques, a good teaching style and maintaining whole-class discipline is effective for children with ADHD. It will be useful to meet with parents/carers and teachers to think about what is already in place, such as reward or token economy systems. There is often a lot of variation in classroom teaching, which can be very helpful for children with ADHD – they find novel situations more stimulating and engaging than those which become repetitive. Thus, wherever possible, adding novelty to classroom tasks is a helpful strategy. Novelty can come in the form of variety in teaching methodologies, methods of illustration and explanation of lesson content and objectives; variety in methods of assessing understanding and progress (not always relying on written tests); and variety in vocal delivery by teachers, avoiding monotony.

Working with teachers as well as parents/carers is likely to maximize the effectiveness of the Young–Smith Programme. This is because strategies that are put in place to support a child with ADHD are more likely to lead to successful outcomes if they are consistently in place across situations, including the school setting. They may not work in exactly the same way in school, but oftentimes they can be adapted in some way to be appropriate and helpful in this setting. In order to do this you will need to engage with teachers, teaching assistants and other support staff and get them on board. They can help in many ways, not only by delivering specific strategies but also by reinforcing those used at home and monitoring progress and outcomes.

Whilst recognizing that teachers have many competing demands on their time, it is important that they develop a good understanding about the needs of children with ADHD and how to manage, and hopefully limit, the presenting problems that hamper learning and behavioural skills, academic and social progress. When working with teachers it is important to reinforce the need for those engaging with the child to be non-judgemental. It is also important that all adults working in the classroom are aware of the targets that have been set for the child (even home-based targets, as they may often translate to behaviours observed in school), as it is disheartening for a child when great efforts go unnoticed. Working together as a 'teaching team' will avoid this, and communication between members of the 'team' is critical. Lots of teachers and parents/carers find that using a Home School Diary is an efficient way to share information on a daily basis. It may also be helpful for teachers to review the child's programme folder, if this is appropriate. It may be necessary for the therapist to set regular meetings attended by all the professionals involved and parents/carers.

Expectations

In schools, there are expectations regarding acceptable behaviour and academic progress. Children with ADHD are often less mature than their peers due to delays in brain development and this should be considered when setting expectations. Without a doubt, there will be some form of reward system in schools to promote desired behaviour and aid learning, to track the child's progress and to help them feel motivated. Achievement is rewarded by grade marks, recognition, certificates, prizes and so on, and failure punished with sanctions such as detentions. Severe behavioural misdemeanours may lead to fixed-term exclusions from school and, for some, permanent exclusions. Aside from a need for clear goals and expectations of behaviour (which is usually provided in school), children with ADHD require frequent feedback and reward systems, as these are techniques that will motivate them to stay on task and achieve their goals. For teachers, walking around the classroom and 'invading' the personal space of the children from time to time can provide a useful reminder to the children that the teacher is observing them and help keep them motivated to stay on task.

It is important for the therapist to elicit shared perspectives from parents/carers and teachers. One way to do this is to ask how a child might perform in a given situation, what they would evaluate from that, and how they would encourage the child further. Differences of opinion can be explored with open curiosity. The aim is to find evidence to support a realistic expectation of the child's ability to complete a task. A different expectation may arise, for example, in the time required to complete homework after school and/or the level of parent/carer input in helping them to complete homework.

Rewards, Praise and Motivators

Children with ADHD need more motivational prompts to help them with goal-oriented behaviour. In daily life this means that children with ADHD need more external motivators to help them to focus, such as small rewards, praise, feedback and an understanding about immediate consequences. If a reward or outcome seems to be far in the distance to the child, they will be less able to sustain motivation and engagement on a task. They are, therefore, dependent on the support of adults to help them learn and develop skills and techniques that will help them sustain effort and motivation.

It is important to provide feedback as soon as the teacher notices effort and/or successful application of a target behaviour or skill, because this will impress on the child that the two things are connected. Constant and consistent feedback and rewards should be given by all adults working with the child, rewarding effort as well as achievement. This could be simple verbal feedback as described in the parents/carers section of this chapter. For those children who have a Star Chart at home (see parent/carer section of this chapter), if school learning and behavioural targets have been set as goals then it is critical that teachers and parents/carers communicate success, difficulties and obstacles on a daily basis and for the Star Chart to be placed in the Home School Diary where it can be reviewed (and rewarded) by all those involved.

Routine and Novel Occupations

Practice makes perfect, but to succeed skilled thinking and/or skilled behaviours need to be repeated over and over again until they become automatic. When you learn to ride a bike or drive a car, you find it difficult at first. There seems to be so much to remember and you have to remind yourself of what to do. Even so, it takes a lot of practice until you can ride the bike without falling off or drive the car without stalling the engine. With practice, the process becomes more familiar and takes less mental effort. The process of acquiring skills in other areas is exactly the same. Practice and routine will help children to better manage the tasks that they struggle with and support them to make a new skill habitual. In addition, having a clear structure to lessons which is outlined at the outset will help children manage their time and maintain attention. Due to the poor working memory of children with ADHD, it is important that tasks are recorded in a visual form to be referred to at regular intervals. Do not expect them to remember without such prompts.

However, we are all familiar with the monotony of routines. Sometimes a change can help us feel refreshed, look at things with new eyes and feel excited and motivated about them again. A low threshold for boredom is a core enemy for children with ADHD as it will lead them to struggle on long tasks or those that are overly familiar. There are several things that can be done to help, including: switching tasks; mixing up a sequence of tasks so the child does something in a different order; using rewards, feedback and motivators (described earlier in this chapter); taking a brief (timed) break; moving position; setting a timed period for work; working things out aloud before writing them down; and using different coloured pens.

A Direct Resource for Parents/Carers and Teachers

Towards the end of each module there are sections that we have written for parents/carers and teachers who are not actually delivering the Young–Smith Programme directly to the child (or who are involved in its delivery via a therapist) but who wish to learn behavioural management strategies that they can apply in their respective home and school settings. Please do not read only these sections, as you will find helpful information in the rest of the book also.

We encourage parents/carers and teachers to look at programme modules, including the worksheets, which seem relevant to the needs of the child and consider delivering some of them themselves (or identifying someone who would be interested in doing this and who perhaps has more time). The high level of structure and the modular content of the programme mean that one does not need to have undergone years of training and/or developed expertise in delivering cognitive behavioural therapy to be able to deliver the Young–Smith Programme. The structure of the programme means that it is highly supportive in its delivery and we believe that non-healthcare professionals can deliver it with relative ease and confidence. As for those who are familiar with CBT techniques, parents/carers and teachers will need to select a module of interest and thoroughly prepare for its delivery by reading the whole chapter which describes how to deliver the module (it is recommended to read all of it, including the sections for delivery by a therapist), downloading the worksheets and hand-outs, preparing the agenda and folder and so on. The chapters for each module will take you through this step-by-step and tell you exactly what to do.

It is very likely that teachers and parents/carers are already regularly sharing information about the child. For children with ADHD this is even more crucial because a shared protocol is a key factor in the success of effecting change. By using similar strategies across settings, teachers and parents/carers can work together to double the effect of the treatment. Discussions need to be programmed in as opposed to ad-hoc opportunistic meetings at the end of the school day. We strongly advise that parents/carers and teachers specify arrangements to facilitate communication between them, for example, by email and/or regular meetings. A Home School Diary is the most common method for daily contact, and is a perfect tool to communicate targets for intervention, monitor progress and record outcomes between the two settings. It is important to discuss expectations for this arrangement, including agreement for all parties to look at and make comments in the Home School Diary every day and define boundaries, such as when (and when not) to use email communications.

It is helpful for parents/carers and teachers to identify and prioritize targets together; they may share similar perspectives about a child's needs but they may also have contrasting perspectives. They should also share methods of motivation and reward in order that these are consistently applied. Remember to feedback in the Home School Diary any tips or 'breakthroughs' that are discovered to be helpful to the child. If there are obstacles or sticking points (and these are inevitable) then it's important to troubleshoot these together. It is important that expectations of performance and behaviour can be realistically achieved. If expectations are too high you may notice that children avoid the tasks, become oppositional or give up. If expectations are too low (especially for children of high general cognitive ability) they may become demotivated, inattentive and bored. It can be difficult, therefore, to find the right level, so it is helpful to ask yourself the following questions: What is the priority? Where are we up to with a skill and what is the next step or stage? Does this need to be broken down into smaller and more achievable steps or stages? Can we improve confidence and effort by slowly increasing targets? Does the child need direct help and guidance or can they simply be prompted? Have they managed to do what you are asking before and what was helpful then? Are there obstacles (such as environmental factors) that need to be tackled first?

Finally, managing a child with ADHD can take its toll on both parents/carers and teachers. For parents/carers it can feel that life is a battle that can't be won as they struggle to care for a child who may have boundless energy and rapidly shifting emotions. They may feel that they are being pushed to the extreme and feel tired and drained from coping with a child who can't settle down to play quietly in the day or go to sleep in the evening. For teachers, the child with ADHD can be time consuming and frustrating to teach, and the child's behaviour may be perceived as demanding and/or attention-seeking. Teachers are unable to provide sustained individual tuition to one child in the class; they are responsible for teaching and monitoring all of the children in the class. Try to remember that the child usually wants to engage and learn like other children but sometimes it doesn't work out that way; it's a case of can't rather than won't. You will not be able to adequately support the child if you feel stressed out and fatigued. Ensure that you build time into the week to look after yourself – the reward system works for you too! Gain support from other people when you yourself need help or feel you can't cope. Take a break, take time out and/or count to ten. Count to one hundred if need be. It is important that you develop ways to effectively manage your own response to the child, whether this is frustration, anger and/or distress. This can be particularly challenging when managing children who are also oppositional and who respond negatively to boundary-setting. However, patience and consistency can make the difference between the development of positive and negative cycles of interaction; it's not always easy in practice but in the case of the latter this can spiral out of control. It doesn't help anyone to be in a place where there are no winners.

3

Introduction to Buzz and His Family

The aim of this module is to acquaint children with Buzz and his family. All treatment should commence with this module as it introduces the child to the narrative that will be used in CBT exercises throughout the Young–Smith Programme, in which the child will learn about the life and adventures of Buzz. In this session, as for all sessions, the therapist will set an agenda, work through selected worksheets, place work completed in a folder (that the child will take home) and set Home Missions.

There are three worksheets associated with the introductory module and we advise that all three are used; they introduce the child to Buzz and his family (Worksheet 1), introduce positive self-talk (Worksheet 2) and identify a reward system (Worksheet 3). The reward and self-talk strategies are applied in the session, at home and/or at school. All the worksheets are available on the companion website (www.wiley.com/go/young/helpingadhd).

If the worksheets are not being used, the therapist should introduce the child directly to the topic and, in discussion, apply it directly to the life and experience of the child. We suggest that a mid-session break can be offered halfway through the session; this will be particularly important for younger children. Chapter 2 provides generic information on the structure and content of sessions (irrespective of topic); supplementary information is included within this chapter that specifically relates to the delivery of the introductory session(s).

Agenda

At the beginning of the session, show the child the written agenda (see Figure 3.1) that you have prepared prior to the session and go through it, verbally linking the themes and worksheets that you will introduce during the

Helping Children with ADHD: A CBT Guide for Practitioners, Parents and Teachers,
First Edition. Susan Young and Jade Smith.
© 2017 John Wiley & Sons Ltd. Published 2017 by John Wiley & Sons Ltd.
Companion website: www.wiley.com/go/young/helpingadhd

session. In the first session you will start by providing the folder, together with Worksheets 1, 2 and 3, which introduce the child to Buzz, by saying:

> First of all, I am going to give you a special folder where you will keep all the work that we do as we go along. This folder is yours to keep and you can take it home and show it to anyone that you want. If you want, you could take it to school and show it to your teacher! Then we will hear about Buzz. Buzz is a boy who is eight years old and today we are going to get to know Buzz and his family. After that, we will have a short break and you can colour in the worksheet using these crayons. After the break we are going to look at some other worksheets and talk about rewards. I bet you like rewards! Buzz loves to be praised and to receive rewards.

<u>Agenda</u>

Introduce the folder

Buzz and his Family [Worksheet 1]

Break

Buzz and Self-talk [Worksheet 2]

Buzz enters a Competition [Worksheet 3]

Home Missions

Figure 3.1 Example agenda for introductory session(s).

Introducing the Folder

Over time, the folder will be filled with materials used both during and outside of the sessions (e.g., agendas, worksheets, Home Missions). Thus it will become a comprehensive personal resource for revision and sharing. Encourage the child to illustrate their folder with drawings that they can colour in, or by cutting out and pasting favourite images from magazines, comics or the Internet. Additionally, the child could add photographs, paintings or drawings, which they can do at home. This will personalize the folder and make it more meaningful for the child. The therapist, together with other adults who have access to the folder, should comment on their efforts and add stickers and/or drawings of smiley faces to reward the child. Aside from acting as a revision prompt, the folder will also act as a reward system for the child.

In future sessions, the therapist will review the folder with the child to check any Home Missions completed, revise salient information and reinforce important concepts. It is important to comment on the efforts the child has made to illustrate and personalize the folder. Talk about these illustrations and relate these to discussions that you have had previously about the experiences of Buzz and his family, and/or their own experiences. Don't forget to give lots of stickers, ticks and smiley faces! Older children could start and maintain a more 'grown-up' version of the folder in the form of a notebook where they can add notes and materials used in the sessions. They could illustrate the notebook with doodles, favourite pop groups and ticket stubs from weekend activities.

Introduce the folder to the child by saying (adapt this for older children with a notebook):

> Let's look at this folder. As I said before, this is yours to keep and we will put all the work you do in here. You will take the folder home, but you must remember to bring it back with you to each session! You can show it to anyone that you want. It's your folder and you don't want it to look plain and boring. You are not like that at all! So I want you to decorate your folder so it tells people something about the type of person you are and the things that you like. You can draw pictures and colour them in and you can add photographs and cut out pictures you like from magazines. You might want to add things about your house, your family, your school, your pet, your friends, your favourite pop star, favourite food, favourite sport … in fact, you can add anything that you like! Do you have any questions about your folder?

The child may then have questions to ask about the folder which you can answer.

Worksheet 1 Buzz and his Family

Worksheet Description

To download this worksheet, please visit the companion website

Buzz is a boy who lives in a town with his Mum and older brother. He has a dog called Wilma. Buzz thinks he is a bit different to other children as he sometimes struggles to learn new skills and do things like pay attention. At school, Buzz likes learning about new things but he finds the work hard sometimes. His favourite class is Art. Buzz likes going to the park to play with all the other children and he does this every day after school. He loves running around and is always on the move. Every Friday, Buzz goes to Scouts and he has been awarded some badges which he wears on his sleeve. He wants to get some more. Buzz tries hard but he gets over excited and is often told off by his Mum and teachers at school. They say he needs to 'think before he does things'.

(Continued)

Worksheet 1 (Continued)
Worksheet Prompts
Let's think about Buzz and his life. What do you think Buzz is good at? What might make him feel happy or sad? Can you tell me about your family? What is your school like? What do you like about school? What do you like to do outside of school? What are your hobbies and interests? Let's go back to Buzz. What kinds of things might he find difficult? What might he worry about? Do you find some things difficult? What do you worry about?

Worksheet 1 introduces the child to Buzz, his family and his daily activities. It contains a drawing of Buzz and his family, which can be coloured in either during a mid-session break or as a Home Mission. Worksheet 1 aims to foster a therapeutic relationship and promote the child's ability to express him/herself. The worksheet introduces the child to the concepts of skills and challenges, and encourages them to consider these concepts from the perspective of themselves and others.

The therapist should introduce the worksheet format to the child by saying:

> Do you see this picture? This is a little boy called Buzz, and this is his Mum and older brother. Look at his dog! Her name is Wilma. They are standing outside of the house where they all live. Buzz's Mum and Dad don't live together as they split up, but his Dad lives nearby and they see each other often. Each time we meet we will look at a worksheet, like this one, and learn about some of Buzz's activities and adventures. You may also do some of the things that Buzz does. Okay, let's start by reading about Buzz and his family.

Then read the Stimulus Sheet to the child, or, if they wish, they can read it with you. Check that the child was paying attention and has understood. 'Scouts' can be explained as, 'A group for boys where they learn skills together and do activities'. Start up a discussion about what it is like to be a little boy like Buzz. Talk about what Buzz might be good at. Ask the child what he/she thinks makes Buzz feel happy or sad. Then shift the conversation to talking about the child's life and family by working through the guided questions on the Discussion Sheet. Returning to Buzz, ask the child what Buzz might find difficult, and if he/she thinks Buzz has any worries, and what these may be. Encourage the child to then reflect on what they are not so good at and whether they, too, have any worries.

For older children and those for whom the worksheets are not being used, the therapist should commence a discussion about why they think they are attending the sessions and gauge an understanding of the presenting problems. For children who are not very forthcoming, it may be helpful to use the 'some children have/think/do' format by making statements and then asking if they agree with it for them. For example, 'Some children find some classes difficult at school, is that the same for you? Which do you find the most difficult? Why do you think that?' The therapist should then lead the discussion to talk about skills and challenges; 'What does the word "skill" mean? What do you think a skill is? What are your skills? How do you learn new skills? What does the word "challenge" mean? What do you think a challenge is? What kinds of things challenge you? How do you overcome them? How does that usually work out?'

Give praise for the child's effort in the session. If you choose to set Home Missions based on this worksheet we suggest asking the child to do the following:

1) Cut out a photograph or draw a picture of you and your family and stick it on the cover of your folder.
2) Decorate the worksheet by colouring in the picture and/or add to it with pictures on the theme of the story. These could be photographs or pictures in magazines or comics.

If Home Missions are set, remind parents/carers to complete the Home Missions Record Form and to place it in the folder for review at the next session.

Mid-session Break
This should be provided at an appropriate point in the session as outlined in Chapter 2.

Worksheet 2 Buzz and Self-talk

Worksheet Description

To download this worksheet, please visit the companion website

Buzz sometimes tells himself things. He does this by thinking them in his mind or saying them out loud. We call this self-talk. It helps people to do things. Buzz tells himself things like 'Come on, I can do this!' Or sometimes he thinks things quietly to himself like 'I did that really well!' Or he might imagine something, like winning a trophy. Buzz's mum calls these friendly thoughts and when Buzz has these thoughts, he feels good about himself. Sometimes Buzz finds himself having bad thoughts. Buzz's mum calls these enemy thoughts

(Continued)

> **Worksheet 2 (Continued)**
>
> and these thoughts are not helpful. Buzz tells himself things like 'I'm no good at this, I'm giving up!', 'This is stupid, I hate it!', 'Everyone is watching me, they think I look silly!' When Buzz has enemy thoughts, he feels bad about himself. Buzz has learned that he can fight enemy thoughts with friendly thoughts. This means that when he has an enemy thought, he kicks it out of his head with a friendly thought. Let's see if we can help Buzz in his mission to come up with some friendly thoughts.
>
> **Worksheet Prompts**
>
> Look at the grid. Let's match which friendly thoughts will kick out the enemy thoughts. If we get this right, then Buzz will feel better about himself.
> When might Buzz have enemy thoughts like these?
> How does Buzz feel when he has enemy thoughts?
> If Buzz kicks out the enemy thoughts with friendly thoughts, will that change how he feels?
> Do you ever have enemy thoughts about yourself?
> Tell me about that. How did that make you feel?
> Together, let's write out some friendly thoughts that you can use to kick out your own enemy thoughts.

Worksheet 2 aims to introduce the concept of self-talk and how this can influence our emotions and behaviour. It is an introductory, core worksheet because it is important that children develop the skill to self-monitor, recognize and identify negative thoughts, and then replace them with positive and motivational self-talk statements. The exercise therefore teaches the child that thoughts are related to behaviour, and invites them to consider what they say to themselves (in other words, the child's thoughts) and how these thoughts can be helpful or unhelpful. This is presented as a 'battle' between enemy thoughts and friendly thoughts, and the child is taught to identify and 'kick out' enemy thoughts by superimposing them with friendly thoughts. Hence, the child learns to replace negative thoughts that will hold them back in some way with a constructive coping mechanism that will foster positivity and motivation. The child learns how to do this in an exercise grid of thoughts (friendly and enemy) and they are asked to match the self-talk themes that 'kick out' an enemy thought with a friendly thought. These are shown in Table 3.1 (in the worksheet they are mixed up, with friendly thoughts being presented in green and enemy thoughts in red).

Read the Stimulus Sheet to the child, or, if they wish, the child can read it with you. Check that the child has understood. Next, work through the exercise grid together and match the enemy and friendly thoughts (see Table 3.1).

Table 3.1 Exercise grid of enemy and friendly thoughts.

I'm no good, I'll never do this.	This is hard but I can ask for help and keep trying.
Everyone thinks I'm stupid for getting it wrong.	It doesn't matter what other people think. I tried my best.
This is boring, I'm giving up.	If I give up now, I won't get the reward. I'll have a break then try to do a bit more.
We have fallen out and will never be friends again.	I'll ask a teacher what to do to make up with my friend again.
They called me a name. It makes me feel like hitting them.	Hitting someone won't solve the problem and I'll get into trouble, I need to calm down.
I don't want to try because I'll get it wrong.	Most people don't get things just right the first time they try.

The child could do this using different coloured crayons to link up the two types of thoughts. Then look through the grid and talk to the child about the enemy thoughts that Buzz says to himself sometimes. Ask the child to consider what situations may prompt these types of thoughts? When Buzz has these thoughts, how does he feel about himself? How does he think that other people see him? If he 'kicks out' the enemy thought with a friendly thought, how might that make a difference?

Prompt the child to draw parallels with their own life by asking if they have ever had one of the thoughts? Have they had similar thoughts? When? What were the circumstances? How did they make the child feel? Together, think of some friendly thoughts that would 'kick out' the enemy thoughts. Would this have helped the child feel better? Are there situations where the child already 'kicks out' enemy thoughts with friendly thoughts? What about other people (teachers, friends, mother, granddad), have they ever tried to 'kick out' (the child's) enemy thought with a friendly thought? Make a note on the Task Sheet of some helpful friendly thoughts that the child might want to remember. In the session, rehearse 'kicking out' enemy thoughts with these friendly thoughts. Encourage the child to visualize the enemy thoughts being kicked right out of their head by the friendly thoughts!

Give praise for the child's effort in the session. If you choose to set Home Missions based on this worksheet we suggest asking the child to do the following:

1) Decorate the worksheet by colouring in the pictures and bubbles, and/or add to them with pictures on the theme of the story. These could be photographs or pictures in magazines or comics.
2) Choose one or two friendly thoughts from the Task Sheet. Write them on a cue card and put it somewhere where you are most likely to have enemy thoughts (e.g., where you do your homework, or next to your bed at night). This will prompt you to 'kick them out'.

If Home Missions are set, remind parents/carers to complete the Home Missions Record Form and to place it in the folder for review at the next session.

Worksheet 3 Buzz Enters a Competition

Worksheet Description

To download this worksheet, please visit the companion website

There is a competition at school. The children have to think up lots of rewards they would like to have. Rewards don't have to cost money. The person who thinks up the most things will win the competition. If Buzz wins the competition he will be 'top of the class' and his name will go up on the classroom wall as the winner!

Worksheet Prompts

What is a reward?
In each big star, write a small reward that you would like or something positive you could say to yourself when you have done well and tried hard.

The aim of Worksheet 3 is to introduce the child to the concept of positive reinforcement through the development of a reward system. This is an introductory, core worksheet because this exercise will lead to the identification of a range of rewards that can be applied both within and outside of sessions, including for use in a Star Chart. This is an essential tool for increasing self-monitoring, engagement, motivation and learning a sense of achievement.

Read the Stimulus Sheet to the child, or, if they wish, they can read it with you, and check that they have understood the content. Engage the child in talking and thinking about rewards. Bear in mind that rewards can be big and small, tangible and intangible. There is nothing wrong with having large items or goals as rewards, but these need to be realistic; so if the child names a reward that is too big or expensive, direct them to consider how quickly they might get it, for example, 'Do you think this is really something that you could get as a reward? It seems very big to me and it might take a while to get there, perhaps we could think of something different and smaller?' or 'Wow, I bet you would love one of those but it is quite expensive, you would have to talk to your Mum about that! Perhaps we should also think up some other things.' Of course, a reward could be a present but presents do not have to be gifts that cost money. A reward could involve time to do something, like going to the park to play or having a bedtime story.

Rewards do not have to be given by others; the child can learn to self-reward, perhaps by writing in their folder when they think they did something well! It is important, therefore, to have a discussion about what motivates the child and how he/she can reward himself/herself for his/her efforts. If the child is very young or struggling, prepare a bag of paper cut-outs that you can use as a 'lucky dip'. Inside the bag include cut-outs of treats such as watching a DVD, eating some sweets or biscuits, getting pocket money, having a friend to tea after school, reading a book or comic, playing football or having a sleepover. Invite the child to dip into the bag and take one out, and then discuss whether this is something they would like and/or could do. The cut-outs will act as prompts to help the child think up some specific rewards that they might like to have.

Next, on the Task Sheet, ask the child to generate some rewards that they would like to receive when they have done something well and/or made a great deal of effort. It is important to reward effort, even if something is left unfinished. Ensure that the Task Sheet of rewards includes one or two positive self-statements, such as telling him/herself 'well done'.

Give praise for the child's effort in the session. If you choose to set Home Missions based on this worksheet we suggest asking the child to do the following:

1) Decorate the worksheet by colouring in the picture and stars and/or adding pictures on the theme of the story. These could be photographs or pictures in magazines or comics.
2) Read through the Task Sheet of rewards at home with a parent/carer and together extend this list to include new ideas (your parent/carer may also have reward ideas that you might like).
3) Using some of the rewards you have listed, make up a Star Chart (together with your parent/carer) and decide where best to place it (this could be in the folder, on a wall or on the fridge door). See Chapter 2 for information about how to make up a Star Chart.

If Home Missions are set, remind parents/carers to complete the Home Missions Record Form and to place it in the folder for review at the next session. (Note that if the Star Chart involves teacher input, even by simply being in the folder where a teacher might see it, ensure that you follow-up the session with a phone call to parents/carers and/or teachers to introduce the strategy and discuss how the information will be shared between them.

Feedback and Rewards

At the end of the session, appropriate rewards identified from the Worksheet 3 Reward Task should be applied (e.g., the child should engage in positive self-talk). See Chapter 2 for more information about feedback and rewards.

Working with Parents/Carers and Teachers

For information relating to this introductory module, please refer to the relevant generic sections in Chapter 2.

What Can We Do As Parents/Carers and Teachers?

For information relating to this introductory module, please refer to the section 'A Direct Resource for Parents/Carers and Teachers' in Chapter 2.

4

Attention

Attention is a cognitive skill which directs focus and helps people to make sense of their worlds by orienting attention to the stimuli which are most relevant, whilst filtering out or ignoring those which are not. Attention-control processes are varied and complex and play a role in memory, forward planning and organization. Attention has been described through a number of models and theories including Norman and Shallice (1986) and Baddeley (1986). The models propose that a central component serves to modulate attention by directing it as appropriate in the moment, much like an executive in an office who keeps the workers on-task. If this executive role is not effective then information is not attended to, competing information interferes and mistakes are made. Attention skills in the typical population develop as the brain matures and as abilities to attend and select strengthen (Posner, Rothbart, Sheese & Voelker, 2014); however, reported attention difficulties and overall symptoms related to ADHD have been found to remain mostly stable across child development, thought to be due to a person's genetic disposition (Larsson, Larsson & Lichtenstein, 2004; Rietveld, Hudziak, Bartels, van Beijsterveldt & Boomsma, 2004) and brain structure (Valera, Faraone, Murray & Seidman, 2007).

Attention can take on a 'selective' form, in which a person focuses on specific information whilst filtering other information out (e.g., reading a book whilst in a busy classroom). It can also take a 'divided' form by occurring in a situation where there may be multiple tasks which all require attending to simultaneously with efficient switching between them (e.g., playing football which involves watching the ball, predicting movements of one's own team and also of the opposition). A further form of attention is 'sustained' attention; this refers to the ability to focus attention over a longer duration and to remain alert and on-task (e.g., listening to a story). Table 4.1 summarizes these domains of attention and Figure 4.1 lists the DSM-5 (American Psychiatric Association, 2013) items of attention that are assessed in children with ADHD.

Helping Children with ADHD: A CBT Guide for Practitioners, Parents and Teachers,
First Edition. Susan Young and Jade Smith.
© 2017 John Wiley & Sons Ltd. Published 2017 by John Wiley & Sons Ltd.
Companion website: www.wiley.com/go/young/helpingadhd

This chapter will examine attention in children with ADHD and the impact this can have on their functioning in different areas of life. The assessment of attention will be discussed, followed by interventions and strategies for the children and adults around them, using a cognitive-behavioural approach.

Table 4.1 Types of attention.

Selective Attention	A child can stay on task even with distractions present.
Divided Attention	A child can manage two or more tasks at one time.
Sustained Attention	A child can stay on task for a long period of time. The attention of the child in this case does not move away from the task.
Visual Attention	A child attends to what is seen.
Auditory Attention	A child attends to what is heard.

Presentation

Children with ADHD and attention difficulties will experience functional problems in a range of areas. Indeed, for a diagnosis of ADHD these difficulties must have been present by the age of 12, have been present at least 6 months and have resulted in functional problems in a range of domains such as at school, at home and in their social life. As attention is required to effectively remember and learn, listen and observe, and respond appropriately to the environment, functional problems arising from attention difficulties are expressed in poor academic functioning, disruptive behaviour and peer and family relationship problems.

Inattention-
- Often fails to give close attention to details, or makes careless errors in school work, work or other activities
- Often fails to sustain attention in tasks or play activities
- Often appears not to listen to what is being said to him or her
- Often fails to follow through on instructions or to finish school work, chores or duties in the workplace (not because of oppositional behaviour or failure to understand instructions)
- Often impaired in organising tasks and activities
- Often avoids or strongly dislikes tasks, such as homework, that require sustained mental effort
- Often loses things necessary for certain tasks and activities, such as school assignments, pencils, books, toys or tools
- Often easily distracted by external stimuli
- Often forgetful in the course of daily activities

Figure 4.1 DSM-5 diagnostic criteria for ADHD attention symptoms.

Behavioural Functioning

Despite attention being a cognitive skill, it is most commonly expressed through the manifestation of behaviours which are observed by others. Children daydream, become distractible, lose focus and move from task to task. They intend to complete a task or instruction but become distracted by something, including their own thoughts, along the way. This may make them appear oppositional, as if they are choosing not to follow the rules, which of course may also be true at times. However, children with ADHD often do not realize that they are distracted or daydreaming and have gone off-task. To them, they have entered another world or a new activity, and one that is perhaps more appealing. It is not until later that they realize they are behind everyone else, don't understand what they should be doing or are getting things wrong. Sometimes they try to catch up by rushing through tasks and guessing, but speed and accuracy are not good friends. They usually start to feel upset, irritated and frustrated. This can be demoralizing as it is experienced as failure. They do not understand why they are being reprimanded or labelled disruptive, attention-seeking or naughty. They may feel confused and unfairly treated. All they know for certain is that they are different to their peers in some way.

Parents/carers of children with ADHD often report finding themselves constantly reminding and prompting their child to get on with what they should be doing, and find themselves and their child increasingly frustrated, tense and snappy. In parallel, children may express their frustrations at coping with these difficulties and attributions from others through irritability, oppositional behaviour, sadness and/or apathy. In school, teachers must keep a class on-task and support them through the curriculum, and it is essential that teachers learn how to support ADHD children with special educational needs and acquire positive and helpful techniques to engage the child and optimize their interest and attention. Importantly, they must steer around and avoid interactions characterized by conflict, confrontation and/or punitive sanctions.

Academic Functioning

In order to learn effectively, children must pay attention to their environment. They must listen to the teacher, read and absorb information, work cooperatively with peers and carefully observe what others are doing. Deficits in attention impact on learning and remembering, and can hinder the process of important information being taken in by the child from the environment. This means that they may pick up some information but miss other parts because they are distracted and/or they do not attend to relevant information. For example, a child may have difficulty learning maths because they are easily distracted by external factors that make them go off-task (e.g., other children chattering or activities outside the window) or by internal distractors (e.g., feeling bored, restless or daydreaming about lunch). This has nothing to do with their intellectual ability but often leads to a discrepancy between potential and performance. This can reinforce their sense of failure and lower their self-esteem, which in turn weakens their motivation to engage in the learning process. One has to pay attention in order to hold information in short-term memory. Hence, attention problems may lead to difficulty completing tasks that involve multiple steps. For example, calculating a percentage may be difficult because it requires the child to hold and process information in their minds. They may also have difficulty forming and holding a mental plan to complete multiple tasks. When listening to or reading a story, children with ADHD may lose the narrative thread and/or forget the names of key characters, meaning they may lose not only their understanding but also their interest.

Others commonly perceive this in a negative light – as being uninterested, ignoring others, uncooperative or even naughty. People around children with ADHD assume that this is something they are choosing to do (or not do). This perspective is wrong: it's more a matter of *can't* as opposed to *won't*. For children with ADHD there is always a temptation or distraction, and the grass always looks greener on the other side! This means that they often do not complete tasks. Many children with ADHD don't know what it feels like to achieve, to receive praise or feel pride, because they don't get that far – they receive a lot of negative feedback from teachers, parents/carers and peers. They feel that they are told off all the time for not getting their homework done, forgetting the things that they needed for class, talking and disturbing others and letting the team down by missing the ball, to give a few examples. They feel that they are always being compared with other children and are perceived by others in a more negative light.

Interpersonal Functioning

Attentional problems cause children to be disadvantaged in their peer interactions. To engage in a conversational thread one must sustain attention, listen to what is being said and take turns in making a valid contribution. This often involves switching between what is said and heard at the same time, as well as between different topics and speakers. Children with ADHD lose track of the conversation, they forget what has been said and may miss vital information (both verbal and non-verbal). Other children get irritated when they flit from topic to topic. They may be perceived as just wanting to talk and not listen, as being boisterous and loud, as shouting out and pushing in so other children don't get their turn and sometimes as not being very caring when they upset other children. They are perceived as not fitting in and may develop a reputation for being the 'odd' child, unpredictable and emotional, or spiteful. A child who struggles to sustain attention can be challenging to parents/carers and teachers. Parents/carers and teachers often report feeling pushed, rejected or ignored, and this can affect their relationship with the child; sometimes a negative cycle begins, which can be difficult to break.

Coping

Children cope with these problems in a number of ways, and often these are not very helpful in the long run. Being persistently compared with others and not meeting expectations is not a nice feeling, and can lead to anxiety and/or resentment. They may overcompensate by 'playing the clown' in the hope that, by making their peers laugh, they will make friends and be liked. They may cover up their problems by making out that they *won't* do something, as opposed to admitting that for some reason they *can't* do it. They may rush through work and make lots of errors just to get it over with whilst they can. They may put on a lot of bravado by pretending that they don't care about their relationships with peers, siblings, teachers and family, and therefore are not affected by them going wrong. They may pretend that they have stomach ache, for example, so they don't have to play sport (and avoid being the last one chosen for the team) or in more extreme cases, to avoid going to school at all.

Anxiety and attention are closely linked, and the more anxious a child feels the more inattentive that child will become. This can be demonstrated in an example of a child with ADHD who has been chosen to be a shepherd in the school nativity play. The child has lots of lines to learn, has to attend rehearsals and has to remember to come onto the stage at the right cue and say their lines at the right time, all of which requires good concentration. The problem is, the child keeps missing the cue and saying the lines at the wrong time. The teachers and other children become irritated in the rehearsals. The child thinks, 'I'm always getting it wrong. I'm just no good at it.' The child starts to become anxious and develops an expectation that he/she will miss the cue; what happens then is that the child forgets the lines as he/she can't think or concentrate clearly. The child's belief that he/she is no good is reinforced by the prompter having to prompt the lines, and the irritation of teachers and peers. In turn the problems get worse, the child misses more lines, becomes flustered, feels upset and tries not to cry. Things get worse and worse for the child due to becoming increasingly anxious and caught up in a spiral of anxiety. A child who already struggles to maintain attention will find it more difficult when experiencing anxiety, as systems in the brain are attempting to scan for threat stimuli as well as all the other aspects of the environment. In this case, the threat stimuli may be irritation on the teachers' faces and/or a negative reaction from the other children in the play.

Assessment

International guidance on the assessment and treatment of ADHD recommends that a comprehensive assessment procedure is carried out by trained and qualified healthcare practitioners in order to assess ADHD (Sexias, Weiss & Müller, 2012). This often includes a multi-method assessment involving psychometric questionnaires, a clinical interview and observation of the child to assess their difficulties and behaviour in different contexts and settings. It is preferable to obtain multiple perspectives from different people involved in the child's care (including that of the child if possible) and often involves multi-agency liaison. It is important to fully understand the nature and complexity of the child's difficulties across their development, the historic, environmental and psychosocial factors, the child's strengths and weaknesses and the support that it currently receives, in order that a care plan is developed with appropriate interventions that are likely to succeed. In doing this, it is important to be mindful of the comorbid and social problems experienced not only by the child but that may also be present within the family.

Measures

There are many methods for assessing attention in ADHD children, the most commonly used include the Conners' Rating Scales 3rd edition (Conners, 2008) for age six years and over, and the Strengths and Difficulties Questionnaire (SDQ; Goodman, 1997) for age two and upwards. These compare the frequency of a child's perceived functioning with norms obtained from the general population for their age and gender. It is recommended that the perspectives of different raters are obtained in order to gain a broad range of perspectives of the child's functioning across different settings. For example, a parent/carer and teacher may complete the questionnaires for behaviour at home and school. Some measures also include a child version for the young person to self-rate; however, their use depends on the child's reading ability and level of insight. Ratings are also helpful to obtain a baseline assessment of perceived functioning, which is then repeated after intervention to evaluate efficacy at outcome. It is recommended that an adult provide support to children completing self-reported questionnaires. Children with ADHD may misread questions, miss out answers, respond impulsively and/or miscommunicate the rating. However, it is essential that responses not be influenced by leading questions. Children who struggle with reading should always have items read out to them. As for many measures, ratings may be subject to bias and must be interpreted cautiously by a trained practitioner.

Aside from questionnaire based assessments, there are a number of objective psychometric tests that measure attention and related difficulties in children with ADHD, including: the Test of Everyday Attention for Children (TEA-Ch; Manly, Robertson, Anderson & Nimmo-Smith, 1998) for ages six to 16 years; the Brief Rating Inventory of Executive Functioning for five to 18 years (BRIEF; Gioia, Isquith, Guy, & Kenworthy, 2000); the Developmental NEuroPSYchological Assessment (NEPSY-II; Korkman, Kirk & Kemp, 2007) for 3–16 years; and the Behavioural Assessment of Dysexecutive Syndrome in

Children (BADS-C; Emslie, Wilson, Burden, Nimmo-Smith & Wilson, 2003) for 8–16 years. TEA-Ch offers a measurement of the child's attention as rated by their performance on a series of tasks requiring the use of sustained, selected and divided attention. The benefit of children completing performance-based assessments is that it provides more concrete evidence of ability rather than subjective opinion; however, due to the complex nature of skills, they can never be 100% ecologically valid. Normed against children of the same age or ability, these tests can determine whether the child has specific and/or broader functional problems than their peers. Continuous performance tests can be particularly helpful as they assess the ability to sustain attention and related skills such as response inhibition and vigilance; the *Conners' Continuous Performance Test* 3rd Edition (Conners, 2014) is an example of one such performance test.

Clinical Interview

To obtain richer and more descriptive information about the child, it is essential that questionnaire screens and psychometric assessments be supplemented with clinical interviews with those who know the child best. It is good practice for this to be done with both parents/carers and teachers to consider the different settings and contexts in which the child interacts. The interview should comprehensively explore the details of a child's difficulties and associated impairments. Children who are able should also be asked for their own feedback about the struggles they perceive themselves to have, the impact they have on the child's life and how the child copes with them.

Thoughts

It will be helpful to talk to the child about how thoughts may be represented as words or pictures in his/her mind. It can be difficult for younger children to identify and articulate what goes through their mind, and asking whether the child can 'follow' his/her thoughts and ideas or whether they seem to quickly go 'in and out' of his/her mind will assist the therapist. You can explain, 'Sometimes we can think about things, but other times thoughts pop into our minds and disappear quickly. Does that happen to you? Can you tell me about that or give me an example?' Ask the child to describe what it is like for them and, if possible, get some specific examples. 'Can you tell me about that. Did it happen today in class? What were you doing at the time?' This will indicate whether the child can follow their thoughts or experiences, racing or fleeting thoughts that flash in and out of their mind, and/or whether the child becomes distracted by them. For example check with the child, 'So you had thoughts like this when you were doing maths in class. Could you focus on the question until you got to the end? Were you distracted by other thoughts in your mind? What were these thoughts? Did anything else distract you? What about things going on in the room?' Ask the child about the feedback they have received from others, such as 'My teacher says that I don't pay attention in class. My mummy tells me off for not listening.' Older children in particular may be able to link this feedback to their perceived effort and motivation.

Feelings and Physiology

When conducting assessments, the therapist needs to consider differential formulations and contributing factors, which may worsen the child's presentation. Poor attentional control may not relate solely to ADHD but can be present for other reasons, such as anxiety. Do you know if the child is anxious or worried? This can increase restlessness and muscle tension. It may also cause distressing ruminations, a difficulty sustaining focus on the task at hand, and distractibility. This may be associated with a change in medication regime. Furthermore when feeling tired or fatigued, the child will find it difficult to settle; the child is more likely to have poor listening skills and find it hard to sustain attention.

Behaviours

When interviewing parents/carers and/or teachers it is very important to grasp the bigger picture, how distractibility or inattention manifests in the child's behaviour, their ability to complete tasks and learn what it is like to have a sense of achievement. Ask them to describe how the child presents when he/she is off-task, distracted or not appearing to listen or pay attention. This will help to better understand what is going on for the child at such times, whether there are specific triggers for going off-task, whether the child tends to move from task to task, appears bored or seems to be daydreaming, and whether the child is distracted by other activities and/or conversations. It is important to ascertain whether there are activities on which the child can focus well. These may be specific activities of great interest to the child, often fast moving activities that have persistent stimuli and rewards (such as computer games). Children may not have the self-awareness to understand this themselves and it is important for the child to receive positive feedback that he/she has the ability to focus well sometimes, but struggles on other occasions. It may also provide insight into goals of treatment, how the child can be best supported and by whom.

Direct observation to record the child's behaviour and interactions can also be helpful, however, it is important to bear in mind that the presence of an observer will impact on the environment, with the child and his/her peers acting artificially (e.g., by putting on their 'best behaviour'). Ideally, observations would be completed across contexts. A classroom observation, for example, should include recording how often the child is on-/off-task, whether they appear to miss information, what helps to redirect their attention, and how this impacts on their functioning in the environment.

Behaviour Diary

Those caring for the child and the child him/herself can also keep diaries that record frequency and severity of specific difficulties. This can be a great way to capture chaotic situations, which may not have been reported. It involves recording the problem behaviour (e.g., going off-task, what task, when it happened, where it happened, what else was going on at the time), antecedents to the behaviour (what was the lead-up to that behaviour and who was involved) and the consequences of the behaviour (what was the result of the behaviour and who was involved). This record is also known as an 'ABC chart' and functional analysis of the data obtained can give rise to patterns of problem behaviours and antecedent chains. This may inform the practitioner as to what interventions could be tried out and when these may best be applied. The Behaviour Diary should continue to be used after intervention in order to gain information about the success of the treatment. An example of a Behaviour Diary is given in Table 4.2.

Table 4.2 Example of a completed Behaviour Diary for attention.

Day/Time	Antecedent (What was happening just before the behaviour? Who was there? What happened earlier in the day that may be relevant?)	Behaviour (What did you observe? Describe the duration and severity.)	Consequence (What happened next? What was the result?)
Monday 4pm	Joe came home from school. I said it was time to do homework before going out to play.	Joe sat at the kitchen table and after 20 minutes I checked and he had only written the title (not doing the task). He had put the TV on (distracted). Joe got annoyed when I told him to get on with it. He pushed it on the floor (avoiding).	I picked it up and told Joe I would sit with him. I ended up doing more of it than he did. He went out to play when it was done.
Tuesday 4pm	Joe was getting changed after school. He knew he then had to do his maths homework.	Joe said it was too difficult. He asked me to help him. He then did it for 10 minutes and then got up to go and play (avoiding, distracted).	I took Joe's toys off him and said he couldn't have them back until he finished the homework.

This example is a record of a boy called Joe who has ADHD. His Mum completed the Behaviour Diary for a week when he was doing his homework after school. By looking at the record it became clear that Joe was struggling with sustaining his attention and this was made worse when the tasks were complex and when there were distractions in the environment.

CBT Interventions for Attention

If the therapist is treating younger children and/or the worksheets are being used as a basis for treatment, the first session should always commence with Worksheets 1, 2 and 3 to introduce the child to Buzz and his family (Worksheet 1), introduce positive self-talk (Worksheet 2) and identify a reward system (Worksheet 3). The reward and self-talk strategies are applied in the session, at home and/or at school. See Chapter 3 for a suggested outline of how to plan and conduct the introductory session. All the Worksheets are available on the companion website www.wiley.com/go/young/helpingadhd resource page.

The aims of the interventions and worksheets in the attention session(s) are to introduce children to the concept of attention and help them develop skills that will assist them to manage distractions and improve their concentration. The therapist will achieve this by setting an agenda, reviewing Home Missions done between sessions in the folder, working through new worksheets (or just the strategies for older children) and setting new Home Missions. If required, a mid-session break can be offered halfway through the session; this may be particularly important for younger children. Chapter 2 provides generic information on the structure and content of sessions (irrespective of topic); supplementary information is included within this chapter that specifically relates to the delivery of the attention session(s).

Agenda

At the beginning of the session, show the child the written agenda (see Figure 4.2) that you have prepared prior to the session and go through it, verbally linking the themes and Worksheets that you will introduce during the session. For the attention module, introduce Worksheets 4, 5 and 6 by saying:

> Buzz doesn't always pay attention. Sometimes he finds it hard. This means that he gets into trouble sometimes at school and at home. Today we are going to play a game called 'Spot the Difference'. Buzz isn't very good at this game! Let's see how you do it. Then we are going to talk about what happens when Buzz completes a Scout Badge. After that, we will have a short break and you can colour in the worksheets using these crayons. After the break we are going to look at another worksheet and talk about what happens when Buzz has to do his homework.

Attention | 55

> *Agenda*
>
> *Folder Review*
>
> *Spot the Difference [Worksheet 4]*
>
> *Buzz gets his Cycling Badge [Worksheet 5]*
>
> *Break*
>
> *Buzz does his Homework [Worksheet 6]*
>
> *Home Missions*

Figure 4.2 Example agenda for attention session(s).

Folder Review

When reviewing the folder with the child, aside from checking whether the Home Missions are completed, take the opportunity to revise important information and/or concepts, as this will help the child to consolidate the learning points and/or newly acquired skills. Ensure that you make time to look at the illustrations, colourings, paintings, magazine cuttings and/or photographs that the child has added to the folder. Discuss them and try to relate these to discussions about Buzz and his family and/or topics or strategies that have been covered. Aside from acting as a revision prompt, this will also act as a reward system for the child. Praise should be given verbally, but you can also reward by adding stickers, handwritten notes or smiley faces. If Home Missions were set then you should review their Home Missions Record Form for comments and feedback from parents/carers and discuss this with the child.

Worksheet 4 Spot the Difference

Worksheet Description

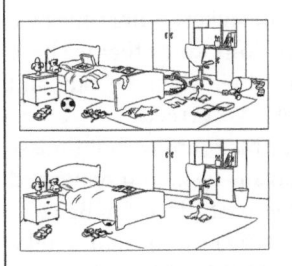

To download this worksheet, please visit the companion website

Every Friday Buzz has to tidy his bedroom. He's not very good at tidying up as he misses things. He's not as good as his Mum at finding what needs to be tidied away.

Let's compare these two pictures to see what's been put away, we'll look first at the 'before' picture and then at the 'after' picture. Put a circle around items in the first picture that he put away.

(Continued)

> **Worksheet 4 (Continued)**
>
> **Worksheet Prompts**
>
> There were ten items that Buzz had put away. Did you find them all?
> Is there anything else Buzz could have put away?
> Together let's write out some ideas of things Buzz can do to help him tidy his room.
> Tell me about what happens if you have to tidy your room at home.
> Now let's look at the things you thought would help Buzz and circle the ones that might also help you.

Worksheet 4 aims to illustrate to the child in a fun and practical way how attention deficits may hamper their performance in daily activities. Attention skills, such as scanning, can be practised. It also gives an opportunity for reflection on a task requiring skills in sustained, selective and visual attention.

The Stimulus Sheet presents two drawings of Buzz's bedroom, each slightly different to the other. The child is told that every Friday Buzz must tidy his bedroom, but he is not very good at doing this as he misses things. The task is for the child to compare two pictures, one before Buzz has tidied up and one after Buzz has tidied up, and identify how many differences they can find. Do not tell the child that there are ten differences in total. Read the story to the child and check they are listening and have understood. First, the therapist asks the child to circle as many items as he/she can find that Buzz has tidied away in 30 seconds. Then, after the 30 seconds are up, the therapist asks the child to take their time and compare the pictures to see if they can see any more. Almost certainly the child will have missed some of the differences.

This can lead to a discussion about 'more haste less speed' because when you rush things you may miss out information. Did the child make any mistakes by circling items that were not different? Did the child do this and then realize the mistake and correct themselves? In this case put a cross through the circle and point out when you rush things you can also make mistakes. Sometimes we know that we have made a mistake and sometimes we don't know that we have made a mistake. The important thing is to take our time, when we can, and check through work when it is finished to ensure that it is correct.

Talk to the child about what might help Buzz to tidy his room without missing things next time and what might help him to stay on-task. You may need to prompt the child by asking, 'Where would be the best place for Buzz to stand if he needs to see his whole bedroom?' 'Would it be best for him to take it slow or rush through it?' 'What might happen if the TV is on at the same time?' 'Could an adult help Buzz stay focused?' and, 'How might making a "Remember Notice" help?' Fill out the Task Sheet with the ideas generated (e.g., making a 'Remember Notice' that prompts them to look for things that should be put in a drawer, things that can be thrown away, things that belong in the dirty linen bin, kitchen, bathroom, etc.; asking someone else to help; checking nothing has been missed by standing in the middle of the room and walking in a circle). Follow up with a discussion about how the child might apply some strategies to complete a similar task him/herself. Ask the child to circle the ones they think would be most helpful to him/her and add some new ones if they are more appropriate to the child's experiences and circumstances. Role-play the suggestions, where possible; for example, the therapist could ask the child to look around the therapy room and make some suggestions about what could be tidied away and where.

Give praise for the child's effort in the session. If you choose to set Home Missions based on this worksheet we suggest asking the child to do the following:

1) Decorate the Worksheet by colouring in the pictures and thought bubbles, and/or add to them with pictures on the theme of the story. These could be photographs or pictures in magazines or comics.
2) Make a cue card that states 'Check my work' and stick it to the wall where you do your school homework to remind you to check through everything before you finish. You could also stick a similar note in your pencil case. The note should make it bright and colourful.
3) With your parent/carer, cut out a photograph or drawing of a treat that you would hope to get when you have finished and checked your homework and pin this to the wall as well. You can swap the picture for the treat when it's time.
4) Look at the list of things you decided in the session that would help Buzz to tidy his own bedroom. Can you try to do this at home?

If Home Missions are set, remind parents/carers to complete the Home Missions Record Form and to place it in the folder for review at the next session.

Worksheet 5 Buzz Gets his Cycling Badge

Worksheet Description

To download this worksheet, please visit the companion website

Buzz has won some badges at Scouts. He has got an Athletics Badge, a Participation Badge and a Membership Award. Today Buzz is trying to get his Cycling Badge. For this he has to complete several tasks, one of which is to remove a wheel from a bike, then find and repair a puncture. He has some instructions written down to help him. Buzz's Mum

(Continued)

Worksheet 5 (Continued)

is there to watch him. She is sitting on a bench nearby and whenever he looks up she waves at him. There are lots of other children cycling and playing around. They are making lots of noise and having fun. The Scout Leader is also nearby and he comes up to Buzz every so often to check Buzz is doing okay. Buzz is very happy as he fixed the puncture and got his Cycling Badge!

Worksheet Prompts

Buzz's Scout Leader told him he must focus on the task. Do you know what focus means?

What kind of things might have distracted Buzz and made it harder for him to focus on the task? Is there anything that made it easier?

Together let's write out some ideas of things Buzz can do to help him concentrate on the task.

Tell me about a time when there was a lot going on whilst you were trying to do an activity and you were distracted (maybe there was a time at school or when you were doing your homework at home). What happened?

Now let's look at the things you thought would help Buzz and circle the ones that might also help you.

Worksheet 5 introduces the concepts of focus and distraction. It provides an opportunity for reflection on how an attention deficit may influence performance. The child is guided to identify strategies that will help Buzz achieve the task and to associate achievement with rule setting and self-regulation.

In the story, Buzz has to complete some tasks successfully to get his Scout Cycling Badge. He needs to follow a set of instructions and concentrate on what he has to do. It's not easy and he is aware that his Mum is watching him and other children are making a noise which is distracting him.

Read the Stimulus Sheet to the child, or, if they wish, they can read it to you. Answer any questions they might have. Check that the child understood the story and was paying attention. You could do this by asking them to summarize the story or asking a specific question such as, 'What is Buzz hoping to do?' or 'What are the other children doing?' 'Scouts' can be explained as 'a group for boys where they learn skills together and do activities'. Go through the discussion points that will help the child to reflect on the situation. These aim to help the child to think about distractions in the environment, their impact on performance and methods that will help them stay focused. If the child seems unclear about the meaning of 'distraction' explain that, 'Distractions are things going on around you that take your attention away from what you should be doing. You can be distracted by things that you see and things that you hear.'

Guide the discussion by clarifying the child's thinking with prompts such as, 'So you think that Buzz might be distracted by his Mum watching, are there other things that might be distractions?' Note whether the child identifies distractions of a particular modality (e.g., visual or auditory) as this may reflect the child's own experience.

Talk to the child about what Buzz might do to help him concentrate on the task. Describe concentration as, 'focusing on the important things around you'. Some ideas are to picture a visual image of the Cycling Badge, work through the instructions step by step, try not to look up and around him or ask the Scout Leader if he can go somewhere quieter instead. At the end of this conversation, fill in the Task Sheet with the ideas generated.

Move the conversation to focus on the child's own experiences of completing activities and/or performing when there were a lot of distractors present. You can prompt the child to think about a place, for example at home or at the shops, or a time when he/she had to do a task, such as a class project, playing sport or doing homework. Ask, 'What was it you had to do? What made this difficult? Were there distractions you could see or hear? Were other people distracting?' Return to the list of ideas on the Task Sheet that the child thought might help Buzz and ask the child to circle the ones they think would be most helpful to them; add some new ones if they are more appropriate to the child's experiences and circumstances.

Role-play the suggestions, where possible; for example, the child could role-play asking someone to be quiet. In this role-play the child should state calmly what he/she would like and why (e.g., 'Please could you be quiet for the next half an hour while I finish my homework'). The therapist should give feedback and rehearse the interaction until the child is confident in its delivery.

Give praise for the child's effort in the session. If you choose to set Home Missions based on this Worksheet we suggest asking the child to do the following:

1) Decorate the Worksheet by colouring in the pictures and thought bubbles, and/or add to them with pictures on the theme of the story. These could be photographs or pictures in magazines or comics.
2) Make a 'Do Not Disturb' notice to put on the door when they are doing their homework or other tasks that they have to concentrate on. Make it bright and colourful so everyone sees it!
3) Make up a 'Remember Notice' and place this where you have to concentrate (e.g., where you do their homework) or somewhere that you will be able to regularly look at it (e.g., in the front of your 'Home School Diary'). The 'Remember Notice' should list the ideas that you came up with in the session that will help you with concentrating, such as:
   - Is it noisy? Can I move somewhere quieter?
   - Ask for the TV or music to be turned down.

- Don't look around, keep looking at what I have to do.
- Take the first step, then take the next step.
- Tell myself 'I can do this', 'Keep calm', 'Focus'.
- If I don't understand, ask for help.

If Home Missions are set, remind parents/carers to complete the Home Missions Record Form and place it in the folder for review at the next session.

Mid-session Break

This should be provided at an appropriate point in the session as outlined in Chapter 2.

Worksheet 6 Buzz does his Homework

Worksheet Description

Buzz is trying to concentrate on his homework. He is finding it hard to settle down and work quietly because lots of thoughts are whizzing through his mind.

Worksheet Prompts

Colour the friendly thoughts in Green. These are the ones that you think might help Buzz to concentrate.

Colour the enemy thoughts in Red. These are the ones that you think make it harder for Buzz to concentrate.

To download this worksheet, please visit the companion website

---

Worksheet 6 introduces the child to the concept of self-talk and encourages the child to identify how positive self-talk can be helpful and negative self-talk can be unhelpful.

Start by reading the Stimulus Sheet to the child, or, if they wish, they can read it with you. Read through each thought on the task sheet and check the child has understood what each one means. You can see if the child understands the impact of helpful and unhelpful thoughts (referred to as friendly and enemy thoughts); this also links and reinforces the skills they learnt in Worksheet 2. For example, 'What might Buzz end up doing if he thinks playing the Xbox is more fun than doing his work?' ... 'I think so too, he might get distracted.' 'What would be the consequence of that?' 'Do you think he would get his work done?' Ask him/her to complete the task, 'I have brought a red and a green crayon with me so that together we can colour the helpful thoughts in green and the unhelpful thoughts in red'.

Give praise for the child's effort in the session. If you choose to set Home Missions based on this worksheet we suggest asking the child to do the following:

1) Decorate the Worksheet by colouring in the pictures and thought bubbles, and/or add to them with pictures on the theme of the story. These could be photographs or pictures in magazines or comics.
2) Take the Worksheet home and stick up the helpful green self-talk statements.

If Home Missions are set, remind parents/carers to complete the Home Missions Record Form and to place it in the folder for review at the next session.

Feedback and Rewards

At the end of the session, appropriate rewards identified from the Worksheet 3 Reward Task should be applied (e.g., the child should engage in positive self-talk). See Chapter 2 for more information about feedback and rewards.

Working with Parents/Carers

This section presents strategies that parents/carers can apply to support the child to improve their attention control. We all experience situations when you don't hear what someone says because you are concentrating on watching something, or you have difficulty taking in something you are reading because there is a lot of noise and activity around you.

It is important to be realistic about what can be achieved. It can be just as helpful to learn strategies to cope better with a child's behaviour as to learn strategies to improve the behaviour itself. In this section we discuss a method of monitoring behaviour using a Behaviour Diary and cognitive-behavioural strategies to support parents/carers to ensure they gain the child's focus, break down information into manageable chunks and check it has been understood, reduce distractions in the environment and sustain attention. When working with parents/carers, the therapist should introduce suggested techniques and strategies; practise and rehearse them in role-plays during the sessions if appropriate (without the child present). Parents/carers should report back to the therapist on how they managed at home. In future sessions, it is important to troubleshoot any obstacles and/or difficulties that arise by thinking of ways to adapt the techniques or strategies so they are successful in helping the child.

A key strategy for changing behaviour and improving cognitive skills is to find motivators to promote success. Children with ADHD tend to respond better to immediate rewards as they have a difficulty with delayed gratification for longer-term rewards (even if these are bigger and better). Methods to motivate success (including the use of a Star Chart) and other topics that are generic to working with parents/carers are described in Chapter 2. Supplementary information that specifically relates to the delivery of the attention session(s) is outlined in this chapter.

Behaviour Diary

In order to home in on specific situations in which the child struggles with their attention, ask parents/carers to complete a Behaviour Diary (described earlier in this chapter) to monitor behaviour. Discuss the information recorded in the diary with parents/carers to gain further insight and understanding about the type of behaviour, its triggers and when it is most likely to present. Over time patterns often emerge that may explain the causes of some behaviours. This can be helpful in determining which interventions may be best introduced to address the problem.

Chunk Information

Attention and memory are related skills, and children who struggle with auditory attention often forget the things they hear. This can cause frustration for both children and parents/carers. Encourage parents/carers to use shorter and simpler pieces of information with their children. A good rule of thumb is to chunk information into no more than two or three things at a time and monitor how their child copes with that. For example, instructing the child to, 'Go upstairs, get ready for school, brush your teeth, then have your breakfast before you need to leave at 7.30am' is likely to be far too much information, especially for younger children. It would be better to say, 'Go upstairs and get dressed' and then when this is complete tell the child to 'Go downstairs and have your breakfast.' With practice, and by observing the outcome, the parent/carer will soon be able to identify what works best for their child.

Use the Child's Name

It helps to add the child's name when talking to them as this directs their attention to the fact that they are being spoken to and need to pay attention. For example, 'What do you think of that idea, Joe?' or 'Joe, I want you to pick up those clothes.' It also serves to emphasize when the parent/carer wishes to communicate important information, such as, 'Joe, I am going to say something important, I need you to listen.'

Summarizing and Concept Checking

There can be uncertainty about whether a child has been fully listening to what has been said or whether the child has grasped the point. This can be overcome by summarizing the information at the end, followed by the parent/carer checking that the child has understood the concept. For example, 'I'm going to give you some instructions, so listen carefully Joe. Firstly put in the flour and then add the egg. OK? Flour first, then the egg. So what do you need to do first? Yes that's right, and then what comes next?' Applying the summarizing and concept checking technique can be role-played with the parents/carers until this comes naturally to them.

Change the Environment

Home can be full of noisy distractions, including Xbox games, music, washing machines, pets, siblings, traffic, neighbours and arguments. Parents/carers need to do two things: firstly, they need to identify the various sources of noise in the house; and, secondly, they need to plan how to minimize excessive noise and/or stimulation at certain times, such as when the child needs to do homework or when winding down for bedtime.

To identify potential distractions, encourage parents/carers to sit quietly and observe what is going on around the child at certain times of day. They could also make a recording on their mobile phone or by setting up a video camera in the corner of a room. Ask them to record what they notice and bring it back to discuss. Then, work out a plan together than can be tried out at home. This may involve: making house rules as to when family members cannot play music or Xbox, or watch TV; identifying a quiet room where homework is to be completed; putting up a 'Do Not Disturb' sign; asking other family members to take the dog for a walk; and/or changing the household routine so noisy chores are done at different times. They should monitor the changes that they make and evaluate success. Note that for some children with ADHD, low-level background noise can be helpful in facilitating concentration because it drowns out other unexpected noise (which is more disruptive against a background of silence). Headphones work best for some children, even in the classroom. In this case, the low-level noise introduced should be unstimulating and consistent, such as quiet music.

Aside from being distracted by a noisy environment, an overload of visual information or activity can also overwhelm a child who is already struggling to pay attention to the right things at the right time. It helps for homework, eating dinner and other activities that require concentration to be attempted in a low-stimulation environment. This can be achieved, for example, by closing the door so the child is not distracted by family members moving between rooms and/or doing other activities. Ensuring a chair is not facing a window or door will also be helpful, as will the removal of potential sources of distraction from the vicinity (e.g., mobile phones, comics).

Visual Cues and Prompts

Visual cues and prompts can be helpful in focusing attention, such as putting up 'Remember Notices' and 'Reward Signs' (the latter being a visual picture or drawing of the reward chosen for completing the task). These visual prompts will help to motivate the child to stay on-task. In everyday life, visual prompts are commonly used to guide our attention in busy environments towards what is important, for example traffic lights, instructions at cash points, reminders to look before crossing roads and in what direction to look, and ladies/men's signs on bathroom doors. When they go out, parents/carers should point out these visual cues and prompts to the child as this will normalize their use. Next, parents/carers should work with the child to think up visual cues and prompts that could be placed in the home. These may cover a range of tasks and situations and be simple instructions or reminders such as 'School bag', 'Flush the chain', 'Get started' or more complex 'Remember Notices' for bathroom routines and bedroom tidying. The cues and prompts must stand out from the background in some way (e.g., bright paper, colourful pictures or illustrations, big and colourful fonts).

Rewards and Praise

A key strategy for increasing a child's ability to sustain attention over time is to find motivators to promote vigilance. It is especially important to use reward techniques and give frequent feedback and praise, as this will help the child to stay engaged and motivated to complete a task to the best of their ability. See Chapter 2 for more details.

Goals, Steps and Check-points

Children with ADHD are better at coping with shorter tasks than longer ones, although even short tasks may seem too demanding for a child with severe ADHD symptoms, especially if the task is perceived as boring. Writing tasks and complex problems that require a lot of thinking can be particularly daunting, especially if the child feels there will be a negative consequence for failing. In order to foster empathy with the child's difficulty, ask the parent/carer to recall a time when they had a big task to do and were feeling tired. Perhaps they felt at a loss to know where to start. What helped them to make it achievable? Did they ask for help? Did they leave it until the next day? What about a task that couldn't be left until the next day? Did they make a start? Did they do a bit at a time?

A strategy to help a child feel they can manage tasks of longer duration is for parents/carers to talk to the child and define the goal and then break it down into a list of smaller steps. Add a check-point next to each step. For example, a writing task can be broken into 10-minute phases or themed sections; tidying up can be broken up into specific areas. The aim is to sustain their attention in smaller phases. The parent/carer should review the stages/steps attempted and where they have been achieved add a check mark next to the check-point (and perhaps a reward, such as a sticker or smiley face). With practice the child should be encouraged to apply the strategy unaided. Older children will be better able to apply the self-monitoring check-point and self-reward processes than younger children.

Self-talk

This is an internal strategy used to direct our thinking. Talk to parents/carers about the 'inner voice' and thoughts; most parents/carers will recognize that they have an on-going internal dialogue that directs their actions and supports a self-monitoring process. Ask parents/carers to help the child to think up self-motivating statements that will help them to stay on track, such as, 'I can do this', 'Stay calm' or 'I'm nearly at the next check-point and can take a break.' It is very important that these statements are identified by the child, but parents/carers should remind the child to apply self-talk (friendly thoughts), especially if they notice that the child is becoming restless, irritable or distressed.

What Can We Do As Parents/Carers?

Table 4.3 outlines a suggested approach, including a list of strategies that can be implemented at home. To maximize the effect of strategies, it is helpful to discuss these with your child's teacher so they may be implemented at both home and school (wherever possible). Lots of parents/carers and teachers find that using a 'Home School Diary' is an efficient way to share information (see Chapter 2).

Aside from reading the current chapter, we suggest that parents/carers read Chapter 2 which provides important background information about the delivery of the Young–Smith Programme. For younger children, we suggest that parents/carers set aside some time to sit down with the child (around 45–60 minutes) and work through the worksheets recommended for each topic. Guidance is found in the 'CBT Interventions' section in each chapter on how to do this. The worksheets introducing Buzz and his family are outlined in Chapter 3. All the materials (worksheets and Home Missions Record Form) are available for downloading from the companion website www.wiley.com/go/young/helpingadhd. For older children (i.e., 12 years-plus), you can dispense with the Buzz worksheets if necessary and instead introduce the child directly to the topic, and, using the discussion prompts on the worksheets, apply this to the child's experience and discuss suggested strategies. Set and support the child to complete suggested Home Missions. Don't forget to give frequent feedback and praise. Make a Star Chart (see Chapter 2), put it in a prominent place and start to use it on a daily basis.

Table 4.3 Home strategies for attention.

Chunk information
- Chunk information into two or three things at a time.
- Use bullet points and lists as much as possible.

Use the child's name
- Say your child's name before giving instructions.

Summarizing and concept checking
- Ask your child to repeat back instructions and/or information.
- Write things down simply.

Change the environment
- Change routines (e.g., using the washing machine) so that there is less going on when your child does homework.
- Make a dedicated plain space (without distractors such as TV or posters) where your child can do homework.
- Make up a 'Do Not Disturb' sign with them. Use it!
- Switch off TV, phones and music when the child is doing homework.
- Make sure other people and pets stay away; this may include you, unless you are needed to help prompt or direct them.

Visual cues and prompts
- Use bright paper or felt tip pens with them to make 'Remember Notices' of things they need to focus on and decide together where to put them up.

Goals, steps and check-points
- Set specific goals for your child to help them focus on the task and sustain attention.
- Break down large tasks/goals that seem overwhelming into smaller steps, for example, writing a story may become five paragraphs or 30 minutes maths homework may become three sets of five questions.
- Give praise after each step or check-point.

Self-talk
- Prompt your child to identify self-motivating statements (friendly thoughts) that will help them stay on task, and prompt the use of these.

Take breaks
- If your child is struggling, suggest they take a short break and then return to the task.
- Encourage your child to monitor this themselves by prompting *'How do you think you are doing?' 'How is your concentration?' 'Do you think you need a quick break?'*

Working with Teachers and Schools

The following section includes strategies for increasing auditory, visual and sustained attention. The school environment is full of distractions. We have all experienced situations when you do not hear what someone says because you are concentrating on watching something, or you have difficulty taking in something you are reading because there is a lot of noise and activity around you. Teachers need to think carefully about how to support young people to pay attention in class. It is important to be realistic about what can be achieved. It can be just as helpful to learn strategies to cope better with a child's behaviour as to learn strategies to improve the behaviour itself. In this section we discuss cognitive-behavioural strategies to support teachers to ensure they gain the child's focus, break down information into manageable chunks and check this has been understood, reduce distractions in the environment and sustain attention.

Teachers and schools will already have structures in place to support many of the interventions introduced in the Young–Smith Programme. It will be useful to link up parents/carers and teachers to encourage an integrated strategy and share success. It is important to troubleshoot any obstacles and/or difficulties that arise by thinking of ways to adapt the techniques or strategies so they are successful in helping the child. Methods to motivate success and other topics that are generic to working with teachers and schools are described in Chapter 2, where there is also supplementary information that specifically relates to the delivery of the attention session(s).

Chunk Information

Attention and memory are related skills, and children who struggle with auditory attention often forget the things they hear. This may cause frustration not only to children, but also to teachers, who may assume the child is being naughty, lazy or oppositional. Encourage teachers to use shorter and simpler phrases, chunking information into no more than two or three things at a time, and monitor how the child copes with that. For example, 'Pick up those papers on the floor, wash the paint brushes and put the paints back in the drawer, then hang up your overalls when you leave the classroom' is likely to be far too much information, especially for younger children with ADHD. It would be better to say 'Pick up the papers on the floor,' then when this is complete tell the child 'Wash the paint brushes and put the paints back in the drawer,' and finally 'Hang up your overalls when you leave.' With practice, and by observing the outcome, the teacher will soon be able to identify what works best for the child.

Use the Child's Name

It helps to add the child's name when talking to them as this directs their attention to the fact that they are being spoken to and need to pay attention. For example, 'What do you think of that idea, Joe?' or 'Joe, I want you to pick up those clothes.' It also serves to emphasize when the teacher wishes to communicate important information, such as, 'Joe, I am going to say something important, I need you to listen.' This technique is commonly used in schools but it may help to inform teachers that the approach can be particularly helpful for children with ADHD.

Summarizing and Concept Checking

There can be uncertainty about whether a child has been fully listening to what has been said and whether the child has grasped the point. This can be overcome by summarizing the information at the end, followed by the teacher (or teaching assistant) checking that the child has understood the concept. For example:

> I'm going to give you some instructions, so listen carefully Joe. You are going to write about our school trip to the farm. I want you to describe the farm and who works there, and the animals you saw. I want you to tell me what you liked best about the day. So tell me what I want you to do' ... 'Yes that's right ... and what else?' 'What comes next?'

This may involve the teacher working with the child to devise a commonly used short script (e.g., 'Could you say that again please?'). If the task involves lengthy instructions, then these should be given in written format. It is useful for summaries of important information to be presented in a bullet point format on the class whiteboard.

Ask for Help or Clarification

Teachers should reassure the child that it is okay for him/her to ask for help and/or clarification if they have missed some information or do not understand what they should be doing. This is better than guessing and getting it wrong. One must be mindful, however, that a child may be reluctant to speak up for fear of getting in trouble, looking silly, interrupting or drawing attention to themselves. In cases where the child is highly sensitive and/or unlikely to communicate that they don't understand, a code could be set up with the child, for example pulling his/her earlobe to subtly indicate a need for help. In order to prevent this being, or becoming, attention-seeking behaviour, however, the teacher should tell the child that they will return to help them at the next convenient moment rather than responding immediately.

Verbal Prompts

Whether provided by teaching assistants or teachers, giving prompts will help an ADHD child remember what they have to do and stay on-task to do it. Prompts can be used to self-monitor, 'What did the teacher ask you to do?', to direct, 'Listen carefully,' and to repeat information when needed, 'The teacher said page 42.'

Visual Cues and Prompts

Instructions for tasks and/or assignments should be displayed prominently as an aide memoire. 'Remember Notices' can be displayed in relevant places, such as a sign in the cloakroom to say 'Hang coats on the peg,' or a note on the door saying 'Take home sports kit.' These can be in words or pictures. They can also be used to prompt school routines.

Change the Environment

Invite teachers to consider developing a quiet low-stimulus space in the classroom if this doesn't exist already. Teachers will already be used to creating quiet classroom environments as far as possible to enhance learning. For the easily distracted child, an individual workstation and/or privacy screens can be useful, especially if they can be moved away when necessary. For children who are very highly sensitive to noise, earphones/ear defenders may be helpful; some children may even have their own. A further option is to sit the child closer to the front, as this will reduce both visual and verbal stimuli from across the classroom and the opportunity for distraction. It is also a good idea not to sit the child facing a window or classroom door where outside activities may be distracting.

'Time Out' Space

The child may be supported by 'Time Out' from the classroom (e.g., by going to a quiet space just outside the classroom where the child, or child and assistant, can go when the classroom is too noisy). Aside from providing a place where a child can read or work quietly with fewer distractions, this can also serve as a space for 'Time Out' for when children become unsettled, disruptive and/or emotional. The child should be given a clear explanation for the use of this space, and care must be taken to prevent the child associating a quiet and productive area with being punished or distressed.

Rewards and Praise

A key strategy to increase the ability to sustain attention over time is to find motivators to promote vigilance. It is especially important to use reward techniques and give frequent feedback and praise, as this will help the child to stay engaged and motivated to complete a task to the best of their ability. Discuss with teachers how praise and rewards can be incorporated into the school day. Token reward systems of building up credits for rewards can be helpful for children with ADHD who need immediate reinforcers. Some children benefit further from a teaching assistant or teacher keeping them on-task with 'ticks' or tokens given up to every minute for a period of time, with a reward at the end.

Goals, Steps and Check-points

Children with ADHD are better at coping with short tasks than longer tasks, although even short tasks may seem too demanding for a child with severe ADHD symptoms, especially if the task is perceived as boring. Writing tasks and complex problems that require a lot of thinking can be particularly daunting, especially if the child feels there will be a negative consequence for failing. A strategy to help a child feel they can manage tasks of longer duration is to specify the goal and then break it down into a list of smaller steps. Add a check-point next to each step. For example, a writing task can be broken down into paragraphs, as in the farm story example described earlier in this chapter, with a check-point at the completion of each section or paragraph. The use of a timer can be helpful so that the child can see clearly how much time there is to complete a step, if this is appropriate to the task. The aim would be to help the child pace him/herself and reduce procrastination, rather than to rush them. Children should receive praise and encouragement after completing each check-point. If they become restless they can be encouraged with motivating statements such as, 'You are doing so well, just three more minutes' or 'Keep going with this story, you are writing it so clearly'. The aim is to sustain their attention in smaller phases, and this technique is especially important to support the child to achieve larger projects that build up over time and require planning and organization.

Check-points can be transferred to a check-list that can be reviewed by the teacher, with each target section being ticked off as it is achieved. Stickers or smiley faces can also be given to reinforce achievement. With practice, the child should be encouraged to apply the strategy unaided. Older children will be better able to apply the self-monitoring check-point and self-reward processes than younger children. They are more likely to have long-term assignments and when sub-tasks have been completed they should be encouraged to tick these against a list to demonstrate progress, as this can be very motivating. Teachers or teaching assistants can discuss at review meetings how this strategy helps and they should liaise with parents/carers to explore how it can be implemented successfully at home.

Self-talk

This is an internal strategy used to direct positive thinking. Talk to teachers about the 'inner voice' and thoughts; most teachers will recognize that they have an on-going internal dialogue which directs their actions and supports a self-monitoring process. Ask teachers to help the child to think up self-motivating statements (friendly thoughts) that will help them to stay on track, such as, 'I can do this', 'Stay calm', or 'I'm nearly at the next check-point and can take a break'. It is very important that the child identifies these statements, but teachers should remind the child to apply self-talk, especially if they notice that the child is becoming restless, irritable or distressed. It will be helpful for successful strategies to be shared with parents/carers.

Fiddle Toys

Some children find it easier to maintain attention if they have a fiddle toy (also known as a fidget toy) to play with. These toys may be sensory tangles, bracelets or stress balls that promote directed movement and tactile input. A tangle, for example, is a series of 90-degree curves that are connected and pivot at each joint. It has no beginning and no end, and the child is able to twist and manipulate the tangle to create variable shapes. Blu-Tack also works well as a fiddle toy and is quiet, cheap and easily available in classroom environments. Fiddle toys are self-regulation tools that enhance learning by supporting the child to focus, attend, feel calm and actively listen. They relieve the stress associated with the child attempting to control the impulse to fidget and go off-task, and help them to reduce feelings of tension and anxiety. They can be introduced as a break activity and/or as a background activity whilst the child is sitting and listening (much in the same way as doodling).

Activity Breaks

To relieve feelings of restlessness and/or the urge to get up and walk around, introduce fidget breaks or stretches. Teachers can make lesson plans, for example, that include interactive elements.

What Can We Do As Teachers?

Table 4.4 outlines a suggested approach, including a list of strategies that can be implemented at school. To maximize the effect of strategies, it is helpful to discuss these with the child's parents/carers so they may be implemented at both home and school (wherever possible). Both teachers and parents/carers find that using a 'Home School Diary' is an efficient way to share information (see Chapter 2).

We suggest that teachers read Chapter 2, which provides important background information about the delivery of the Young–Smith Programme. It is unlikely that teachers will have the time to go through specific worksheets with children, although if parents/carers are unable to do this and it can be arranged with the Special Educational Needs Coordinator, this would be helpful. Guidance is found in the 'CBT Interventions' section in each chapter on how to do this. The initial worksheets, introducing Buzz and his family, are outlined in Chapter 3. All the materials (worksheets and Home Missions Record Form) are available for download from the companion website, www.wiley.com/go/young/helpingadhd. For older children (i.e., 12 years-plus), one may dispense with the Buzz worksheets and instead introduce the child directly to the topic, applying the discussion prompts on the worksheets to the child's experience and discussing suggested strategies. Set the suggested

Table 4.4 School strategies for attention.

Chunk information
- Chunk information into two or three pieces at a time.
- Write information down in simple ways and use bullet points on the board.

Summarizing and concept checking
- Say the child's name before giving instructions.
- Ask the child to repeat back information to check understanding.

Ask for help or clarification
- Encourage the child to tell the teacher if they can't focus and/or don't understand.
- Encourage children to put their hand up and ask the teacher if they think they have missed and/or don't understand something.

Visual cues and prompts
- Use bright paper and colours to attract to key notes on 'Remember Notices'.
- For highly sensitive children, work out a 'code' to communicate they need assistance.

Change the environment
- Arrange a quiet space in the classroom and section it off using aids such as screens.
- Position the child where they can clearly see and hear the teacher.
- Position the child away from windows and doors.
- Keep distracting items out of reach, but remember that a 'fiddle toy' can sometimes promote concentration.
- Sit the child with peers who are able to remain on task and can support the child as role models.
- Arrange a quiet space outside of the classroom that can be used for 'Time Out'.

Goals, steps and check-points
- Set specific goals for the child to help them focus on the task and sustain attention.
- Break down large tasks/goals that seem overwhelming into smaller steps, e.g. writing a story may become 5 paragraphs or 30 minutes maths homework may become 3 sets of 5 questions.
- Give praise after each step or check-point.

Activity breaks
- If the child is struggling, suggest a short break and then to return to task.
- Encourage the child to self-monitor by asking *'How do you think you are doing?'* or *'Can you manage a bit more or do you need a quick break?'*

Staff collaboration
- Ensure that all staff know and understand what strategies are being used and why.

Home Missions and support the child to complete them. Don't forget to give frequent feedback and praise. If a Star Chart is used (see Chapter 2) then this could be put in the 'Home School Diary' where parents/carers can also review it on a regular basis.

References

American Psychiatric Association. (2013). *Diagnostic and statistical manual of mental disorders* (5th ed.). Washington, DC: American Psychiatric Association.

Baddeley, A. D. (1986). *Working memory.* Oxford: Clarendon Press.

Conners, C. K. (2008). *Conners 3rd edition.* Toronto: Multi-Health Systems.

Conners, C. K. (2014). *Conners Continuous Performance Test 3rd edition.* Toronto: Multi-Health Systems.

Emslie, H., Wilson, F. C., Burden, V., Nimmo-Smith, I., & Wilson, B. A. (2003). *The behavioural assessment of dysexecutive syndrome in children.* London: Harcourt Assessment.

Gioia, G. A., Isquith, P. K., Guy, S. C., & Kenworthy, L. (2000). *Behavior rating inventory of executive function (BRIEF).* Odessa, FL: Psychological Assessment Resources.

Goodman, R. (1997). The strengths and difficulties questionnaire: A research note. *Journal of Child Psychology and Psychiatry and Allied Disciplines, 38*(5), 581–586.

Korkman, M., Kirk, U., & Kemp, S. (2007). *NEPSY-II: Clinical and interpretive manual.* San Antonio, TX: Psychological Corporation.

Larsson, J. O., Larsson, H., & Lichtenstein, P. (2004). Genetic and environmental contributions to stability and change of ADHD symptoms between 8 and 13 years of age: A longitudinal twin study. *Journal of the American Academy of Child and Adolescent Psychiatry, 43*(10), 1267–1275.

Manly, T., Robertson, I. H., Anderson, V., & Nimmo-Smith, I. (1998). *Test of everyday attention for children (TEA-Ch).* London: Pearson Assessment.

Norman, D. A., & Shallice, T. (1986). Attention to action: Willed and automatic control of behaviour. In R. J. Davidson, G. E. Schwartz, & D. Shapiro (Eds.), *Consciousness and self-regulation: Advances in research and theory* (4th ed.) (pp. 1–18). New York: Plenum Press.

Posner, M. I., Rothbart, M. K., Sheese, B. E., & Voelker, P. (2014). Developing attention: Behavioral and brain mechanisms. *Advances in Neuroscience, 2014.* doi: 10.1155/2014/405094.

Rietveld, M. J. H., Hudziak, J. J., Bartels, M., van Beijsterveldt, C. E. M., & Boomsma, D. I. (2004). Heritability of attention problems in children: Longitudinal results from a study of twins, age 3 to 12. *Journal of Child Psychology and Psychiatry and Allied Disciplines, 45*(3), 577–588.

Sexias, M., Weiss, M., & Müller, U. (2012). Systematic review of national and international guidelines on attention deficit hyperactivity disorder. *Journal of Psychopharmacology, 26*(6), 753–765.

Valera, E. M., Faraone, S. V., Murray, K. E., & Seidman, L. J. (2007). Meta-analysis of structural imaging findings in attention-deficit/hyperactivity disorder. *Biological Psychiatry, 61*(12), 1361–1369.

5

Hyperactivity

Hyperactivity is a physical state of heightened energy levels, above and beyond the cognitive and developmental stage of the child. It has been linked to the neural pathways and neurotransmitters in the brain that are responsible for goal-directed behaviours and sustained attention, and is also associated with certain diets. There is support for a small but significant treatment effect of polyunsaturated fatty acid supplementation, specifically omega supplements (Sonuga-Barke et al., 2013).

Hyperactive behaviour will be present in a range of environments to greater or lesser degrees, depending on the context and social expectations around behaviour. Indeed, cultural expectations and perspectives on childhood behaviour may contribute to how hyperactivity is perceived (James & Taylor, 1990; Timmi & Taylor, 2004). Additionally, environmental context will be a factor: for example, social norms suggest that a child can be very active in a park, whereas behaviour should be controlled in a library. Figure 5.1 describes the DSM-5 (American Psychiatric Association, 2013) symptoms of hyperactivity that are assessed in children with ADHD.

This chapter will examine hyperactivity in children with ADHD and the impact this can have on their functioning in different areas. The assessment of hyperactivity will be discussed, followed by interventions and strategies for children and the adults around them, using cognitive behavioural models.

Presentation

It is not uncommon for people to hold negative attitudes about a child with ADHD because they assume the child can control their hyperactive behaviour. In seeking an explanation for this 'bad behaviour', people may assume that the child is attention seeking or being deliberately oppositional by refusing to comply with rules (e.g., to remain seated and be quiet). They may be perceived as boisterous and out-of-control children, and these behaviours are often blamed

Helping Children with ADHD: A CBT Guide for Practitioners, Parents and Teachers,
First Edition. Susan Young and Jade Smith.
© 2017 John Wiley & Sons Ltd. Published 2017 by John Wiley & Sons Ltd.
Companion website: www.wiley.com/go/young/helpingadhd

> **Hyperactivity-**
> - Often fidgets with or taps hands or feet, or squirms in seat.
> - Often leaves seat in situations when remaining seated is expected.
> - Often runs about or climbs in situations where it is not appropriate (adolescents or adults may be limited to feeling restless).
> - Often unable to play or take part in leisure activities quietly.
> - Often "on the go" acting as if "driven by a motor".

Figure 5.1 DSM-5 diagnostic criteria for ADHD hyperactivity symptoms.

on bad parenting practices. These opinions are not merely incorrect, they are damaging. Hyperactive children with ADHD are not extraverted and oppositional children who have the ability to adapt to situations as needed. They are children who want to stay still, but cannot. They say, 'I have to fidget, my hands can't help it' and they often feel frustrated by their restlessness, knowing that it leads to trouble, especially at school. It is also very unhelpful that these erroneous perceptions place the blame on parents/carers; it is very important to recognize that parenting style does not cause hyperactivity. It can be very difficult to manage a child with ADHD on a daily basis. To those people who believe that poor parenting practices are to blame – we remind them that adults have ADHD too, and their restless behaviours cannot be due to poor parenting.

Behavioural Functioning

Children with hyperactivity struggle to comply with a range of everyday demands and expectations. This is most typically observed in quiet places or where strict, low levels of physical activity are expected (e.g., in the cinema, library, assembly or hospital). Children may present as if they are 'driven by a motor', in need of constant movement, chatting, fidgeting, squirming, shuffling and fiddling with hands and objects, frequently getting up and down, or climbing and switching position. Their behaviour affects the feedback and approval they receive from others and their ability to learn and participate effectively in activities. It may cause them to feel distressed, especially if they are aware of these factors and feel unable to control their behaviour. On a positive note, as children mature, physical hyperactivity tends to decrease, although a subjective sense of inner restlessness often remains.

Academic Functioning

When children first go to school they experience few academic demands and lots of freedom to play and explore the environment. However, as they progress through the academic years they are expected to manage their behaviour for increasingly long periods. They are expected not only to remain seated and on-task during practical activities, but also whilst listening or completing cognitive tasks. Children who do not remain seated and/or who are constantly fidgeting are not able to stay on-task and focus. They may also distract others, both peers and/or teachers. This leads to impairments in their ability to learn and acquire new skills, and ultimately prevents them from reaching their potential. Furthermore, their behaviour may attract criticism or blame.

Interpersonal Functioning

Hyperactive behaviour is not only exhausting for the child with ADHD; it is exhausting for those who interact with them, especially those who prefer low levels of noise and physical activity. Conflict may occur when the needs and desires of family members clash. Parents/carers feel that they must always be on guard, watching, supporting and managing the behaviour of their child with ADHD, and this can be tiresome. Siblings may feel envious of the support and attention given by parents/carers. At school, peers may avoid the child who appears to be unable to follow the rules and behave appropriately, for fear of getting into trouble through association. Hyperactive children with ADHD may also be unattractive playmates due to their overly boisterous behaviour, rough and tumble play, and, in some circumstances, reckless and/or risky behaviour due to not knowing when to stop.

Coping

Some families apply a strategy of avoidance by not going to places where the negative behaviours stand out. This may help in the short term but not in the long run, as children don't learn when and how to adapt their behaviour appropriately across settings. Furthermore, it is important to expose the child to these settings in order to prevent the development of social anxiety resulting from aversive experiences. Hence, it is helpful to find ways for the child to learn how to improve behaviour, for instance by going to places at quieter times, and/or find ways to channel the hyperactivity to focused and positive activities. Once success has been achieved, gradually move to going out at more challenging times (e.g., when it is busier). Some settings are more suitable than others, such as those that include sport activities, outdoor games, cycling and trampolines, as they allow for excess energy to be channelled in constructive ways.

Sleep

Bedtime routines and sleep patterns are often completely disrupted for a child with ADHD, and without a good night's sleep a child is even less likely to sustain concentration, manage their emotions and control their behaviour. Parents/carers can also lose sleep whilst trying to manage the child in the night, developing sleep deprivation which leads to stress, low mood and reduced capacity to cope.

Assessment

International guidance on the assessment and treatment of ADHD recommends that a comprehensive assessment procedure is carried out by trained and qualified healthcare practitioners in order to assess ADHD (Sexias, Weiss & Müller, 2012). This often includes a multi-method assessment involving psychometric questionnaires, a clinical interview and observation of the child to assess their difficulties and behaviour in different contexts and settings. It is desirable to obtain multiple perspectives from different people involved in the child's care (including that of the child if possible), often requiring multi-agency liaison. To develop a care plan that is likely to succeed, it is important to fully understand the nature and complexity of the child's difficulties across their development, including historic, environmental and psychosocial factors, the child's strengths and weaknesses and the support that they currently receive. In doing this, it is important to be mindful of any comorbid and social problems experienced by the child, but also within the family.

Measures

Many assessments of ADHD include items relating to hyperactivity: the most commonly used include the Conners' Rating Scales 3rd Edition (Conners, 2008) for age six upwards and the Strengths and Difficulties Questionnaire (SDQ; Goodman, 1997) for age two upwards. These compare the frequency of a child's perceived functioning with norms obtained from the general population for their age and gender. It is recommended that different raters' perspectives are obtained in order to establish a broad outlook of the child's functioning across different settings and contexts. For example, a parent/carer and teacher may complete the questionnaires for behaviour at home and school. Some measures also include a child version for self-rating, though, of course, their use depends on the child's reading ability and level of insight. Rating is also helpful for obtaining a baseline assessment of perceived functioning which is may be repeated after intervention to evaluate efficacy at outcome. The Conners' Rating Scales 3rd Edition and SDQ can both be repeated. An adult should support children completing self-report questionnaires: children with ADHD may misread questions, miss out answers, respond impulsively and/or miscommunicate the rating. However, it is essential that responses are not influenced by leading questions. Children who struggle with reading should always have items read out to them. As is the case for for many measures, ratings may be subject to bias and must be interpreted cautiously by a trained practitioner.

Clinical Interview

We suggest the therapist first meets with the child's parents/carers and teachers to determine which situations are most problematic, and to ascertain the impact of the child's difficulties on their functioning and quality of life.

The therapist should enquire whether there are particular contexts or times when the child presents with more severe hyperactive symptoms. What makes it worse? What makes it better? What seems to help and what does not? Ask about specific situations across settings (such as at home, in class, with friends, with strangers) and how the presentation may vary in social settings (such as in church, at the cinema, when shopping). Record these situations in a table like the example in Table 5.1. When assessing for hyperactivity, it is important to bear in mind that behaviour may not be dysfunctional in every context, as some situations, such as sports, require high energy and movement. The aim should be to assess hyperactivity that is dysfunctional and causes impairment.

Table 5.1 Example of a completed hyperactivity record.

Situation	How impairing is hyperactivity in this situation? 0 = not at all, 10 = severe	How stressful is it to manage? 0 = not at all, 10 = severe	What have you tried so far, and what has helped/not helped?
Cinema	8 – Can't sit through the whole movie, worries people will reprimand him.	7 – We know that it will happen and it is sometimes not worth going.	We try to sit at the back so that people's views aren't blocked.

Thoughts

It is also useful to gain the child's perspective by talking to them about their difficulties. Children will have their own views and insights. There are specific techniques to externalize the problem, so helping the child feel less blamed and more able to answer objectively and honestly. For example, you can ask, 'Does hyperactivity ever get in the way of what you are doing?' 'When is hyperactivity *around* the most?' 'Who gets most annoyed with hyperactivity?' 'Do you ever get told off when hyperactivity *is around?*.' Perspectives can then be compared between the child, parents/carers and teachers.

Feelings and Physiology

When conducting assessments, the therapist needs to consider differential formulations and contributing factors, which may worsen the child's presentation. Hyperactivity symptoms may not relate solely to ADHD but be present for other reasons:

- *Anxiety*. Nervous energy and tension may present as hyperactivity. Do you know if the child is anxious or worried? This can increase restlessness and muscle tension.
- *Fatigue*. We all know the feeling of irritability when tired, and children may be more active and restless when tired, rather than quieter.

- *Avoidance of task*. Children may be less settled when faced with a difficult or boring task, leading them to appear hyperactive. This behaviour may be reinforced by task removal or time out, resulting in them not doing the task that they had found aversive.
- *Medication*. It should be investigated whether hyperactivity relates to medication (e.g., a change in medication and/or medication regime)
- *Diet*: Some foods have been associated with hyperactivity. A diet free from additives and/or supplemented with fish oils or vitamins may help reduce hyperactive behaviour.

Behaviour

Those who are regularly involved in the care of children who are hyperactive often feel stressed and exhausted. Every day may seem to be a battle because they have to be permanently on guard and monitoring the child's behaviour. A measure of carers' stress levels may be helpful, and this may be repeated to assess progress and outcome of treatment. This may be a simple recording of stress made each week; a stress monitor of 0–100 %, with 0 % being no stress at all and 100 % feeling extremely stressed. Formal questionnaires, such as the Parent Stress Index (Abidin, 1995), are also widely available and are often used to measure aspects of stress, distress and coping in relation to traits in the child.

A Behaviour Impact Scale completed by Joe's Mum is presented in Table 5.2, giving a detailed summary of how Joe's Mum feels. She describes feeling overwhelmed and stressed and, though she is sometimes successful in managing her son's hyperactive behaviours, she is not routinely applying strategies. Hence, she has not figured out what are the best strategies for Joe and those that she does use are not always effective.

Table 5.2 Example of a completed Behaviour Impact Scale.

Behaviour: Hyperactivity	Not at all	A little	Sometimes	Quite often	All the time
How much time do you spend worrying about your child's behaviour?				✓	
Does this behaviour disrupt family life?				✓	
Do you feel stressed when you are with your child?					✓
Can you confidently and calmly manage your child's behaviour?			✓		
Do you apply strategies to manage your child's behaviour?		✓			
Do the strategies work?			✓		

Parents/carers often find that their child's activity levels worsen at bedtime, a period where we usually unwind and decrease our activity. In such cases, it is important to assess the bedtime routine (times and activities), daily exercise, medication timings and other household routines. This may reveal obstacles to successful sleep hygiene – for example, video games before bed, bright lighting, sharing a room with a noisy sibling, play fighting before bed and late-night snacking. An information guide on sleep strategies 'And So to Bed....' can be downloaded from the Psychology Services website (www.psychology-services.uk.com/resources).

Behaviour Diary

Diaries that record frequency and severity of specific difficulties can be kept at home or school by those caring for the child, and by the child him- or herself. This can be a very good way to capture chaotic situations which may not otherwise have been reported. The diary should record the hyperactive behaviour (e.g., what the child is doing, when it happened, where it happened, what else was going on at the time), antecedents to the behaviour (what was the lead-up to that behaviour and who was involved) and the consequences of the behaviour (what was the result of the behaviour and who was involved). This Behaviour Diary is also known as an 'ABC chart', and functional analysis of the data obtained can reveal patterns of problem behaviours and 'antecedent chains', which may inform the practitioner as to what interventions could be tried out and when they may best be applied. An example of a Behaviour Diary is given in Table 5.3.

Table 5.3 Example of a completed Behaviour Diary for hyperactivity.

Day/ Time	Antecedent (What was happening just before the behaviour? Who was there? What happened earlier in the day that might be relevant?)	Behaviour (What did you observe? Describe the duration and severity.)	Consequence (What happened next? What was the result?)
Friday 4pm	On his way home from school, Joe and his friend were both feeling excited as they were going to play football in the park. His big brother said he would take them to the park when he got home from school (about half an hour later).	Joe came home full of energy. He would not sit down when I asked him but kept running around the lounge and jumping on the sofas. I told him if he carried on he would not be allowed to go to the park. He got very upset when I said this and started to shout and scream at me.	I sent Joe outside to wait for his brother in the back garden because he was being loud and disruptive in the house. He wanted to take his football with him but I said no as he needed to calm down.

This example is a record of a boy called Joe who has ADHD. The Behaviour Diary was completed by his Mum and in this example there are a number of possible triggers for the hyperactive behaviour. Joe had just come out of school where he would have been expected to manage his activity levels, and he was excited about playing football in the park. Having to wait for his brother to come home from school probably made the situation worse. It was only half an hour, but it seemed to be a very long time for Joe. Waiting is difficult for children with ADHD. Joe couldn't do what he wanted immediately, but instead had to control his behaviour, and when he was reprimanded he started to scream and shout. His Mum couldn't tolerate his behaviour, so she sent him outside. This may be a positive outcome as he could let out his activity levels in a safe place. Joe's Mum might want to use this strategy earlier in future, as this may avoid the reprimand and the shouting and screaming.

However, the example is just one episode, whereas the purpose of a Behaviour Diary is to record several episodes over time, from which a pattern may emerge. For example, if records indicated that Joe had consumed a fizzy drink before episodes of hyperactivity, then one may conclude that the behaviour seems to be associated with dietary intake. An intervention might be to remove fizzy drinks from Joe's diet and evaluate the result.

School and home observations and Behaviour Diaries can be combined to further understand the nature, severity and contributing factors to hyperactive behaviours. When observing the child in class, record a Behaviour Diary by making specific notes on what is happening in the classroom (the situation), the specifics of the behaviour and the outcome of the behaviour (the consequences), including how others respond. Try to observe the child in different settings (e.g., during an academic lesson, a practical lesson, at break time, at home, at a leisure activity/club). Note any successes in supporting the child as well as any difficulties.

CBT Interventions for Hyperactivity

If the therapist is treating younger children and/or the worksheets are being used as a basis for treatment, the first session should always commence with Worksheets 1, 2 and 3 to introduce the child to Buzz and his family (Worksheet 1), introduce positive self-talk (Worksheet 2) and identify a reward system (Worksheet 3). The reward and self-talk strategies are applied in the session, at home and/or at school. See Chapter 3 for a suggested outline of how to plan and conduct the introductory session. All the worksheets are available on the companion website resource page www.wiley.com/go/young/helpingadhd.

The aims of the interventions and worksheets in the hyperactivity session(s) are to introduce children to the concept of hyperactivity and improve their skills in recognizing and coping with it. The therapist will achieve this by setting an agenda, reviewing any Home Missions done between sessions, working through new worksheets (or just the strategies for older children) and setting new Home Missions. If required, a mid-session break can be offered halfway through the session; this may be particularly important for younger children. Chapter 2 provides generic information on the structure and content of sessions (irrespective of topic); supplementary information is included within this chapter that specifically relates to the delivery of the hyperactivity session(s).

Agenda

At the beginning of the session, show the child the written agenda (see Figure 5.2) that you have prepared prior to the session and go through it, verbally linking the themes and Worksheets that you will introduce during the session. For the hyperactivity module, introduce Worksheets 7 and 8 by saying:

> Buzz sometimes gets in trouble at school for fidgeting. In the first story today, Buzz falls off his chair and the teacher is annoyed. We will think together about what could be done to help Buzz. After that, we will have a short break and you can colour in the worksheet using these crayons. After the break we are going to look at another worksheet and talk about what happens at bedtime, because Buzz can't always get to sleep.

Agenda
Folder Review
Buzz at School [Worksheet 7]
Break
Buzz at Bedtime [Worksheet 8]
Home Missions

Figure 5.2 Example agenda for hyperactivity session(s).

Folder Review

When reviewing the folder with the child, aside from checking whether the Home Missions are completed, take the opportunity to revise important information and/or concepts, as this will support the child in consolidating the learning points and/or newly acquired skills. Ensure that you make time to look at the illustrations, colourings, paintings, magazine cuttings and/or photographs that the child has added to the folder. Discuss them and try to relate these to discussions about Buzz and his family and/or topics or strategies that have been covered. Aside from acting as a revision prompt, this will also act as a reward system for the child. Praise should be given verbally, but you can also reward by adding stickers, handwritten notes or smiley faces. If Home Missions were set then you should review the Home Missions Record Form for comments and feedback from parents/carers and discuss this with the child. See Chapter 2 for more information about the folder review and Home Missions.

Worksheet 7 Buzz at School

Worksheet Description

To download this worksheet, please visit the companion website

Buzz is in trouble again with his teacher. All the children are supposed to sit down quietly while the teacher tells them a story. The teacher is going to give them a test afterwards to see how much they remember. Buzz finds it very difficult to sit still and he starts to wriggle about like a worm. He isn't listening to the teacher anymore, but is thinking about the ice cream his Mum said she would buy him on the way home. Buzz can't wait for his ice cream. He feels so restless he can't sit still any longer. He starts to fidget and swing on his chair. After a while it topples over and he ends up on the floor! Now none of the children are listening to the story! The teacher is very cross.

Worksheet Prompts

Do you ever wriggle about like a worm? Can you show me?
What was stopping Buzz from listening to the story? Has that ever happened to you?
Why was Buzz in trouble with the teacher? When Buzz fell on the floor, how did he feel?
How did the other children respond?
Together let's write out some ideas of all the things Buzz can do to help himself in this situation.
Now let's look at the things you thought would help Buzz and circle the ones that might also help you.

Worksheet 7 illustrates the relationship between hyperactivity and attention problems. It also introduces the potential for distraction and/or disturbing others and so preventing them achieving a task, and how this may be perceived from a social perspective. The scenario is thus considered from the child's, peer's and teacher's perspectives. Methods to reduce restlessness and help the child to remain seated and focused are identified and discussed.

In the story, Buzz goes to school and is struggling to sit still and concentrate during story time. Read the Stimulus Sheet to the child, or, if they wish, they can read it with you. Check that the child has understood the story and answer any questions they might have. Using the Discussion Sheet, talk through the points with the child to help them think about the situation. The first point is to help them consider whether they have similar difficulties to Buzz. They may say that they don't wriggle around like a worm, but that they do shuffle, get up a lot or play with their hands, for example. You can ask them to show you and/or comment on any restlessness/hyperactivity you have observed in the session. Next ask the child, 'What was stopping Buzz from listening to the story?' The aim is to help the child to identify that both internal factors (like imagining the ice cream and feeling impatient) and external factors (like the expectation to sit down quietly) can impact on activity levels. You may need to prompt the child by asking, 'Was Buzz thinking of something?' 'What was Buzz meant to be doing?'

Encourage the child to think about situations when they had a similar experience. This doesn't have to be exactly the same as Buzz's situation, but may include a time they struggled to stay still. Ask them, 'What happened and how did you feel?' 'What did the teacher do?' Move the conversation on to thinking about what made Buzz get into trouble with the teacher. You may need to ask, 'What was it that Buzz and the class should have been doing?' 'Why was it important to listen to the story?' Direct the child to consider how the other children responded, such as laughing, being distracted or feeling annoyed. Direct the child to consider how Buzz felt when he fell off the chair and became the centre of attention – perhaps silly, stupid, embarrassed or self-conscious.

Talk to the child about what might help Buzz in that sort of situation. Write these ideas on the Task Sheet (e.g., ask for 'time out', remind himself of what he should be doing, take some deep breaths to keep calm, apologize or play with a fiddle toy). The child might come up with ideas of what Buzz might do that may not be a good solution, for example, leave the classroom without asking. Check with the child if they have had these experiences, how they felt, what they did and how that worked out. Follow up with a discussion about the ideas and which of them might be most helpful. Ask the child to circle the ideas they think would be most helpful to them; add some new ones if they are more appropriate to the child's experiences and circumstances. Role-play the suggestions, where possible; for example, the therapist could practise with the child asking if they could have a short break.

Give praise for the child's effort in the session. If you choose to set Home Missions based on this Worksheet we suggest asking the child to do the following:

1) Decorate the Worksheet by colouring in the pictures and thought bubbles, and/or add to them with pictures on the theme of the story. These could be photographs or pictures in magazines or comics.

2) Share the ideas about how to control behaviours with parents/carers and/or teachers. Practise these in the week.

If Home Missions are set, remind parents/carers to complete the Home Missions Record Form and to place this is the folder for review at the next session.

Mid-session Break

This should be provided at an appropriate point in the session, as outlined in Chapter 2.

Worksheet 8 Buzz at Bedtime

To download this worksheet, please visit the companion website

Worksheet Description

Buzz does not like going to bed. His head is full of all sorts of exciting thoughts and he finds it hard to go to sleep. This means that he often feels tired in the morning. He goes to bed when his Mum tells him but really he stays awake. His Mum tells him off if he gets out of bed, so he pretends he needs something (like a drink, or the toilet, or he's forgotten to tell his Mum something).

Worksheet Prompts

What do you think will happen if Buzz keeps going to bed late and feels tired in the morning?
Do you have any ideas about what might help Buzz to calm down and get to sleep?
Tell me about your bedtime routine.
Do you ever have trouble getting to sleep or staying asleep?
Together let's write out some ideas for things that Buzz can do to help him go to sleep.
What gets in the way of a good night's sleep? What helps you to sleep well?
Now let's look at the things you thought would help Buzz and circle the ones that might also help you.

The Worksheet 8 bedtime task aims to acknowledge sleep problems and link sleep difficulties with symptoms of hyperactivity. Children are asked to discuss their own sleep patterns and routines, including factors that help them to sleep better. Through discussion, sleep hygiene practices should be introduced that can be implemented by both the child and parents/carers.

In the story, Buzz has difficulty getting to sleep at night. He lies in bed thinking about the day he has had and what will happen the next day. Because he feels restless, he often makes excuses to get out of bed. Read the Stimulus Sheet to the child, or, if they wish, they can read it with you. Check the child has understood the story and answer any questions they have. Prompt a discussion by asking, 'What do you think will happen if Buzz keeps going to bed late and feels tired in the morning?' This can prompt conversations about fatigue, being late to school and feeling emotional and less in control. Discuss with the child why they think it is important for Buzz, or for him/her, to get enough sleep. You can explain that, 'The brain and the body need time to rest and grow and they do this when we are sleeping, so sleep is very important. It helps people to concentrate and control their feelings and behaviour better and face the day.'

Once the importance of sleep is understood, ask the child, 'What might help Buzz to wind down so he can get a good night's sleep?' The child is likely to already have some ideas that they haveheard from adults, or may have discovered themselves. Make sure you correct any misunderstandings (or desires!) that would not be helpful, such as playing computer games in bed until you fall asleep. Ask the child about their own bedtime routine. The child will most likely be able to tell you about this, but you can also prompt by asking, 'What time do you start getting ready for bed?' 'What order do you do things in?' If the child has siblings ask how their routine compares and how he/she feels about any differences (as some children think differences are unfair). Then summarize what he/she has told you, for example, 'So you put your pyjamas on at 7 p.m. after your little brother has got changed. He goes to bed earlier than you. You go back downstairs but you aren't allowed to play computer games after this time. Sometimes you read a story with your Mum.'

Move the conversation on to ask the child if they ever have any trouble getting to sleep. If the child tells you that they struggle to get to sleep until late at night, you can ask what sorts of things go through their mind, how they are feeling and what they are doing in this time. If they wake up in the night, find out why. Explore with them what they do, or what they have been told to do, if they wake up and can't get back to sleep. Remember to gently correct any misunderstandings and also discuss these with parents/carers. For example:

> You told me that if you wake up in the night you play on your tablet and this helps you get back to sleep. Something that I have learnt, and other children have told me, is that this actually makes them stay awake longer. We know that sleep is very important and we want you to sleep well. We need to figure out something different for you to do that will help you get back to sleep.

On the Task Sheet write out ideas for what might help Buzz sleep better. Include things like calm breathing, plumping up the pillows so he is comfy and settling down with a cuddly toy or comforter. Ask the child to circle the ones they think would be most helpful to them; add some new ones if they are more appropriate to the child's experiences and circumstances. Role-play the suggestions, where possible; for example the child could practice some calm breathing or asking their sibling to turn the TV down a bit. The therapist should give feedback and rehearse the interaction until the child is confident in its delivery.

Give praise for the child's effort in the session. If you choose to set Home Missions based on this worksheet we suggest asking the child to do the following:

1) Decorate the Worksheet by colouring in the pictures and thought bubbles, and/or add to them with pictures on the theme of the story. These could be photographs or pictures in magazines or comics.
2) Write out your own bedtime routine and decide how it could be changed so you sleep better.
3) Share the ideas you have with their parents/carers and practise some of the ideas to make positive changes.

If Home Missions are set, remind parents/carers to complete the Home Missions Record Form and to place this is the folder for review at the next session.

Feedback and Rewards

At the end of the session, appropriate rewards identified from the Worksheet 3 Reward Task should be applied (e.g., the child should engage in positive self-talk). See Chapter 2 for more information about feedback and rewards.

Working with Parents/Carers

This section presents strategies that parents/carers can apply to support the child to control feelings of restlessness and reduce and/or cope with the child's hyperactivity.

It is important to be realistic about what can be achieved. It can be just as helpful to learn strategies to cope better with a child's behaviour as to learn strategies to improve the behaviour itself. In this section we discuss a method to monitor behaviour using a Behaviour Diary and present behavioural strategies that include engagement of the child in physical activities, generating dedicated activity opportunities ('wiggle space'), introducing methods to support the child to calm down by means of planned breaks and calm breathing techniques. We also discuss the need to frame requests in a positive way and to reinforce positive responses and behaviours. We discuss specific interventions for sleep problems, including the need to introduce a consistent sleep routine, and suggest methods to help the child settle at night. We present cognitive strategies that will support parents/carers to pre-plan for challenging situations and settings and engage in positive self-talk. Parents/carers are also advised to monitor their own stress levels and responses.

When working with parents/carers, the therapist should introduce suggested techniques and strategies; practise and rehearse them in role-plays during the sessions if appropriate (without the child present). Parents/carers should report back to the therapist on how they managed with these techniques at home. In future sessions, it is important to troubleshoot any obstacles and/or difficulties that arise by thinking of ways to adapt the techniques or strategies so they are successful in helping the child.

A key strategy to change behaviour and improve cognitive skills is to find motivators to promote success. Children with ADHD tend to respond better to immediate rewards, as they have difficulty with delayed gratification for longer-term rewards (even if these are bigger and better). Methods to motivate success (including the use of a Star Chart) and other topics that are generic to working with parents/carers are described in Chapter 2. Supplementary information that specifically relates to the delivery of the hyperactivity session(s) is outlined in this chapter.

Behaviour Diary

In order to home in on specific situations in which the child is hyperactive, ask parents/carers to complete a Behaviour Diary (described earlier in this chapter) to monitor behaviour. Discuss the information recorded in the diary with parents/carers to gain further insight and understanding about the type of behaviour, its triggers and when it is most likely to present. Over time, patterns emerge that may explain the causes of some behaviours. This can be helpful in determining which interventions should be introduced to address the problem.

Physical Activity

Sometimes it is more realistic to direct and shape a child's problematic behaviour than attempt to stop it completely. In this case, direct the child towards an appropriate activity or place that they can be active (but not at bedtime!). Help parents/carers to develop creative ideas that work for their family, such as: riding their bike in the garden; going on the trampoline; taking the recycling out; running up the garden and back; walking five times up and down the hallway; standing up and doing stretches; or hand and/or feet shakes. Other ideas include pressing their hands together, clenching and unclenching fists, push ups against the wall and scribbling on a notepad. The aim is to direct the energy to focus on something and/or to do a helpful task. Children should receive praise and encouragement in order to reinforce their efforts.

Wiggle Space

Another method is to designate a wiggle space for children at home. A wiggle space may be a corner of a room or a place in the child's bedroom or hallway. He/she may want to put out a sign to indicate the space. The wiggle space can be used both as a place to promote calm after physical activity and/or a temporary space for activity in a place that minimizes disruption to others in the home. Children should also know that there is a time limit to using the wiggle space, to prevent it becoming a place to avoid homework or chores.

Breaks

Sometimes children become restless when they have been doing the same thing for a while. This may not seem like very long to you, but for a child with ADHD it may feel like forever. Parents/carers should offer breaks at these times, as getting up and doing something else in a structured way may prevent the child becoming disruptive and/or oppositional. After a few minutes the child should be redirected to the original task and aim to complete it. A break might include a physical activity, such as getting a drink or switching tasks. It could also be an activity break, like five minutes on the gym ball, a series of wall presses and star jumps or walking to get fresh air and coming back. This can be adapted when children are out and about; try to plan ahead so parents/carers have some ideas about what might work.

Positive Requests and Reinforcement

Research has shown that children respond better to sanctions of praise than reprimands. Thus, negative commands should be replaced with positive requests. This means exchanging comments to not do something, such as, 'get down', 'stop that', 'don't run', 'don't touch', to statements of desired behaviour, such as 'come here', 'remember to stay as still as you can', 'try not to shuffle just until this bit is over', 'go outside for five minutes and run around'. Negative commands may stop a specific behaviour, but they are not constructive. Positive requests are more informative, and for the child they resolve the problem of figuring out what is expected of them.

Calm Breathing

When the body is over-aroused and restless, there are techniques that can be applied to calm down. One technique you can teach parents/carers to use with their children is as follows: breathe in for three through your nose and out for three through your mouth.

Practise the technique with both parents/carers and the child, demonstrating that the technique is to use the diaphragm so that the abdomen expands, rather than the shoulders rising.

Sleep Routines

A sleep hygiene guide 'And So to Bed...' is available for parents/carers on the Psychology Services Website (www.psychology-services.uk.com/resources). Night times, when children are expected to be calm and restful, can become battles in the household. It is essential that sleep routines and good practice be followed to aid restfulness as much as possible. Talk to parents/carers about their child's routine and sleep, and help them to think about areas where improvements or changes could be made. For example, keeping noisy siblings away, reducing stimulating activities in the evening and ensuring that they have plenty of exercise in the day to physically tire them. In the lead up to bedtime, forbid the use of electronic devices (such as laptops, computers, tablets, mobile phones) as the light emitted from these devices interferes with the natural production of melatonin which facilitates sleep.

Games

The 'sleeping animal game' requires the child to choose and act out an animal that is asleep. You can ask the animal to sleep for increasing amounts of time (such as one minute, three minutes, five minutes) while the parents/carers watch for signs of movement. If the child remains still, they get a point. If they move, the parent/carer gets the point. Parents/carers should be encouraged to comment on their child's performance, 'Wow you are staying so still, I am watching really carefully to get my point' and 'You did that brilliantly, I never saw you move at all.' Children like positive reinforcement from parents/carers and it can open up conversations to aid understanding, 'So when did you feel like moving the most?' It is important that parents/carers set realistic aims and do not use the game unfairly. If the game is being played at bedtime, the parent/carer should not give feedback if the child seems to have fallen asleep – in case they wake them!

Self-talk

Talk to parents/carers about how they can remind and prompt their child to manage their own activity with helpful self-talk (friendly thoughts). This could include ideas like, 'I know I can manage a few more minutes, then I will have a break' or a funny rhyme like, 'When my feet start to shake, it's time to take a break.'

Signs and Places

You can work with parents/carers to help them become more aware of their child's needs by noticing the early signs of hyperactivity in a situation and managing it before it becomes destructive. Some environments are more challenging than others as they require you to be still, quiet and/or spend long periods of time sitting, such as in church, a museum or at the dinner table. By being aware of difficult places, parents/carers can make a management plan (include the child's input in making the plan) and prompt its execution.

Beliefs and Feelings

Support the parents/carers you work with to look after themselves too. Parents/carers who are tired and stretched sometimes start feeling that their child is testing them on purpose. This type of thought is negative and unhelpful. It is more likely to result in punishment rather than tolerance and understanding. The child may pick up on this and feel 'not good enough', anxious or even angry, and these feelings may play out in relationships within the family.

What Can We Do As Parents/Carers?

Table 5.4 outlines a suggested approach, including a list of strategies that can be implemented at home. To maximize the effect of strategies, it is helpful to discuss these with your child's teacher so they may be implemented at both home and school (wherever possible). Lots of parents/carers and teachers find that using a 'Home School Diary' is an efficient way to share information (see Chapter 2).

We suggest that parents/carers read Chapter 2, which provides important background information about the delivery of the Young–Smith Programme. For younger children, we suggest that parents/carers set aside some time to sit down with the child (around 45–60 minutes) and work through the worksheets recommended for each topic. Guidance on how to do this is found in the 'CBT Interventions' section in each chapter. The worksheets introducing Buzz and his family are outlined in Chapter 3. All the materials (worksheets and Home Missions Record Form) are available for downloading from the companion website, www.wiley.com/go/young/helpingadhd. For older children (i.e., 12 years-plus), you can dispense with the Buzz worksheets if necessary, and instead introduce the child directly to the topic, and, using the discussion prompts on the worksheets, apply this to the child's experience and discuss suggested strategies. Set Home Missions and support the child to complete them. Don't forget to give frequent feedback and praise. Make a Star Chart (see Chapter 2), put it in a prominent place and start to use it on a daily basis.

Table 5.4 Home strategies for hyperactivity.

Physical activity
- Add sport, exercise and physical activity into the daily routine.
- Engage your child in physical activities during task breaks.
- Consider having a small trampoline or gym ball to use at home.
- Redirect your child to a place in which they can use up energy, such as a jog in the garden.
- Remind your child they can take time out and do star jumps or wall presses.

Wiggle space
- Create a wiggle space at home where the child will be undisturbed.

Breaks
- Watch out for when your child is becoming tired or bored and quickly implement a break and/or a change of activity.

Positive requests and reinforcement
- Give positive and directed requests rather than negative commands.
- Try to be patient and don't lose your temper.

Calm breathing
- Prompt your child to do some simple calming breathing.

Sleep routine
- Ensure your child has a good sleep routine that promotes restfulness.
- Forbid the use of electronic devices in the lead up to bedtime.
- Create a consistent sleep routine.

Self-talk
- Identify (and prompt) positive self-talk (friendly thoughts) to help them cope.

Signs and places
- Be familiar with early warning signs that your child is becoming restless.
- Consider if anything is contributing to activity levels, such as anxiety.
- Make a management plan with your child.

Working with Teachers and Schools

In class, children are often expected to sit quietly whilst they learn. Hyperactive children are therefore hampered in their ability to learn. This section presents strategies that teachers can apply to support the child to control feelings of restlessness and reduce and/or cope with hyperactivity.

It is important to be realistic about what can be achieved. It can be just as helpful to learn strategies to cope better with a child's behaviour as to learn strategies to improve the behaviour itself. In this section we discuss a method to monitor behaviour using a Behaviour Diary and present behavioural strategies that include engagement of the child in physical activities, generating dedicated activity opportunities ('wiggle space'), introducing methods to support the child to calm down with planned breaks, and the employment of calm breathing techniques. We also discuss the need to manage the responses of other children who may become upset and/or disturbed by the hyperactive behaviours of the child, together with a need to frame requests in a positive way and reinforce positive responses and behaviour. We present cognitive strategies that will support teachers to pre-plan for challenging situations and settings and engage in positive self-talk. Teachers are also advised to monitor their own stress levels and responses.

Teachers and schools will already have structures in place to support many of the interventions introduced in the Young–Smith Programme. It will be useful to link up parents/carers and teachers to encourage an integrated strategy and shared success. It is important to troubleshoot any obstacles and/or difficulties that arise by thinking of ways to adapt the techniques or strategies so they are successful in helping the child. Methods to motivate success and other topics that are generic to working with teachers and schools are described in Chapter 2. Supplementary information that specifically relates to the delivery of the hyperactivity session(s) is outlined in this chapter.

Physical Activity

In the classroom it is sometimes more realistic to direct and shape the child's behaviour than attempt to stop it completely. This may also avoid escalations and arguments. For example, when a teacher notices that a child is becoming restless they can suggest the child changes the activity and/or moves to a place where they can be more active. It is not possible to be prescriptive about this, as the therapist will need to work with the teacher to think of ideas that will work in their specific environment. Some suggestions for consideration are: walk up and down a corridor, stand up and do stretches and/or hand and feet shakes, thumb twiddling, walking their feet under the desk, pressing their hands together, clenching and unclenching fists, chewing on a pencil topper or using a special wobble cushion which is placed on their seat. The aim is to direct and focus the energy and place boundaries around it. Children should receive praise and encouragement for doing this, in order to reinforce their efforts.

Wiggle Space

A more formal method is to allocate wiggle space, which could be a designated part of the room. This can be used to promote calm after physical activity and/or as temporary space for activity on the spot that minimizes disruption to other people. Children should also know that there is a time limit to using the wiggle space, to avoid it becoming a place to avoid schoolwork.

Breaks

Sometimes children become restless when they have been doing the same thing for a while. This may not seem very long to you, but for a child with ADHD it may feel like forever. It is important for teachers to be aware of this and to develop an understanding about what the child is typically able to manage. Teachers are then able to plan for breaks (or changes in activities) before a problem develops. Getting up and doing something else in a structured way may prevent the child becoming disruptive and/or oppositional. After a few minutes the child can return to the original task and aim to complete it.

Positive Requests and Reinforcement

Research has shown that children respond better to praise than reprimands. Thus, negative commands should be replaced with positive requests. This is usually well practised in schools. The therapist should encourage teachers to reflect on how they ask the child to do things, how they will direct their attention and engage them in a task, and how they will then praise and reward their efforts. Discuss with teachers how they use positive requests to help children understand what is expected of them. An example is to change the command, 'Stop distracting people, you should get on with your work', to a more specific request, 'The thing to do next is answer number three', combined with an immediate reinforcement of praise. For the child with ADHD, this resolves the problem of figuring out what is expected of him/her; this is especially helpful when the child is feeling overwhelmed and unsure what to do or how to respond.

Calm Breathing

When the body is over aroused and restless there are techniques that can be applied to calm down. One such technique you can introduce to teachers is as follows:

breathe in for three through your nose and out for three through your mouth.

Practise the technique with teachers, demonstrating that the technique is to use the diaphragm so that the abdomen expands, rather than the shoulders rising. This is a simple technique that teachers can use with the child.

Responses of Others

Teachers will be mindful that they must attend to the needs of all the children in their classroom. It is helpful to discuss how best to manage responses of the other children in class if they are distracted and/or disturbed by the child with ADHD. For example, peers may respond by laughing at the child, they may ridicule or humiliate the child, mimic or goad the child. Sometimes the ADHD child's behaviour may be reinforced by attention from peers, leading them to 'play the clown' and/or engage in other attention-seeking behaviours. It is important that teachers remain calm and in control.

Self-talk

Talk to teachers about how they can remind and prompt the child to manage their own activity with helpful self-talk (friendly thoughts). This could include ideas like, 'I know I can manage a few more minutes, then I will have a break' or a funny rhyme like, 'When my feet start to shake, it's time to take a break.'

Signs and Places

You can work with teachers to help them be more aware of the child's needs by noticing the early signs of hyperactivity in a situation and managing it before it becomes destructive. By recognizing early warning signals, the teacher can intervene early to prevent any escalation into over-excited, oppositional and/or confrontational behaviours. Some places and contexts are likely to be more challenging for the child with ADHD, such as assembly, the library, test conditions, story times and quiet writing time. By recognizing the difficult times and places, teachers can develop contingency plans to support the child. Nevertheless, it is important that teachers have realistic expectations; even with acceptable fidget strategies and breaks, a child with ADHD may not manage to be restful for the same length of time as their non-ADHD peers.

Beliefs and Feelings

Support the teachers you work with to look after themselves too. Teachers sometimes feel tired or stretched with their daily schedule and management of a large number of children. In these moments a child with challenging behaviour or needs may seem too demanding, leading to negative attitudes towards the child and/or lowered tolerance. It is essential to support teachers who are thinking or feeling like this to help them identify what they can do to help themselves, such as talking to their manager and/or peers.

What Can We Do As Teachers?

Table 5.5 outlines a suggested approach for teachers, including a list of strategies that can be implemented at school. To maximize the effect of strategies, it is helpful to discuss them with the child's parents/carers so that similar or complementary strategies are implemented at home and school (wherever possible). Lots of teachers and parents/carers find that using a 'Home School Diary' is an efficient way to share information (see Chapter 2).

Table 5.5 School strategies for hyperactivity.

Signs and places
- Be familiar with early warning signs that the child is becoming restless.
- Make a management or contingency plan you can apply if the child becomes restless.
- Discuss this with the child and plan how you will communicate with each other.

Other influential factors
- Consider whether any other factors might be contributing to the behaviour, such as anxiety.
- Consider whether the child may be restless due to a need, like being hungry or thirsty.

Physical activity
- Breaks should be timed and at the end of the break the child should return to the class activity.
- Engage the child in physical activities during breaks.
- Maximize active learning tasks and physical exercise.
- Consider having a gym ball in class (e.g., in the wriggle or time-out space).
- If short breaks are required then lesson notes may need to be taken.

Wiggle space
- Create a wiggle space in the classroom where the child will be undisturbed.

Calm breathing
- Prompt the child to do some simple calming breathing.

Self-talk
- Identify (and prompt) positive self-talk (friendly thoughts) to help them cope.

Staff strategies
- If the child is disruptive or gets out of hand, keep calm and in control. Be fair but firm.
- Give positive and directed requests rather than negative commands.
- Try to be patient and don't lose your temper.
- Ensure that all staff know and understand what strategies are being used and why.

We suggest that teachers read Chapter 2, which provides important background information about the delivery of the Young–Smith Programme. It is unlikely that teachers will have time to go through specific worksheets with children, although if parents/carers are unable to do this it would be helpful to make arrangements with the Special Educational Needs Coordinator. Guidance on how to do this is found in the 'CBT Interventions' section in each chapter. The worksheets introducing Buzz and his family are outlined in Chapter 3. All the materials (worksheets and Home Missions Record Form) are available for downloading from the companion website, www.wiley.com/go/young/helpingadhd. For older children (i.e., 12 years-plus), one may dispense with the Buzz worksheets if necessary, and instead introduce the child directly to the topic, and, using the discussion prompts on the worksheets, apply this to the child's experience and discuss suggested strategies. Set Home Missions and support the child to complete them. Don't forget to give frequent feedback and praise. If a Star Chart is used (see Chapter 2) then this should be put in the 'Home School Diary' so parents/carers can also review it on a regular basis.

References

Abidin, R. (1995). *Parenting stress index* (3rd ed.). Odessa, FL: Psychological Assessment Resources.

American Psychiatric Association. (2013). *Diagnostic and statistical manual of mental disorders* (5th ed.). Washington, DC: American Psychiatric Association.

Conners, C. K. (2008). *Conners 3rd edition*. Toronto: Multi-Health Systems.

Goodman, R. (1997). The strengths and difficulties questionnaire: A research note. *Journal of Child Psychology and Psychiatry and Allied Disciplines*, 38(5), 581–586.

James, A., & Taylor, E. (1990). Sex differences in the hyperkinetic syndrome of childhood. *Journal of Child Psychology and Psychiatry and Allied Disciplines*, 31(3), 437–446.

Sexias, M., Weiss, M., & Müller, U. (2012). Systematic review of national and international guidelines on attention deficit hyperactivity disorder. *Journal of Psychopharmacology*, 26(6), 753–765.

Sonuga-Barke, E. J. S., Brandeis, D., Cortese, S., Daley, D., Ferrin, M., Holtmann, M., et al. (2013). Nonpharmacological interventions for ADHD: Systematic review and meta-analyses of randomized controlled trials of dietary and psychological treatments. *American Journal of Psychiatry*, 170(3), 275–289.

Timmi, S., & Taylor, E. (2004). ADHD is best understood as a cultural construct. *British Journal of Psychiatry*, 184(JAN), 8–9.

6

Impulsivity

Impulsivity is associated with executive functioning skills such as planning, judgement, goal-directed behaviour, inhibition and attention. Children are naturally more impulsive than adults and adolescents as they do not have the experience or skills to foresee the consequences of their actions or the ability to plan ahead. This means that they may repeat things that have previously caused them difficulties or even harm. Children are learning and their brains are developing; hence, within reason, this is a normal function that improves with age.

Impulsivity can be grouped into responses that are premature, mistimed or difficult to suppress, each type meaning that the action is less functional or optimal than it could be (Dalley & Rosier, 2012). It is believed that impulsivity is mediated by disrupted levels of serotonin and dopamine across parts of the brain, including those systems that activate and inhibit behaviour and those that respond to reward. This can be experienced as a person saying what comes to mind before thinking it through, expressing feelings in the moment as they are experienced despite social consequences and acting on thoughts and desires without having thought about their implications and consequences. The thought-to-action process is 'speedy', often leading to inappropriate behaviour and poorly executed outcomes that in some cases may cause harm. However, impulsivity may be a positive trait that allows a person to seize the moment or act spontaneously. The difference between impulsivity and spontaneity relates to degree and timing; the former is often associated with harm being caused to self or others and is therefore seen to be a dysfunctional trait.

This chapter will examine impulsivity in children with ADHD and the impact this can have on their functioning in different areas of life. The assessment of impulsivity will be discussed, followed by interventions and strategies for children and the adults around them based on cognitive behavioural models.

Helping Children with ADHD: A CBT Guide for Practitioners, Parents and Teachers,
First Edition. Susan Young and Jade Smith.
© 2017 John Wiley & Sons Ltd. Published 2017 by John Wiley & Sons Ltd.
Companion website: www.wiley.com/go/young/helpingadhd

Presentation

Children with ADHD are typically more impulsive than their peers in many ways. They often act and speak without any thought about the impact of their behaviour. Because they struggle to inhibit their responses, they require closer adult supervision. It is like living without an internal brake to slow down or make an emergency stop. More often than not, this has negative consequences and leads them to engage in risk-taking and/or addictive behaviours. DSM-5 (American Psychiatric Association, 2013) includes three items for ADHD that relate to impulsivity (see Figure 6.1).

Impulsivity-
- Often blurts out answers before questions have been completed
- Often has difficulty awaiting turn
- Often interrupts or intrudes on others

Figure 6.1 DSM-5 diagnostic criteria for ADHD impulsivity symptoms.

Behavioural Functioning

Because children with ADHD tend to act without thinking, they may not follow rules or think about the potential consequences of their actions. This can get them into trouble at school, and may also mean they exhibit dangerous or reckless behaviour, such as running out in the road, wandering away from their parents/carers side when something takes their interest nearby and touching things which are dangerous, such as electrical items. They may not have a sense of danger in hazardous places, and this can be stressful for those supervising children with ADHD. Often, children with ADHD have a history of minor injuries and/or presentations at accident and emergency services. The core problem for children with ADHD, however, is that they do not learn from their mistakes. Impulsivity inevitably gets children into trouble for 'misbehaving' and/or being careless or oppositional. Adults around these children can find themselves challenged by such behaviours, as everyone involved feels out of control, frustrated and unsure what to do to make positive changes.

Academic Functioning

The school day is difficult for the impulsive child. Impulsivity can lead them to call out in class without putting their hand up or waiting for the question to be completed and interrupting others. This is irritating for both peers and teachers. Impulsive children often make frequent, silly and unnecessary errors as they give the first answer that springs to mind. They respond so rapidly that there is no time to self-monitor or double-check their answer. Sometimes they self-correct, but sometimes they do not; it depends on the task and context, for example, in timed tests they are less likely to check work as they favour speed over accuracy. Even if children with ADHD are allocated additional time in exams, when checking their answers they may make poor use of this time by scanning rather than reading answers carefully and consequently miss errors. In addition, children with ADHD may not expand on answers as they favour speed over depth and detail. Due to the cumulative effect of inattention and impulsivity, it is common for children with ADHD, therefore, to have lower achievement than their academic potential suggests.

Interpersonal Functioning

The acquisition of social skills is a critical aspect of development that includes a complex set of processes which take place intuitively in children without ADHD. Social development involves children learning to fit in and cooperate with peers, and establish roles and social groups. Impulsive behaviour often negatively impacts on social interactions and communications, and those with ADHD may withdraw from social contact and the learning that this encourages. Impulsive and socially inappropriate behaviours will hamper progress, as reactive verbal and behavioural outbursts may lead to misunderstandings and interpersonal conflict. It may also encourage the adoption of undesirable behaviours and the adoption of roles within the social group such as that of the 'class clown'. Consequently, relationships may be superficial and based more on attention-seeking than on true reciprocity in social interactions.

Children with ADHD may be perceived as oppositional, especially if adults around them believe that they are deliberately being rude or difficult 'to get attention' or 'to push people's buttons'. It is not uncommon for children with ADHD to be reprimanded or punished (e.g., with detention), which can be very distressing for them as they feel rejection, regret, embarrassment and shame about upsetting others. The problem is that they can't control their behaviour; the operative work being 'can't', rather and 'won't'. As one little boy once said, 'I want to be good, but my body won't let me.'

Social and academic failure are strongly associated with low self-esteem, which may not in itself be apparent in the overt behaviours that are observed in school, but which may chronically undermine both social and academic development. Some children internalize their difficulties and present with anxiety, low mood and/or depression.

Coping

'Emotional Regulation' is the ability to manage one's own internal emotional states and responses. Children with ADHD have impaired ability to inhibit their responses to emotional states or, at times, understand them. This means that their tolerance can be very low and they are likely to express frustration and anger more readily than their peers. Their emotional response to negative sanctions and/or consequences may be amplified, with increased agitation, sadness and helplessness, leading to temper tantrums, low self-esteem and/or withdrawal. In order to avoid the feeling of being out of control, some children may use denial ('I meant to do it'), asserting that they chose their action. They may minimize consequences and/or act as if they don't care ('So what, it doesn't matter').

Assessment

International guidance on the assessment and treatment of ADHD recommends that a comprehensive assessment procedure is carried out by trained and qualified healthcare practitioners in order to assess ADHD (Sexias, Weiss & Müller, 2012). This often includes a multi-method assessment, involving psychometric questionnaires, a clinical interview and observation of the child to assess difficulties and behaviour in different contexts and settings. It is preferable to obtain multiple perspectives from different people involved in the child's care (including that of the child, if possible), often requiring multi-agency liaison. To develop a care plan with appropriate interventions that are likely to succeed it is important to fully understand the nature and complexity of the child's difficulties across their development, including historic, environmental and psychosocial factors, the child's strengths and weaknesses and the support that they currently receive. In doing this, it is important to be mindful of any comorbid and social problems experienced by the child but also within the family.

We suggest the therapist first meets with the child's parents/carers and teachers to determine which symptoms are the most problematic and the impact of any difficulties on the child's functioning and quality of life. The assessment (and treatment) of risky, reckless and/or dangerous behaviours should always be prioritized, as should consideration of anxiety, depression and social dysfunction.

Measures

Generic ADHD assessments, such as the Conners' Rating Scales 3rd Edition (Conners, 2008) for age six upwards and the Strengths and Difficulties Questionnaire (SDQ; Goodman, 1997) for age two upwards, include an assessment of impulsive behaviours. Ratings are provided by parents/carers and teachers based on observation and knowledge of the child, which are then compared against norms for the child's age and gender. These are useful measures that will provide a pre-treatment baseline which can be repeated at intervals during intervention to assess outcome. An adult should support children completing self-report questionnaires: children with ADHD may misread questions, miss out answers, respond impulsively and/or miscommunicate the rating. However, it is essential that responses are not influenced by leading questions. Children who struggle with reading should always have items read out to them. As is the case for many measures, ratings may be subject to bias and must be interpreted cautiously by a trained practitioner.

There are a number of objective psychometric measures that specifically measure impulsivity or inhibition in children, such as the Test of Everyday Attention for Children (TEA-Ch; Manly, Robertson, Anderson & Nimmo-Smith, 1998), the Delis–Kaplan Executive Function System (DKEFS; Delis, Kaplan & Kramer, 2001), the Brief Rating Inventory of Executive Functioning (BRIEF; Gioia, Isquith, Guy & Kenworthy, 2000) and the Behavioural Assessment of Dysexecutive Syndrome in Children (BADS-C; Emslie, Wilson, Burden, Nimmo-Smith & Wilson, 2003).

Clinical Interview

Through discussion with parents/carers and teachers, and observation of the child, it may be possible to determine in which situations impulsivity is most problematic and what impulse-control strategies are currently being used, either effectively or ineffectively.

Thoughts

There are various cognitive strategies that are applied to help children to stop, think, reduce impulsive responding and engage in a consequential thinking process. These may be introduced from a young age as a routine drill, for example, when crossing the road saying 'look left, look right, look left again and if it's all clear march across'. Hence it is important to establish if the child uses any self-talk techniques to guide their own behaviour by asking, 'Do you ever say things in your head to help you with these problems?' Children have usually heard of strategies such as 'count to three' or 'stop and think'. Do they implement such strategies? Identify strategies that are helpful and strategies that are unhelpful, or even maladaptive. Notice if the child tends to respond with comments such as 'What's the point?' or 'It doesn't work!', as this will signal their readiness and motivation to learn new skills. It is important to impress upon the child, and those providing care, that they can all do things to make life easier.

Feelings and Physiology

Impulsivity may be experienced in a number of ways. You should ask both parents/carers and the child, 'Do feelings ever seem to build up quickly, as if they go from 0 to 100?' 'Does your child react to these feelings, or to situations, immediately?' The therapist can enquire as to whether the child can describe the feeling of disinhibition or impulsivity, for example they may be able to explain, 'It's really fast. I just do things' or 'I feel like a volcano, it just happens'. Enquire whether the child tries to resist the urge to do something. Ask whether this is successful or unsuccessful. Try to ascertain whether there are certain situations or contexts that make it more successful. This is important as you can introduce positive mediators in treatment.

Behaviours

The therapist should aim to establish how the impulsive child presents across settings and situations. Ask parents/carers to describe the most problematic behaviours and ascertain whether there is a level of danger or risk associated with these behaviours. Follow this up by asking if the child has ever been in trouble, been injured or has injured someone else as a consequence of their impulsive behaviour. Impulsivity may not just be expressed by physical behaviours, but also by verbal interactions characterized by the child lacking the ability to inhibit their thoughts, leading to hurtful and upsetting things being said. Assess the contribution of the child's emotional state to such behaviours and interactions –are they associated with emotional reactivity and/or interpersonal conflict? Assess insight by asking the child, 'Have you ever done something without thinking?' 'Has this ever got you in trouble?' 'Have you ever hurt yourself doing something without thinking?' 'Have you upset someone you care about by saying something hurtful and wish you had not?' Determine how other people respond; for example, what helps the situation? have the family stopped going places? does the child get reminded about safety? has supervision been increased?

Observations may help to further understand the nature, severity and contributing factors impulsive behaviours, along with any contributing factors. Ideally observations would be completed across contexts. Try to observe the child in different settings (e.g., during an academic lesson, a practical lesson, at break time, at home or at a leisure activity/club). Such observations are helpful to determine how the child engages with activities, remains on-task, or employs diversionary tactics to avoid work and/or activities. Observation of the child's performance relative to that of their peers will be helpful to indicate peer engagement during unstructured activities at intervals, breaks and lunchtimes. Note successful as well as unsuccessful behaviour-management strategies applied by others. A degree of objectivity can be attained by using school data such as recorded incidents of rule violations, detentions and school exclusions. Positive endorsements such as rewards and achievements should also be noted.

Behaviour Diary

A Behaviour Diary will be useful to assess whether there are patterns that contribute in some way to the behaviour being expressed. This involves parents/carers and/or teachers listing the situations when the child behaves with apparent impulsivity, and recording the antecedents and consequences of the behaviour. Behaviour Diaries are also known as 'ABC charts'. As a practitioner, you will need to determine what is developmentally typical for the child's age and ability, and what may constitute as a difficulty above and beyond that. To help these decisions it is also important to consider comorbid problems and how parents/carers and/or teachers respond to the behaviour. An example of a completed Behaviour Diary for a child named Joe is presented in Table 6.1. It is important to determine risky behaviours that require immediate management, together with those presenting most frequently, in order to prioritize their treatment.

Table 6.1 Example of a completed Behaviour Diary for impulsivity.

Day/ Time	Antecedent (What was happening just before the behaviour? Who was there? What happened earlier in the day that might be relevant?)	Behaviour (What did you observe? Describe the duration and severity.)	Consequence (What happened next? What was the result?)
Monday 12 p.m.	In maths class. Joe's favourite lesson. He is very enthusiastic about maths and looks forward to the lesson.	Joe shouted out continuously when asked to answer questions in class. Joe can work appropriately and complete questions on paper when his teaching assistant sits with him and prompts him to slow down. The problem arose when he had to give verbal answers. When shouting out he gave the wrong answers.	The teacher reprimanded Joe for shouting out and not allowing other children to answer. Other pupils became irritated because they weren't getting the opportunity to answer.
Monday 4 p.m.	At home, after school. Joe was in the kitchen. He was hungry and couldn't wait for dinner.	Joe said he wanted to help. He grabbed a hot tray that had just been taken out of the oven. I told him not to do this but he didn't take any notice.	Joe burnt his hand and cried.

CBT Interventions for Impulsivity

If the therapist is treating younger children and/or the worksheets are being used as a basis for treatment the first session should always commence with Worksheets 1, 2 and 3 to introduce the child to Buzz and his family (Worksheet 1), introduce positive self-talk (Worksheet 2) and identify a reward system (Worksheet 3). The reward and self-talk strategies are applied in the session, at home and/or at school. See Chapter 3 for a suggested outline of how to plan and conduct the introductory session. All the worksheets are available on the companion website, www.wiley.com/go/young/helpingadhd.

The aims of the interventions and worksheets in the impulsivity session(s) are to introduce children to the concept of impulsivity and help them develop skills that will support them to manage their behaviour and improve their ability to slow down and consider consequences. The therapist will achieve this by setting an agenda, reviewing Home Missions completed between sessions, working through new worksheets (or just the strategies for older children) and setting new Home Missions. If required, a mid-session break can be offered halfway through the session; this may be particularly important for younger children. Chapter 2 provides generic information on the structure and content of sessions (irrespective of topic); supplementary information is included within this chapter that specifically relates to the delivery of the impulsivity session(s).

Agenda

At the beginning of the session show the child the written agenda (see Figure 6.2) that you have prepared prior to the session and go through it, verbally linking the themes and worksheets that you will introduce during the session. For the impulsivity module, introduce Worksheets 9 and 10 by saying:

Agenda

Folder Review

Buzz goes to Hospital [Worksheet 9]

Break

Buzz at the Theme Park [Worksheet 10]

Home Missions

Figure 6.2 Example agenda for impulsivity session(s).

In this story Buzz has an accident. He doesn't look before crossing the road and has to go to hospital. We will think together about how he could have stopped that happening. After that, we will have a short break and you can colour in the worksheet using these crayons. After the break we are going to look at another worksheet and talk about what happens when Buzz goes to a theme park for the day with his family.

Folder Review

When reviewing the folder with the child, aside from checking whether the Home Missions are completed, take the opportunity to revise important information and/or concepts, as this will help the child to consolidate the learning points and/or newly acquired skills. Ensure that you make time to look at the illustrations, colourings, paintings, magazine cuttings and/or photographs that the child has added to the folder. Discuss them and try to relate these to discussions about Buzz and his family and/or topics or strategies that have been covered. Aside from acting as a revision prompt, this will also act as a reward system for the child. Praise should be given verbally, but you can also reward by adding stickers, handwritten notes or smiley faces. If Home Missions were set then you should review the Home Missions Record Form for comments and feedback from parents/carers and discuss this with the child. See Chapter 2 for more information about the folder review and Home Missions.

Worksheet 9   Buzz goes to Hospital

Worksheet Description

To download this worksheet, please visit the companion website

Buzz is a fast runner and he has been asked to play football for his local team called the Home Rangers. It is an important day and Buzz is very excited. Buzz sees the team waiting for him in the park, which is the other side of a busy road. There is a crossing further down the road, but Buzz can't wait to join the team and he runs across the road without looking. Buzz doesn't notice the boy on his bicycle who crashes into him. The boy falls off his bike and hurts his arm. Buzz breaks his leg. They both have to go to hospital. Buzz is very sorry.

Worksheet Prompts

Why did Buzz not walk down to the crossing?
What should Buzz have thought about before rushing across the road? What should he have done?

(Continued)

> **Worksheet 9 (Continued)**
>
> Can you think of any other situations when Buzz might not stop and think?
> Tell me a story about a time that you did not stop and think? How did it turn out?
> What should you have done? Would it have ended differently or better?
> Together let's write out some ideas of the things that Buzz can do to help him stop and think.
> Now let's look at the things you thought would help Buzz and circle the ones that might also help you.

Worksheet 9 introduces the concept of impulsivity. Children are introduced to the term 'stop and think' and the consequences of impulsive behaviours. They then apply Buzz's experience to themselves by discussing scenarios when they have acted without thinking. In this exercise the child will develop skills and compensatory strategies that will reduce impulsive and reckless behaviours.

Read the Stimulus Sheet aloud to the child, or, if they wish, they can read it to you. Answer any questions they might have. Check that the child understood the story and was paying attention. In the story, Buzz rushes across a road and is hit by a bicycle. He was lucky he was not hit by a car or did not sustain greater injury. If children are concerned, you can explain that Buzz and the boy were hurt but they were not fatal injuries. It did mean that Buzz couldn't play football for a while. The situation could have been more dangerous and that is why you will be thinking together about what Buzz could have done differently.

First, direct the child to consider why the accident happened by asking, 'What happened to cause Buzz's accident? Why did Buzz not use the crossing?' If the child answers that the crossing was too far away, you can confirm that Buzz probably did think that, but ask, 'Was there another reason?' Encourage the child to consider that Buzz was doing things quickly or impatiently. Then, encourage them to reflect on what they think Buzz should have done instead. The child is likely to have ideas about crossing roads, such as looking both ways or going to a safe place, even if they are not used to doing this on their own. Move the conversation on to consider other situations where the child imagines Buzz might struggle to stop and think.

This should then lead naturally to a discussion of the child's experiences. If they struggle with this, prompt them with common examples like, 'How about when you have complicated maths problems, or when you line up to go out to break?' 'Have you ever been told by your parents/carers to walk with them rather than running ahead?' Together think of some ideas that might have helped Buzz, and write them on the Task Sheet (e.g., double-check, ask for help, think about what might happen, count to five). The final step is for the child to consider how Buzz could have behaved differently (drawing on their own experiences) and how those ideas might help them. 'If you went a bit more slowly with your work, what do you think would happen, instead of making lots of mistakes?' 'Yes, I think you're right, hopefully you would get more right and get a sticker.' Prompt the child to think of things that would help them to take more time when doing homework, such as making a 'STOP and THINK' sign and pinning it to the wall where they do their homework.

Give praise for the child's effort in the session. If you choose to set Home Missions based on this Worksheet we suggest asking the child to do the following:

1) Decorate the Worksheet by colouring in the pictures and thought bubbles, and/or add to them with pictures on the theme of the story. These could be photographs or pictures in magazines or comics.
2) Make a 'STOP and THINK' sign. This could be decorated and displayed as a poster where you do your homework, in the bedroom or somewhere prominent like the fridge. A small version could also be made for your desk at school or put in your bag or pocket, and act as a reminder.
3) (For children who identify specific settings where they are impulsive, e.g., when crossing busy roads.) Make a self-instructional guide to follow in situations where you are impulsive. Write down a set of instructions to remind yourself of what to do, such as 'dangerous road, stop, wait for Mum', 'walk don't run', 'hold hands', 'look left, look right, look left again and if its all clear march across'. This can be supported by self-praise and praise from others when noticed. You should ask your parent/carer to help you with this to make sure you don't miss any steps. You should then practise in the week.
4) Try out one or more of the ideas from the worksheet that might help you with waiting. Ask your parents/carers and/or teachers to help try out the strategies and implement the ideas.

If Home Missions are set, remind parents/carers to complete the Home Missions Record Form and to place it in the folder for review at the next session.

Mid-session Break

This should be provided at an appropriate point in the session as outlined in Chapter 2.

Worksheet 10 Buzz at the Theme Park

Worksheet Description

To download this worksheet, please visit the companion website

As a treat, Buzz's Mum took him and his brother to a theme park. Buzz was very excited about the day out. It took a long time to drive there and his brother got annoyed as Buzz kept fidgeting in his seat and interrupting him when he was talking. When they arrived the park was very busy and there were long queues for the rides. Buzz was impatient to go on a ride and he kept running up the line to try and get to the front. A man told Buzz off for pushing in. Buzz's Mum got annoyed and said they would leave if he didn't wait his turn.

Worksheet Prompts

Who was feeling annoyed with Buzz and why?
How do you think Buzz felt inside and why?
Do you find it hard to wait your turn?
Tell me about a time when you found it hard to wait. What happened?
Together let's write out some ideas for things Buzz can do to help him wait.
Now let's look at the things you thought would help Buzz and circle the ones that might also help you.

Worksheet 10 aims to encourage children to develop insight into their impulsive behaviours and how others may perceive them. In the exercise, children develop skills in predicting when difficult situations may arise and methods to self-regulate and manage their behaviour. In addition, the exercise offers the opportunity to develop skills to resolve interpersonal difficulties.

The story is about Buzz becoming over-excited about a visit to a theme park. Because he is so excited, his ADHD symptoms become more marked and he has difficulty controlling his behaviour. Read the Stimulus Sheet to the child, or, if they wish, they can read it with you. Check that the child understood the story and was paying attention, and answer any questions they might have. If the child has never visited a theme park, check that they have an understanding of what it is like. Most children have visited a theme park at some time, or something similar such as a fair or fete that includes rides and/or a bouncy castle. Also ensure that the child has understood the terms introduced in the story, such as 'impatient'.

Direct the child to consider Buzz's feelings of anticipation and excitement by asking, 'What was happening in the car on the way there?' 'How was Buzz feeling about the trip out?' Talk about how Buzz's feelings of excitement affected his behaviour (fidgeting, interrupting). Move on to the Discussion Sheet, asking who became annoyed with Buzz and why (his brother, his Mum, the man in the queue). The child may have opinions on whether it was okay for others to feel annoyed or not. You can help the child to reflect on this by asking things like, 'Do you think they knew why Buzz was feeling impatient?' Remember to summarize regularly, 'That's right, the man in the queue was annoyed.' 'How do you think Buzz was feeling inside?' You can give prompts like, 'What does it feel like in your body if you feel like that?' or 'That's a great description, do you know a name for that feeling?

Move the conversation on to the child's own experience of waiting. If he/she has difficulty recalling situations, suggest some common examples such as waiting for lunch at school or waiting to pay at the supermarket. After this, work together to think of ideas that could have helped Buzz keep himself amused and occupied so the wait didn't seem so bad, 'Is there something Buzz could have been doing whilst waiting?' Write these ideas on the Task Sheet. Finally, ask the child to circle any of these ideas that could help them when they themselves are struggling in a waiting situation. Add any extra ideas for themselves that they mention, such as having an activity to do, talking to someone and letting someone know if it is difficult to wait. If the child suggests that there should never be any waiting, acknowledge that might be nice but in life there are times when everyone has to wait (perhaps they can think of some times when they keep others waiting!).

Give praise for the child's effort in the session. If you choose to set Home Missions based on this worksheet we suggest asking the child to do the following:

1) Decorate the worksheet by colouring in the pictures and thought bubbles, and/or add to them with pictures on the theme of the story. These could be photographs or pictures in magazines or comics.
2) Think up situations when you find it very difficult to wait. Write these down and show it to your parents/carers and teachers.
3) Try out one or more of the ideas from the worksheet that might help you with waiting. Ask parents/carers and/or teachers to help you to try out the strategies and implement the ideas.

If Home Missions are set, remind parents/carers to complete the Home Missions Record Form and to place this is the folder for review at the next session.

Feedback and Rewards

At the end of the session, appropriate rewards identified from the Worksheet 3 Reward Task should be applied (e.g., the child should engage in positive self-talk). See Chapter 2 for more information about feedback and rewards.

Working with Parents/Carers

This section presents strategies that parents/carers can apply to manage the child's impulsive behaviour. These are largely behavioural strategies but they often include a cognitive component.

It is important to be realistic about what can be achieved. It can be just as helpful to learn strategies to cope better with a child's behaviour as to learn strategies to improve the behaviour itself. In this section we discuss a method to monitor behaviour using a Behaviour Diary and discuss behavioural strategies that aim to reduce impulsivity and risk-taking behaviours. We present ways to rehearse new skills in a graduated hierarchy of challenging tasks that aims to improve problem behaviours in specific situations and contexts. In addition, we discuss cognitive strategies that aim to support the child to improve planning skills, cope with periods of waiting and delayed gratification and reduce errors in schoolwork. When working with parents/carers, the therapist should introduce suggested techniques and strategies; practise and rehearse them in role-plays during the sessions if appropriate (without the child present). Parents/carers should report back to the therapist on how they managed at home. In future sessions, it is important to troubleshoot any obstacles and/or difficulties that arise by thinking of ways to adapt the techniques or strategies so they are successful in helping the child.

A key strategy to change behaviour and improve cognitive skills is to find motivators to promote success. Children with ADHD tend to respond better to immediate rewards, as they have difficulty with delayed gratification for longer-term rewards (even if these are bigger and better). Methods to motivate success (including the use of a Star Chart) and other topics that are generic to working with parents/carers are described in Chapter 2. Supplementary information that specifically relates to the delivery of the impulsivity session(s) is outlined in this chapter.

Behaviour Diary

In order to home in on specific situations in which the child struggles with being impulsive, ask parents/carers to complete a Behaviour Diary (described earlier in this chapter) to monitor behaviour. Discuss the information recorded in the diary with the parents/carers to gain further insight and understanding about the type of behaviour, its triggers and when it is most likely to present. Over time patterns emerge that may explain the causes of some behaviours. Using this, discuss with the parents/carers what interventions can be introduced earlier on to avoid a problem developing.

Planning Ahead

Using the Behaviour Diary, work with parents/carers to help them predict difficult and/or challenging situations. These might include social situations, waiting and/or public spaces with lots of distractions when a child might run off.

Encourage parents/carers to consider why these situations are most challenging in relation to impulsivity, and what they can do to plan ahead for them. Ideas might include: having to hand activities for the child; taking the Star Chart and extra supports out with them; talking to the child beforehand to prepare them; setting rules and/or boundaries; letting people around them know what to expect; obtaining queue-jump passes; and having an extra adult accompany them (especially if the situation is particularly risky). Encourage parents/carers to think about a pending situation, decide what they can do to minimize problems, and put their ideas into practice. Discuss how they got on in future sessions and troubleshoot problems that arose. This will help parents/carers feel more confident and in control and help the child learn how to control his/her behaviour in specific settings. As a result, everyone has a more positive experience.

Managing Risk

A priority for parents/carers is to identify and manage potential risks; most have experienced a child rushing towards a busy road, burning his/her fingers on a hot plate, jumping into water that is too deep or climbing on things that are unstable. Aside from planning ahead and ensuring adequate supervision is on hand, discuss with parents/carers the need to 'read' situations as they arise by persistently assessing and re-assessing the environment. This will give them the opportunity to avoid risky situations from arising, for example, by removing hot or sharp objects from reach. Teach parents/carers to 'read' a pending situation out loud, for example, 'We are approaching a busy road. You need to hold my hand so that you can stay safe.' Explain the rationale for this behaviour, explicitly stating the risk and alerting the child to consequences they might not have thought about or understood, 'We don't want to get run over, so let's check carefully to the left, to the right, to the left again, and when it is all clear we march across so we reach the other side safely.' This simultaneously models a cognitive strategy of consequential thinking and a behavioural strategy for the child to follow when unaccompanied.

STOP and THINK

This is a specific technique that can be taught to the child to interrupt impulsive and automatic responses, and instead promote a process that guides them to consider alternative behaviours and their potential outcomes. It can be applied to help the child to slow down their pace and to consider consequences. The STOP and THINK technique can be associated with a mnemonic around the word STOP, as follows:

> **S**top
> **T**hink: What might happen if you do that?
> **O**ptions: What could you do instead?
> **P**roceed: Go

Aside from teaching the technique to parents/carers and the child (using real-life issues or challenges), the therapist must identify a signal to trigger the process. This may differ depending on the situation, and could be triggered by parents/carers raising a hand to indicate STOP (with a more subtle version being used in public places). Other triggers could also be identified, such as road signs, but also verbal cues by simply saying 'stop'. Children could also make up a cue card and place this in salient places. The therapist should work out, together with parents/carers, how best to introduce the technique, how to trigger the process and get the child's attention and what outcomes they want the child to consider. The technique will teach the child that they can engage in a functional decision-making process. Parents/carers must ensure that they reinforce and reward their child for engaging with the process. You can suggest that parents/carers model the technique to the child by doing it out loud; this is a technique that works with practice and it is important to be consistent.

Alternatives and Distractions

Waiting can be an aversive experience for children with ADHD, as they struggle with delayed gratification and find it hard to manage boredom. You can work with parents/carers to think about ways they can keep their child busy during times of waiting. Ideas could include having a puzzle book, an impromptu game to play together (such as 'I spy with my little eye ...'), a handheld game, or fiddle toy. Activities could also be functional helping tasks, such as assisting parents/carers to unload the supermarket trolley.

Graded Practice

Develop a programme to increase the child's tolerance for delayed gratification, and, in turn, this will also reduce impulsive behaviours. For example, children often get bored when going to a restaurant for lunch or dinner, as the wait for their food to arrive seems intolerable. Many restaurants have resolved this by offering children paper placemats and crayons so they can complete puzzles and/or colour in pictures. However, it is not possible to control the wait time, so parents/carers can be taught a graded practice technique that can be used at home to 'train' children to tolerate longer wait times. First, identify the length of time the child can tolerate waiting for dinner to be served at home, and then gradually extend the wait time by a few minutes each week. Introduce distractions to support the child. This will help the child to build-up a tolerance to the frustration of waiting. If the child isn't able to manage the wait, parents/carers should reduce the time and start again. The idea is that the child begins to associate waiting with a reward (fun activity, nice dinner) rather than something aversive.

Small Steps

Consider tasks when the child is commonly impulsive and, with parents/carers, think about how to break them down into smaller steps to be systematically worked through, rather than rushing ahead to the finishing line. This encourages a slower and more controlled process. The key is to write out the steps, giving praise and rewards at interim steps as well as once the task has been completed. Remember to check that parents/carers are being realistic in their expectations.

Double-checking

A hazard of impulsivity is making mistakes and errors due to rushing and not planning ahead. Encourage parents/carers to support the child to double-check, for example, by matching what they have done with a list of what was needed, reading through instructions and checking they understand rather than guessing and rushing ahead. Parents/carers should also model the double-checking process by doing it themselves and speaking out loud.

What Can We Do As Parents/Carers?

Table 6.2 outlines a suggested approach, including a list of strategies that can be implemented at home. To maximize the effect of strategies, it is helpful to discuss them with your child's teacher so they can be implemented at both home and school (wherever possible). Lots of parents/carers and teachers find that using a 'Home School Diary' is an efficient way to share information (see Chapter 2).

We suggest that parents/carers read Chapter 2, which provides important background information about the delivery of the Young–Smith Programme. For younger children, we suggest that parents/carers set aside some time to sit down with the child (around 45–60 minutes) and work through the worksheets recommended for each topic. Guidance is found in the 'CBT Interventions' section in each chapter. The worksheets introducing Buzz and his family are outlined in Chapter 3. All the materials (worksheets and Home Missions Record Form) are available to download from the companion website, www.wiley.com/go/young/helpingadhd. For older children (i.e., 12 years-plus), you can dispense with the Buzz worksheets if necessary and instead introduce the child directly to the topic, and, using the discussion prompts on the worksheets, apply this to the child's experience and discuss suggested strategies. Set Home Missions and support the child to complete them. Don't forget to give frequent feedback and praise. Make a Star Chart (see Chapter 2), put it in a prominent place and start to use it on a daily basis

Table 6.2 Home strategies for impulsivity.

Planning ahead
- Be prepared!
- Identify challenging and risky situations.
- Prepare your child by talking to them about the situation beforehand.
- Set explicit rules and boundaries that your child agrees to.
- Prepare other adults and gain their support.
- Plan constructive activities to avoid boredom.
- Obtain queue jump passes.
- Use the Star Chart and reward systems.

Managing risk
- Ensure there is sufficient supervision.
- Persistently assess and re-assess the environment.
- Remove items of risk from sight and reach.
- Model the process by explaining the risk and the rationale for adopting appropriate behaviour.

STOP and THINK
- Teach the STOP and THINK process by using the STOP mnemonic.
- Identify a signal to trigger the process (both verbal and visual).
- Make up cue cards and place them where they might be helpful at home.

Alternatives and distractions
- Keep your child occupied if they feel bored or have to wait.
- Develop a repertoire of games and activities that can quickly be applied.
- Always keep a book, puzzle, fiddle toy and/or hand held game in your bag.

Graded practice
- Rehearse difficult situations at home.
- Gradually build-up tolerance to waiting through home-based exercises.

Small steps
- Break tasks down into smaller steps, write out the steps.
- Give interim praise/rewards as well as on completion of the task.

Double-checking
- Cross check what's been done against a task list to ensure nothing has been missed.
- Check instructions have been understood.

Working with Teachers and Schools

The following section includes strategies to manage the child's impulsive behaviour and ways to help them begin to recognize the ways they think and cope. In the classroom, children are expected to be able to wait and work in slow and methodical ways. In this section we discuss behavioural strategies that aim to reduce impulsivity and risk-taking behaviours. In addition, we discuss cognitive strategies that aim to improve planning skills, cope with periods of waiting and delayed gratification and reduce errors in schoolwork. It is important to be realistic about what can be achieved. It can be just as helpful to learn strategies to cope better with a child's behaviour as to learn strategies to improve the behaviour itself. There are numerous times when impulsive behaviour can become problematic, therefore the aim of the chapter is to find ways of managing these times whilst helping the child to acquire and develop skills to control impulsive responses.

Teachers and schools will already have structures in place to support many of the interventions introduced in the Young–Smith Programme. It will be useful to link up parents/carers and teachers to encourage an integrated strategy and share success. It is important to troubleshoot any obstacles and/or difficulties that arise by thinking of ways to adapt the techniques or strategies so they are successful in helping the child. Methods to motivate success and other topics that are generic to working with teachers and schools are described in Chapter 2. Supplementary information that specifically relates to the delivery of the impulsivity session(s) is outlined in this chapter.

Planning Ahead

Teachers are very good at planning ahead and preparing for every eventuality. During school trips they have additional help from fellow teachers and often from volunteer parents/carers as well. Remind teachers that children with ADHD are prone to impulsive and reckless behaviours, especially if the child becomes very excitable (such as on a school trip) when their ADHD symptoms are likely to be exacerbated.

Managing Risk

Teachers may be concerned about a child's impulsive behaviour because of the negative or dangerous potential consequences that could arise, especially in classrooms with scientific equipment, tools or sports equipment, and when out on school grounds or on school visits. Schools usually have risk-assessment procedures in place, and these work well and afford the child with ADHD every opportunity and encourage inclusive learning in a safe environment. Teachers will, however, need to consider whether the child with ADHD requires additional (perhaps individual) supervision for some activities (such as using Bunsen Burners in science classes). It is also important to set rules and boundaries and to explain the rationale for them, for example, 'We are going to be using glue today and because it can damage clothes we must all put on our overalls and be very careful where we put it. This means that we don't wave the glue brush around like a magic wand or hold it near people's faces and hair.'

STOP and THINK

Teachers can also apply the STOP and THINK technique described in the parent/carer section of this chapter. Teachers may trigger the technique by using the same visual or verbal sign used by parents/carers at home and/or by placing a sign to cue the technique at the front of the classroom (and tap it as needed to draw attention to it). Teachers can apply the technique by using a whole-class approach, as well as modelling it by doing it out loud themselves to demonstrate the thinking process.

Alternatives and Distractions

Waiting can be an aversive experience for children with ADHD, as they struggle with delayed gratification. Teachers might consider having additional small tasks to keep children with ADHD busy while they are waiting. Ideas could include adding in a break, having a reading book, providing a fiddle toy or doing a job in the classroom (e.g., taking something somewhere which would also incorporate movement).

Answering Questions and Taking Turns

Teachers are already well trained in supporting children in answering questions and taking turns, but it should be reinforced how crucial this is for a child with ADHD, as interrupting and turn taking can be difficult. Teachers can support the child by rewarding their efforts to follow social rules and being able to have a turn or answer a question. They may need additional reminders about why this is important (e.g., to prevent their peers becoming annoyed if answers are called out by accident).

Small Steps

Teachers can encourage a slower and more controlled approach to tasks by encouraging the child to break it into smaller steps. For example, when children are excited about playing outside at break-time in winter because there is snow on the ground, the teacher can prompt the children to change into their outdoor clothes before they go outside. Rather than rushing off and out of the door the process is broken down, with the teacher telling the children to 'Go to the cloakroom, put on your boots, coat, scarf, hat and gloves.' Teachers commonly use this method in a whole-class manner to prompt desired behaviours. It is important that the child is informed of the rationale and potential consequences if they rush ahead, 'We don't want you to catch a cold, or ruin your shoes and get into trouble at home.'

Double-checking

One hazard of impulsivity is making mistakes and errors due to rushing and not planning ahead. Teachers can also apply the double-checking technique described in the parents/carers section of this chapter.

What Can We Do As Teachers?

Table 6.3 outlines a suggested approach for teachers, including a list of strategies that can be implemented at school. To maximize the effect of strategies, it is helpful to discuss them with the child's parents/carers so that similar or complementary strategies are implemented at home and school (wherever possible). Both teachers and parents/carers find that using a 'Home School Diary' is an efficient way to share information (see Chapter 2).

Table 6.3 School strategies for impulsivity.

Planning ahead
- Be prepared! Consider potential risks and how they might be minimized.
- For school trips, consider how many children with ADHD might be on the trip and what additional resources may be needed.
- Set explicit rules and boundaries that the child agrees to.
- Prepare other adults and gain their support.
- Obtain queue jump passes.

Managing risk
- Ensure there is sufficient supervision.
- Persistently assess and re-assess the environment.
- Remove unnecessary items of risk from sight and reach.
- Monitor the use of items that present potential risk.
- Model the process by explaining the risk and the rationale for adopting appropriate behaviour.

STOP and THINK
- Teach the STOP and THINK process by using the STOP mnemonic.
- Make up cue cards and place them where they might be helpful at school.
- Identify a signal to trigger the process (both verbal and visual).

Alternatives and distractions
- Keep the child occupied if they feel bored or have to wait.
- Develop a repertoire of games and activities that can quickly be applied.
- Introduce a break or physical activity.

Small steps
- Break tasks down into smaller steps, specify them verbally.
- Write them out and put up as 'Remember Notices'.
- Give interim praise/rewards as well as on completion of the task.

Double-checking
- Cross check what's been done against a task list to ensure nothing has been missed.
- Check instructions have been understood.

Staff collaboration
Ensure that all staff know and understand what strategies are being used and why.

We suggest that teachers read Chapter 2, which provides important background information about the delivery of the Young–Smith Programme. It is unlikely that teachers will have time to go through specific worksheets with children, although if parents/carers are unable to do this it would be helpful to make arrangements with the Special Educational Needs Coordinator. Guidance on how to do this is found in the 'CBT Interventions' section in each chapter. The worksheets introducing Buzz and his family are outlined in Chapter 3. All the materials (worksheets and Home Missions Record Form) are available for download from the companion website, www.wiley.com/go/young/helpingadhd. For older children (i.e., 12 years-plus), one can dispense with the Buzz worksheets if necessary and instead introduce the child directly to the topic, and, using the discussion prompts on the worksheets, apply this to the child's experience and discuss suggested strategies. Set Home Missions and support the child to complete them. Don't forget to give frequent feedback and praise. If a Star Chart is used (see Chapter 2) then this could be put in the 'Home School Diary' where parents/carers can also review it on a regular basis.

References

American Psychiatric Association. (2013). *Diagnostic and statistical manual of mental disorders* (5th ed.). Washington, DC: American Psychiatric Association.

Conners, C. K. (2008). *Conners 3rd edition*. Toronto: Multi-Health Systems.

Dalley, J. W., & Roiser, J. P. (2012). Dopamine, serotonin and impulsivity. *Neuroscience, 215*(July), 42–58.

Delis, D. C., Kaplan, E., & Kramer, J. H. (2001). *Delis–Kaplan Executive Function System (D-KEFS)*. San Antonio, TX: The Psychological Corporation.

Emslie, H., Wilson, F. C., Burden, V., Nimmo-Smith, I., & Wilson, B. A. (2003). *The behavioural assessment of dysexecutive syndrome in children*. London: Harcourt Assessment.

Gioia, G. A., Isquith, P. K., Guy, S. C., & Kenworthy, L. (2000). *Behavior rating inventory of executive function (BRIEF)*. Odessa, FL: Psychological Assessment Resources.

Goodman, R. (1997). The strengths and difficulties questionnaire: A research note. *Journal of Child Psychology and Psychiatry and Allied Disciplines, 38*(5), 581–586.

Manly, T., Robertson, I. H., Anderson, V., & Nimmo-Smith, I. (1998). *Test of Everyday Attention for Children (TEA-Ch)*. London: Pearson Assessment.

Sexias, M., Weiss, M., & Müller, U. (2012). Systematic review of national and international guidelines on attention deficit hyperactivity disorder. *Journal of Psychopharmacology, 26*(6), 753–765.

7

Anxiety

Anxiety is a state of increased arousal affecting our physiological response, thought and behaviour. It should be kept in mind that anxiety is a normal and functional trait that occurs when reacting to stress or a perceived threat. If a person were in a cage with a tiger, for example, the autonomic arousal associated with anxiety would prepare them for 'fight or flight'. It is dysfunctional, however, when that level of extreme arousal occurs when preparing to speak in front of the class, sit a school quiz or exam or manage interactions with adults and peers etc. There are predisposing factors that increase the risk of a person developing anxiety, including psychosocial factors which place stress on the family, parenting style and family history of anxiety.

Up to 50 % of children with ADHD suffer with comorbid anxiety, which is associated with higher levels of inattention, impulsivity, school worries and lower social competence (Pliszka, 1998; Bowen, Chavira, Bailey, Stein & Stein, 2008). These children may be less responsive to treatment solely with ADHD medication and require a multi-modal approach (Jensen et al., 2001). Hence, ADHD and comorbid anxiety may have a particularly debilitating impact on the developing child, with anxiety impacting not only on individual performance and function, but also on quality of life.

This chapter will examine anxiety in children with ADHD and the impact this can have on their functioning in different areas of life. It will discuss assessment of anxiety, followed by interventions and strategies for children and the adults around them using cognitive behavioural models.

Presentation

The hallmark of anxiety is negative thinking (cognitive), physiological arousal and avoidance (behavioural responses). It is associated with working memory deficits (e.g., inattention and concentration problems). Hence, children with

Helping Children with ADHD: A CBT Guide for Practitioners, Parents and Teachers,
First Edition. Susan Young and Jade Smith.
© 2017 John Wiley & Sons Ltd. Published 2017 by John Wiley & Sons Ltd.
Companion website: www.wiley.com/go/young/helpingadhd

ADHD and comorbid anxiety have 'double the trouble', with their cognitive symptoms becoming more marked (Ferrin & Vance, 2014). Figure 7.1 presents the anxiety cycle for children with ADHD within a cognitive behavioural framework. Early and negative neurodevelopmental experiences, together with their ADHD symptoms, may lead children to have negative beliefs about themselves, poor self-efficacy and low self-esteem. When faced with challenging situations they are uncertain about their abilities and fear failure and/or rejection.

Neuropsychological deficits
Inattention, impulsivity, poor planning, poor memory, and poor organisation

Early experience
Negative interactions, reprimands, criticisms, blame, misunderstandings, and failure

Beliefs
I am not good enough
I am not liked
There is something wrong with me

Situation requiring performance, skills, or socially appropriate behaviour

Thought: I can't do it
Feeling: Anxiety
Intervention: Give up, withdraw, and avoid situations
Outcome: Negative

Thought: I can't do it
Feeling: Anxiety
Intervention: Draw upon resilience, positive self-talk, motivating self-statements, and seek guidance and support from others
Outcome: Positive

Future Expectation
Failure

Future Expectation
Success and increased self-efficacy

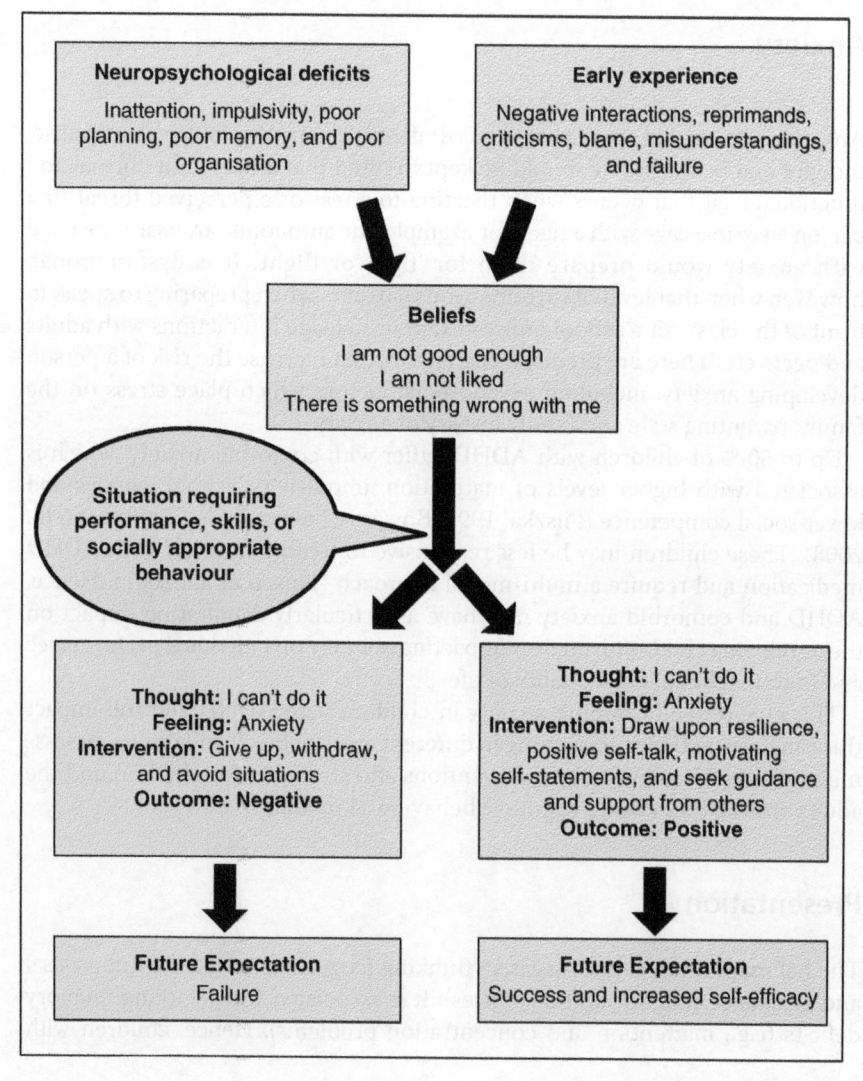

Figure 7.1 Cognitive Behavioural Therapy formulation of anxiety in children with ADHD.

In response to these feelings, the intervention applied will direct the future. Withdrawal and avoidance will result in temporary relief away from the source of the anxiety and perceived threat, but this means the child has not achieved the goal and may miss out on opportunities to further develop their skills and resilience. The cycle repeats itself: situation, anxiety, withdrawal; a self-fulfilling prophecy arises, with the child deliberately avoiding future similar situations. The expectations of others, and indeed of the child itself, are low. Anxiety further impacts on the child's appraisal of the future, as this is based on past evaluations, leading to worries that things will go badly, they will be judged, reprimanded or fail.

The process can be interrupted with an intervention that fosters engagement and resilience, and motivates achievement. This can be achieved by both cognitive interventions (positive self-talk, motivating self-statements) and behavioural interventions (facing up to the situation rather than avoiding it, gaining support from others). This leads to a future expectation of success and belief in yourself. The goal may not be perfectly achieved, but it has been reached as the child has not avoided and failed the task. The problem for children with ADHD is that their symptoms become exacerbated when feeling anxious, and they become more inattentive, hyperactive and impulsive.

Anxiety further impacts on memory and organization and increases restlessness, leading to dysfunctional coping processes, such as aimlessly expending energy by running around in circles and/or engaging in attention seeking behaviours. Thus a vicious cycle of ADHD, anxiety and failure occurs. Hence, anxious children with ADHD are more disadvantaged than anxious children without ADHD, not least because their ADHD deficits cause them to be less likely to attend to helpful stimuli, such as advice or support provided by others. It is very important that they develop strategies to counteract symptoms of anxiety when they arise.

Behavioural Functioning

Anxiety may present in many different situations and/or settings, for example, at home and school, in extra-curricular social activities (e.g., sports and youth clubs), in social interactions, when there are clear expectations they will perform to a set standard and when trying to meet the expectations of others. Negative experiences become aversive experiences and, in turn, children do their best to avoid them. The 'flight' response may present in children making excuses to miss school (or other social situations) by pretending to be sick, or in more severe cases openly refusing to attend school.

Young people are faced with a series of challenges and dilemmas which are part of growing up, such as a desire to 'fit in', achieve good grades, make friends, and learn how to communicate effectively. Sometimes, managing academic and social milestones can feel overwhelming and stressful. Children with

ADHD face the same daily challenges as their peers (desiring social approval, developing their identity, making it through school, living in a family and managing daily hassles of life); however, they may perform less competently than their peers of the same developmental level, leaving them susceptible to feelings of anxiety, vulnerability, difference and insecurity. They may suffer more experiences of failure, misunderstanding, stigma, lack of control and negative judgement of others, and, as a result, fall out easily with friends and family. Some children respond with bravado and/or by putting on a 'macho' front to convince people around them that they do not care what people think about them or how they behave. In some cases, the child may display low levels of empathy and mask their feelings of underlying anxiety with an aggressive and confrontational interpersonal style.

Academic Functioning

In school, children are constantly evaluated. They are expected to perform academically, socially and behaviourally, and to maintain standards set by teachers and governments at all times. The consequence of not performing adequately is negative feedback to parents/carers, disapproval, punishment and social rejection by peers. Children are told that this will impact negatively on their future.

Children with ADHD make more errors, they miss important information and they sometimes make unwise decisions or take inappropriate actions. The pressure to succeed, achieve and meet high standards may make them anxious. At school they often become stressed about small things (especially if they feel they are being evaluated) such as planning a story, organizing their school bag, listening to the teacher giving instructions, taking turns in a game or waiting to answer a question. These may seem like everyday activities, but they require skills that children with ADHD struggle with. In turn, their anxiety will exacerbate symptoms of ADHD, which further hampers their performance and skills, leading them to make more mistakes and feel less in control of their behaviour.

Interpersonal Functioning

Children with ADHD often struggle to apply the essential skills needed to interact effectively with peers, other adults around them and family members. They may worry a lot about how they 'fit in' and come across. They may lack insight into their behaviour, feel that they are being unfairly criticized and blame others for their struggles. Social anxiety, which increases self-consciousness and self-focused thought, distracts the child's attention from important information and stimuli around them. Important information is already missed due to natural inattention in ADHD and is further impacted on by the distractions of self-consciousness and self-focus. This results in a cumulative effect of missed information and can lead to misunderstanding situations, interpersonal conflict and further experience of negative interactions and views of self. It also increases anxiety as children begin to notice and over-evaluate their efforts to interact and may fail to listen to what others say, leaving others feeling unheard or not understood. Failed attempts at establishing, sustaining and repairing peer relationships can cause them to either withdraw from social contact or to adopt the role of the 'class clown', and thus succeed in securing the attention they desire, but at the expense of their own academic progress and disruption to the learning of others.

Coping

An increased experience of failure will inevitably lead to feelings of low self-efficacy and low self-esteem. Children with ADHD are less able to cope with these negative emotions because they have poor problem-solving skills because their symptoms cause them to be less able to accurately appraise a problem, generate solutions, plan, organize and follow through with the best solution (see Chapter 11). Withdrawal and avoidance ('flight' mode) of the anxiety-provoking situation is a quick and effective 'fix'. Responding in 'fight' mode, however, may also bring problems for the child with ADHD who has difficulty with self-regulation, leading to irritability and aggression, increased attention to perceived threat stimuli and misappraisal of the intentions and responses of others. In turn, the child is less likely to attend to supportive and helpful interventions.

As some children mature they may learn to manage their anxiety symptoms by over-control. This is more common in young people of high intellectual ability who set rigid rules to which they adhere in order to overcompensate for their difficulties. This may lead to perfectionistic traits and the setting of unrealistically high expectations. These traits may include rigidity over matters of order, repetitive behaviours in an attempt to 'undo' or make up for errors or mistakes, over-checking, arriving early, seeking reassurance, overfamiliarity and inappropriate generosity and/or personal disclosures to gain social approval and popularity. Parents/carers and teachers may also encourage this overcompensation, and in turn this may increase anxiety as pressure is experienced to keep up and try harder, which in the long run cannot be maintained without stress and exhaustion.

Assessment

International guidance on the assessment and treatment of ADHD recommends that a comprehensive assessment procedure is carried out by trained and qualified healthcare practitioners in order to assess ADHD (Sexias, Weiss & Müller, 2012). This often includes a multi-method assessment, involving psychometric questionnaires, a clinical interview and observation of the child to assess difficulties and behaviour in different contexts and settings. It is preferable to obtain multiple perspectives from different people involved in the child's care (including that of the child, if possible), often requiring multi-agency liaison. To develop a care plan with appropriate interventions that are likely to succeed it is important to fully understand the nature and complexity of the child's difficulties across their development, including historic, environmental and psychosocial factors, the child's strengths and weaknesses and the support that they currently receive. In doing this, it is important to be mindful of any comorbid and social problems experienced by the child but also within the family. Clinical assessment can be supported by classroom observations and reports of how the child performs in unstructured situations, such as on the playground during breaks and lunchtimes.

Measures

There are many assessments of anxiety for children. Commonly used ones include the Strengths and Difficulties Questionnaire (SDQ; Goodman, 1997), for age two upwards, to review emotional symptoms, and the Revised Children's Anxiety and Depression Scale (RCADS; Chorpita, Yim, Moffitt, Umemoto & Francis, 2000), which measures anxiety across a range of diagnostic presentations, including generalized, social and panic disorders, for age six upwards. These are rated by parents/carers and teachers based on observation and knowledge of the child; child self-report measures are also available. The ratings are then compared against norms for the child's age and gender. These measures provide a baseline, which can then be repeated throughout intervention. The Spence Children's Anxiety Scale (Spence, 1998) is a measure of anxiety normed on children aged eight years and over; it is available in a format for rating by parents/carers/self; a parent preschool version is also available. Due to the length of the RCADS and the Spence Children's Anxiety Scale, an adult should support children completing self-reported questionnaires: children with ADHD may misread questions, miss out answers, respond impulsively and/or miscommunicate the rating. However, it is essential that responses are not influenced by leading questions. Children who struggle with reading should always have items read out to them. As for many measures, ratings may be subject to bias and must be interpreted cautiously by a trained practitioner.

Clinical Interview

An assessment should include interviews with both the child and their parents/carers in order to better understand the presenting problem. Sometimes anxiety is a side effect of medication, so it is important to establish onset and potential triggers. A range of areas to cover and possible questions include:

> 'When did the anxiety start?' 'Can you remember the first event?' 'Do you know what triggered it?' 'What situations cause the child to feel

anxious?' 'How distressing is it both for the child and the people around him/her? (Rate on a 5-point scale with 0 = not at all distressing and 5 = extremely distressing.)' 'What does the child do to manage symptoms of anxiety?' 'How does the child usually behave in the situation? (Look out for avoidance behaviours and reassurance seeking.)' 'How do others respond?' 'What do others do? (This can include friends, parents/carers, teachers and siblings.)'

It is important to determine if adults think ahead to predict whether a situation will arise and what plans they make, if they give reassurance, encourage the child to face the situation rather than withdraw or help the child to avoid it in some way. What is the impact on the child at home, school and when out? What do they hope will be different?

During the interview, identify specific situations that cause anxiety, for example: listening to instructions; following instructions; planning and organizing school equipment; performing, such as speaking out loud or remembering lines; social situations; when placed in situations with people who don't understand ADHD; situations when the child wants to make a good impression; and having to adhere to rules. The problem may be triggered at specific times, such as when having to wait quietly (e.g., when in a queue, or waiting for their turn in a game), as waiting is aversive for children with ADHD. By the end of the interview, the clinician should have a 'picture' of when anxiety is present, how this may be associated with their ADHD symptoms' severity and presentation, how it is understood in the family and school and the current coping strategies which may improve or maintain it.

Thoughts

Anxiety is maintained by negative thinking and/or the expectation of a negative response from others. Thoughts such as, 'I can't do it', 'It will go wrong', 'I will get reprimanded' and 'I won't like it' increase feelings of anxiety and stress. The child's perception is that the resources required for the situation are greater than the resources it has. To a certain extent this may be an accurate judgement as children are developing their personal and social skills, and some acquire them faster than others. Children with ADHD are additionally hampered by a lack of confidence and poor self-efficacy due to past experiences and negative feedback from others.

Feelings and Physiology

Children (especially younger children) are still acquiring language with which to express their feelings, and language and communication impairments are common in children with ADHD. They may not describe their feelings as 'anxiety' but use words like stress, worries, tense, panicky, uncomfortable and/or dread. They notice physiological symptoms, such as feeling shaky or sick, or say they have a headache. You should encourage children to use creative and individual ways of expressing their feelings in metaphors and drawings. You can also 'give' them language by suggesting words to describe their anxiety.

Remember that children can find the experience of these symptoms of anxiety to be as distressing as the thoughts or situation. In some cases, children experience such severe anxiety that they self-harm, commonly with cutting. However, it is unlikely that children will make links between thoughts, feelings and behaviours, and this is not necessary for successful intervention. For younger children, the intervention is more likely to focus on behaviours, whereas older children might apply cognitive interventions and may be helped by learning that thoughts, feelings and behaviours are related to the anxiety, and actually serve to maintain it.

Anxiety increases arousal, which may present in a child as irritability and frustration (and in some cases aggressive behaviour). Thus, the presence of irritability, restlessness and a low threshold for frustration and aggression should also be explored during the assessment. Children may appear restless, snappy, impatient and unable to cope with unexpected demands, tasks or problems. It is therefore important for the therapist to determine whether the root cause is an underlying anxiety, as this will influence the interventions selected to address the problem. If it is not, then interventions presented in Chapter 8 (frustration and anger) might be more appropriate (and/or others depending on the presentation) but if underlying anxiety is present or suspected, then interventions in the current chapter should be included.

Behaviours

Avoidance is the most common behaviour problem. This means, for example, that a child who has to perform in the school play becomes anxious and forgets the words, then avoids rehearsals because they worry it will happen again. It can be severe, with some children having such negative experiences at school that they avoid it with truancy, feigning illness or blunt school refusal. It is, therefore, important to assess the current coping strategies (both effective and ineffective) that are applied by the child, parents/carers and teachers. Avoidance may well reduce anxiety, but in the long run it maintains anxiety as the child does not acquire new skills and learn that they can cope in an anxiety-provoking situation.

A support method commonly applied by adults is to reassure the child to help him/her feel better; however, the child may come to overly rely on this reassurance. We suggest the therapist explores the anxiety-provoking situation but also other similar situations, identifying the positive, helpful strategies are used successfully in other circumstances. What helps the child stay cool and calm? Is there a 'safe place' in school that the child can retreat to when feeling anxious before facing a situation? When did the child face an anxiety-provoking situation that worked out okay? Who is best at helping them when they need to face a worrying situation? What approach does that person take?

Creative Methods

When children feel emotional they might find it hard to express their feelings in words. In such cases we suggest the therapist draws a large 'anxiety bag' on a piece of paper and discusses with the child their understanding of anxiety. What different words do they know? Have they heard of worries? What are the things that they feel upset or scared about? Do they know someone else who has worries? What are they? Ask the child, with your help, to fill the bag with their anxiety; this may be in words or drawings and pictures that capture what anxiety means to them. This may include how the child notices it in their body, situations that they are wary of and what goes through their mind. To maintain balance, the conversation should include what the child does with worries, who helps them and when and under what circumstances they feel relaxed, calm and happy.

CBT Interventions For Anxiety

If the therapist is treating younger children and/or the worksheets are being used as a basis for treatment, the first session should always commence with Worksheets 1, 2 and 3 to introduce the child to Buzz and his family (Worksheet 1), introduce positive self-talk (Worksheet 2) and identify a reward system (Worksheet 3). The reward and self-talk strategies are applied in the session, at home and/or at school. See Chapter 3 for a suggested outline of how to plan and conduct the introductory session. All the Worksheets are available on the companion website, www.wiley.com/go/young/helpingadhd.

The aims of the interventions and worksheets in the anxiety session(s) are to introduce children to the concept of anxiety, teach them how to recognize it in their bodies and help them to understand situations that cause it. A further aim is to help them understand the relationship between ADHD and anxiety, and acquire cognitive and behavioural skills to manage it. The therapist will achieve this by setting an agenda, reviewing Home Missions completed between sessions, working through new worksheets (or just the strategies for older children) and setting new Home Missions. If required, a mid-session break can be offered halfway through the session; this may be particularly important for younger children. Chapter 2 provides generic information on the structure and content of sessions (irrespective of topic); supplementary information is included within this chapter that specifically relates to the delivery of the anxiety session(s).

Agenda

At the beginning of the session, show the child the written agenda (see Figure 7.2) that you have prepared prior to the session and go through it, verbally linking the themes and Worksheets that you will introduce during the session. For the anxiety module, introduce Worksheets 11 and 12 by saying:

> Today we are learning about how Buzz coped when he went camping for the first time! He was feeling a bit nervous. After that, we will have a short break and you can colour in the worksheet using these crayons. Then we will read a story about Buzz being in the school play and think together about a time when you have had to do something you felt worried about.

Agenda

Folder Review

Buzz goes Camping *[Worksheet 11]*

Break

Buzz and the School Play *[Worksheet 12]*

Breathing Exercise (optional)

Home Missions

Figure 7.2 Example agenda for anxiety session(s).

Folder Review

When reviewing the folder with the child, aside from checking whether the Home Missions are completed, take the opportunity to revise important information and/or concepts, as this will support the child to consolidate the learning points and/or newly acquired skills. Ensure that you make time to look at the illustrations, colourings, paintings, magazine cuttings and/or photographs that the child has added to the folder. Discuss them and try to relate these to discussions about Buzz and his family and/or topics or strategies that have been covered. Aside from acting as a revision prompt, this will also act as a reward system for the child. Praise should be given verbally but you can also reward by adding stickers, handwritten notes or smiley faces. If Home Missions were set then you should review their Home Missions Record Form for comments and feedback from parents/carers and discuss this with the child.

Worksheet 11 Buzz goes Camping

Worksheet Description

The Scouts are going camping at the weekend. It sounds great fun as the Scouts will play games all day, make a camp fire in the evening and sleep in a tent! Buzz can't wait, especially as he may be able to get a new Camping Badge on his sleeve. Two days before the camping weekend Buzz starts to feel worried. It's the first time that Buzz has been away from home. He knows that he will miss Wilma, his family and his bed! There will be other Scout groups there as well and he's also worried about meeting lots of new children and whether they will like him. As the weekend gets nearer Buzz starts to get a tummy ache.

To download this worksheet, please visit the companion website

Worksheet Prompts

What are worries?
How is Buzz feeling?
What does your body do when you feel anxious or nervous?
Can you tell me about a time when you felt like Buzz?
What do you do to keep calm when you are worrying?
What can other people do to help you when you feel worried?
Together let's write out ideas of all the things Buzz can do to help him feel better.
Now let's look at the things you thought would help Buzz and circle the ones that might also help you.

Worksheet 11 is about anxiety control. The exercise introduces the concept of anxiety as 'worries'. It provides the child with an opportunity to voice their own worries and feelings of anxiety through the experience of Buzz, thus increasing self-reflection and awareness. The exercise draws on challenges that children with ADHD may face, such as making and maintaining friendships and social group interactions. Through the discussion, the child is led to consider functional anxiety management strategies, including social support that can be applied to reduce feelings of anxiety.

Read the Stimulus Sheet or, if the child wishes, they can read it to you. Answer any questions they might have. Check that the child understood the story and was paying attention. ('Scouts' can be explained as, 'A group for boys where they learn skills together and do activities.') In the story Buzz is going on a camping weekend. Although he is looking forward to going, he has some worries about being away from home. He has never been away from home before. As the weekend gets closer, his anxiety increases and he has worrying thoughts about meeting new people and making new friends, and he starts to experience physical symptoms of anxiety that he recognizes as tummy ache. You can help the child explore the story by checking they have understood and listened, 'Where will Buzz be sleeping? Can you remember who Wilma is?' The child may have a story about their own camping, games or pet.

Start by asking the child what they think worries are. If the child is unfamiliar with the word 'anxious' then explain what this is. The aim is to help the child begin to recognize that worries are thoughts or pictures that are in the mind. Younger children may not be able to recognize these yet without assistance, whereas older children are more likely to generate suggestions of their own. Write these down together in big thought bubbles. After this, direct the child to the next task of identifying how Buzz was feeling. There are many feelings that would fit. We suggest having a big piece of paper available so that they can all be written down, for example, excited, scared, nervous, anxious, worried and happy. You can validate their answer by highlighting the feelings they have named and saying, 'That's right, Buzz probably had lots of feelings all at once, like being excited to go camping, sad to leave Wilma and worried about leaving home, being somewhere new and making new friends.' After this, ask, 'How do you feel in your body if you are scared or worried?' It is important that an explicit link is made between having worries and feeling anxious.

Next, help the child reflect on a time they might have felt like Buzz (e.g., going to school, being somewhere new, talking in front of people, being in a competition). Listen to the child's story. This should then lead on to talking about what they already do to help themselves feel calm. Children are likely to have varied levels of skills in this area and some may say, 'I don't know' whilst others may already have strategies. You can always prompt them with some ideas such as, 'When you have been worried have you ever taken some deep breaths? Talked to someone about it? Maybe told yourself it would be okay?'

Finally, encourage children to consider what other people do for them. Younger children may find this easier in the context of the examples they have given. Remember to summarize, 'You felt worried about sleeping in your own room and you told yourself you could do it, and then your mum came in to check on you.'

Returning to the story about Buzz, work together to help the child fill in the Task Sheet with things Buzz can do to help in his situation. For example, he could find out exactly what is planned for the weekend, look up the campsite on the Internet, talk to the Scout Leader, arrange for home contact (if required), pack some things from home (photographs, favourite toy, comforter), take a letter from home that can be opened whilst away and use positive self-talk (friendly thoughts) by telling himself 'It will be okay, I can do this' or 'It will be fun.' Then revise the list of strategies generated for Buzz and circle ideas that might also help the child when they have worries.

Give praise for the child's effort in the session. If you choose to set Home Missions based on this worksheet we suggest asking the child to do the following:

1) Decorate the worksheet by colouring in the pictures and thought bubbles, and/or add to them with pictures on the theme of the story. These could be photographs or pictures in magazines or comics.
2) Be an Anxiety Detective – keep a record in a notebook of any worries you have during the week or times you felt nervous or anxious. Bring it to the next session (so the therapist can explore what caused them and identify coping strategies that might help).
3) Try out one or more of the ideas from the Worksheet that might help you with worrying. Ask parents/carers and/or teachers to help to try out the strategies and implement the ideas.

If Home Missions are set, remind parents/carers to complete the Home Missions Record Form and to place this is the folder for review at the next session.

Mid-session Break

This should be provided at an appropriate point in the session, as outlined in Chapter 2.

Worksheet 12 Buzz and the School Play

Worksheet Description

To download this worksheet, please visit the companion website

Buzz has a part in the school play. The play will be shown at the end of term in front of the whole school, teachers and families. As the day gets closer, Buzz starts to feel very nervous. Last year he forgot his lines and the teacher had to prompt him several times. He felt very stupid as everyone was watching. The more he looked at the audience, the less he was able to concentrate and remember his lines. Buzz has been practising lots, both at home and at school. He wants to do a good job this time. The 'big day' has arrived and he's so worried he feels a bit sick. It feels like there are butterflies flying around in his tummy. Buzz doesn't want to do it any more.

(Continued)

> **Worksheet 12 (Continued)**
>
> **Worksheet Prompts**
>
> Tell me all the things that Buzz seems worried and nervous about.
> What does he think might happen?
> What happens to Buzz's concentration when he is worried?
> What will happen if Buzz drops out of the play?
> How does Buzz feel inside? Have you ever felt like that?
> Together let's write out some ideas of the things Buzz can do to make him feel better.
> Now let's look at the things you thought would help Buzz and circle the ones that might also help you.

Worksheet 12 aims to help children consider how anxiety may negatively impact on their performance. They are also directed to consider the relationship between anxiety and ADHD symptomology. Children are introduced to the negative cycle of anxiety, with past behaviour/experience influencing their anticipation of future behaviours and how this, in turn, may result in a downward spiral of self-fulfilling prophecies and/or withdrawal and avoidance. The dysfunctional consequences of avoidance should be discussed with the child and alternative positive strategies identified that will support successful task achievement.

The story is about feeling anxious about performing well in the school play. Buzz forgot his lines last year and he is worried that this will happen again. Although he has been practising, on the day he is so anxious that he feels sick and doesn't want to do it. He is frightened that everyone watching will laugh at him or think he is stupid. Read the Stimulus Sheet to the child, or, if they wish, they can read it with you. Check that the child has understood the story and answer any questions they might have. Encourage the child to recount stories about the plays at their school, especially if they had a part and felt anxious. Begin by helping the child to consider what Buzz was feeling anxious about. You could direct them by asking, 'What is Buzz worried about happening again?', 'What happened last time that might make Buzz anxious?', 'Do you think Buzz is feeling nervous about how many people are there?' If the child has specific ideas about what Buzz's worries might be, you could write these down together, for example: 'He's thinking "Oh no, what if it goes wrong!" or "I can't do it". This will link in with the child reflecting on what Buzz thinks might happen.

Move on to asking, 'What happens to Buzz's concentration when he is worried?' You can summarize this by saying, 'When people are worried they find it more difficult to concentrate and pay attention to the things they need to. This is because they are thinking about their worries instead.' Older children may be able to make a link between why this is more problematic for children who already struggle with attention control.

Discuss the potential outcomes if Buzz were to drop out of the play, for example, disappointing himself and his class, teachers and family. He would let everyone down as they would have to find a replacement at short notice and the replacement child would not have much time to rehearse. If the child thinks it would be a good idea for Buzz to drop out of the play because he will feel better, help them reflect on this as a short-term solution. In the end he might feel annoyed and disappointed with himself, and it isn't a solution to overcoming his worries. This can be a good starting point for generating ideas about what Buzz can do to manage his feelings, such as using positive self-talk (friendly thoughts) that helps him to feel more confident. Other ideas could be to talk to the teacher, do additional practice and rehearsal or do something to calm his nerves and relax (such as take deep breaths, distract himself from negative thoughts by talking to someone or counting in his head).

Introduce the child to breathing and relaxation techniques and practise these together. A typical breathing and relaxation exercise is included in the psychoeducational booklet 'So I have ADHD', which can be downloaded from the Psychology Services Website, www.psychology-services.uk.com/resources. It is helpful to do this with parents/carers present so they also learn how to do this at home.

Give the child praise for their effort in the session. If you choose to set Home Missions based on this worksheet we suggest asking the child to do the following:

1) Decorate the Worksheet by colouring in the pictures and thought bubbles, and/or add to them with pictures on the theme of the story. These could be photographs or pictures in magazines or comics.
2) Practise the breathing and relaxation techniques at home with parents/carers.
3) Come up with some self-talk statements (friendly thoughts) for keeping calm. An example would be 'I can give this my best try'. Make these into a colourful poster. Bring them to the next session, and show them to parents/carers and teachers.

If Home Missions are set, remind parents/carers to complete the Home Missions Record Form and to place this is the folder for review at the next session.

Feedback and Rewards

At the end of the session, appropriate rewards identified from the Worksheet 3 Reward Task should be applied (e.g., the child should engage in positive self-talk). See Chapter 2 for more information about feedback and rewards.

Working with Parents/Carers

This section presents strategies that parents/carers can apply to support the child to reduce and/or cope with periods of anxiety and worry.

It is important to be realistic about what can be achieved. It can be just as helpful to learn strategies to cope better with a child's behaviour as to learn strategies to improve the behaviour itself. Children will feel anxious and worried many times in different situations and this is normal. Sometimes, however, anxiety can impact negatively on behaviour, performance and health.

When working with parents/carers, it is important to help them to have a good understanding of anxiety and how this impacts on the child's ADHD symptoms. You can talk to them about how past experiences will lead children to make expectations about what will happen in future similar situations and how, in turn, this affects how they think, feel and behave. Explain how this leads to a vicious cycle of expectation and behaviour, and how this becomes increasingly worse, with some situations being completely avoided with the belief, 'I was only okay because I avoided it.' Parents/carers may not be aware that anxiety and worries exacerbate ADHD symptoms by increasing inattention and restlessness and preventing clear thinking, leading to greater risk of impulsive responding and, in turn, attracting the attention of others. This could be a good thing if children gain recognition and support, but it could also be a bad thing if it means they are more likely to be reprimanded for errors and failures.

In this section we discuss the need for parents/carers to set realistic expectations, as well as the behavioural strategies they can apply to support the child to face anxiety-provoking situations, control feelings of restlessness and apply breathing and relaxation techniques. Cognitive techniques are also discussed to support the child in applying a solution-focused problem-solving approach, and to use self-talk and positive self-statements to help them at times of stress. When working with parents/carers, the therapist should introduce suggested techniques and strategies; practise and rehearse them in role-plays during the sessions if appropriate (without the child present). In future sessions, parents/carers should report back to the therapist on how they managed when using them at home. It is important to troubleshoot any obstacles and/or difficulties that arise by thinking of ways to adapt the techniques or strategies so they are successful in helping the child.

A key strategy to change behaviour and improve cognitive skills is to find motivators to promote success. Children with ADHD tend to respond better to immediate rewards as they have difficulties with delayed gratification for longer-term rewards (even if these are bigger and better). Methods to motivate success (including the use of a Star Chart) and other topics that are generic to working with parents/carers are described in Chapter 2. Supplementary information that specifically relates to the delivery of the anxiety session(s) is outlined in this chapter.

Realistic Expectations

Some children become stressed or anxious if they feel they can't meet the expectations of their parents/carers. It is essential to help parents/carers develop realistic expectations of their child's capabilities (both strengths and weaknesses) and what the child can manage and/or achieve. Sometimes it can be hard for parents/carers to know whether the child is unable to do something or is choosing not to; this is especially the case when a child is adept at masking their problems with bravado and/or procrastination. A realistic appraisal of a child's capabilities will mean that realistic goals can be set that the child is likely to achieve. This is a 'win–win' situation.

Facing not Avoiding (Graded Hierarchy)

A successful way to overcome feelings of anxiety is to face up to anxiety-provoking situations; this is done using a graded hierarchy that gradually reintroduces the child to the situation using small and manageable steps. The aim is to increase confidence and coping, and develop skills for facing such situations in the future. This is especially important for children who are reluctant to engage or who rigidly avoid situations. By doing this in small and manageable steps, children and their parents/carers are more likely to have positive experiences and achieve success. Explain to parents/carers how a graded hierarchy can be developed using a ladder metaphor, starting with easy situations that become increasingly difficult as you move higher up the ladder. This is done by the parent/carer working together with the child to rate how anxious they believe they would feel in these situations, for example, the easiest might be rated as 1/10 for anxiety and the biggest challenge might be rated as 10/10. The child is then encouraged to take the first step in the graded hierarchy by facing the easiest situation.

Facing anxiety-provoking situations requires preparation, so discuss with parents/carers how they might prepare their child to face the situation, for example, 'What could make it easier? What would make it harder? What could they say to themselves to help? Could they get someone to help them?' The first step must always be the least challenging and then you gradually introduce more challenges (for example, going somewhere with a parent/carer, going with a friend and a comforter, going with a friend, taking a comforter, going on your own). Rehearse the technique with parents/carers in the session and ensure that they remember to identify and introduce cognitive strategies to help the child achieve each step. Remind parents/carers that the Star Chart, praise and rewards are very important methods that will keep the child feeling positive and motivated and reinforce their efforts.

Restlessness

Children might not be open about their worries. Remind parents/carers that anxiety can increase feelings of restlessness and hyperactive behaviours.

If children seem more fidgety or active than usual, they might consider whether this stems from an underlying worry or anxiety. When developing strategies to support a child to face up to anxiety-provoking situations, include strategies that address feelings of restlessness if there are any (see Chapter 5).

Breathing and Relaxation

Introduce the child to breathing and relaxation techniques. A typical breathing and relaxation exercise is included in the psychoeducational booklet 'So I have ADHD', which can be downloaded from the Psychology Services Website, www.psychology-services.uk.com/resources. Parents/carers should practise the techniques with their child to help them gain control of physiological symptoms. Remind parents/carers that the more children practise these techniques, the more natural they will become. We suggest that good times to practise include before bed, when travelling and before or after school. Parents/carers should also prompt the child to apply these techniques if the child is complaining about physiological symptoms that are associated with anxiety.

Problem-solving

Parents/carers may not be aware that anxiety can be caused by not knowing how to cope with a situation. Thoughts like, 'What am I going to do?' increase anxiety and lead to avoidance behaviours or unwise, impulsive decisions. This is particularly true for children with ADHD who already have difficulties with problem-solving, decision-making and following through with solutions; comorbid anxiety makes matters worse, leaving them feeling overwhelmed. When this problem seems to present, consider including appropriate strategies outlined in Chapter 11.

Self-talk

Parents/carers have an important role in helping their child to develop positive self-talk and use positive self-statements (friendly thoughts). Explain to parents/carers that a child's self-talk will develop from the messages the child hears from the adults around them regarding their competence and the abilities of others to cope with situations. Self-talk also develops from the child's own efforts and parents/carers should prompt them with positive examples. We suggest you discuss some examples of self-talk (both positive and negative) and their influence on the anxiety state by considering the differential impact these will have on the behaviour of the child. For example, 'I feel a bit nervous but I'll give it my best go' will motivate a child to engage with the situation, whereas, 'I'll never do this, I'm scared and want to quit' will not. It is easy for children with ADHD to lose track of positive thoughts when they feel anxious, as lots of negative thoughts flood their mind. Encourage parents/carers to model positive self-talk and statements in front of the child and to consider ways to develop their own positive self-talk and statements. They should also prompt the child to use the techniques when the child appears anxious. Self-talk can be reinforced by reassurance and positive statements by others.

Role Model

Parents/carers are important role models for their children. Children may 'learn' to be anxious about the things that worry their parents/carers. Thus, it can be helpful to identify what these are, how they manage them (and in particular how expressive or demonstrative they are in their response), as well as how they experience the anxieties of their child. Parents/carers must recognize that they can model adaptive functioning to their children by facing their own anxieties and applying helpful strategies, such as using self-talk to foster a positive attitude, using positive self-statements to guide them through functional behaviours and/or a constructive problem-solving approach, and applying breathing and relaxation techniques. Parents/carers should be encouraged to do it out loud by giving themselves instructions to cue the use of techniques, as in this way the child who 'learns' about anxiety from parents/carers will simultaneously learn how to combat it.

What Can We Do As Parents/Carers?

Table 7.1 outlines a suggested approach, including a list of strategies that can be implemented at home. To maximize the effect of strategies, it is helpful to discuss them with your child's teacher so they can be implemented at both home and school (wherever possible). Lots of parents/carers and teachers find that using a 'Home School Diary' is an efficient way to share information (see Chapter 2).

We suggest that parents/carers read Chapter 2, which provides important background information about the delivery of the Young–Smith Programme. For younger children, we suggest that parents/carers set aside some time to sit down with the child (around 45–60 minutes) and work through the Worksheets recommended for each topic. Guidance is found in the 'CBT Interventions' section in each chapter. The worksheets introducing Buzz and his family are outlined in Chapter 3. All the materials (Worksheets and Home Missions Record Form) are available for download from the companion website, www.wiley.com/go/young/helpingadhd. For older children (i.e., 12 years-plus), you can dispense with the Buzz Worksheets if necessary and instead introduce the child directly to the topic, and, using the discussion prompts on the Worksheets, apply this to the child's experience and discuss suggested strategies. Set Home Missions and support the child to complete them. Don't forget to give frequent feedback and praise. Make a Star Chart (see Chapter 2), put it in a prominent place and start to use it on a daily basis.

Table 7.1 Home strategies for anxiety.

Realistic expectations
- Consider both strengths and weaknesses of your child.
- Set targets that your child is able to achieve so that they experience success.
- Consider whether your child masks underlying problems with bravado and/or procrastination.

Facing not avoiding
- Support your child to face anxiety-provoking situations by devising a graded hierarchy of steps together with the child.
- Rate each step and place in a sequential order (lowest to highest).
- Work through each step and suggest techniques that will help them to remain calm and achieve the step.
- Give praise and rewards for effort and achievement.

Restlessness
- Remember that anxiety may increase restlessness and some strategies from Chapter 5 might also help.

Breathing and relaxation
- Practise breathing and relaxation techniques together.
- Prompt your child to use them when feeling anxious.

Problem-solving
- Help your child solve problems that they are feeling stressed or worried about. See strategies in Chapter 11.

Self-talk
- Together, think up some positive self-talk statements (friendly thoughts) and self-instructions your child can apply to help manage feelings of anxiety.
- Prompt the child to use them when feeling anxious.

Role model
- Be a role model to your child by using strategies yourself.
- Do this out loud so your child can observe and learn what you do.

Working with Teachers and Schools

School can induce anxiety in children for many reasons, whether it is to do with schoolwork, separation from parents/carers or getting along with others. It is not uncommon for children to feel anxious in school settings where they are expected to behave cooperatively and acquire new skills.

However, frequent and/or severe anxiety may impair their functioning and affect their performance by decreasing their ability to concentrate, memorize information and organize their thoughts and behaviour. It can also hamper their ability to think ahead and predict situations or even to stay in the classroom. Classrooms are places where children are expected to sit down quietly and stay still for long periods of time whilst they learn and follow rules. Hence, for children with ADHD and comorbid anxiety, the school day can feel extremely challenging and stressful; anxiety and worries exacerbate ADHD symptoms by increasing inattention and restlessness and preventing clear thinking, leading to greater risk of impulsive responding. In turn, this means they are more likely to disturb, distract and irritate their class peers and teachers and receive reprimands for 'bad behaviour'.

When working with teachers it is important to help them develop a good understanding of anxiety and how it impacts on a child's ADHD symptoms. Explain how anxiety prepares the body for 'fight or flight' as this will explain why anxiety, agitation and restlessness often co-occur. You can talk to teachers about how past experiences will lead children to make predictions about what will happen in future similar situations. In turn, this affects how they think, feel and behave. Explain how this leads to a vicious cycle of prediction, expectation and behaviour, and how this becomes increasingly worse with some situations being completely avoided with the belief, 'I was only okay because I avoided it.'

Parents/carers and teachers often need to work together to address school-based worries. Common school worries for children with ADHD relate to keeping up with the work, not understanding the work, getting reprimanded for not following rules, getting along with other children, losing things and generally being disorganized. Children may perceive themselves as being unfairly targeted as they are doing their best but this is not good enough. They may develop a sense of hopelessness and give up. It should be kept in mind that immediate rewards (and praise) work best with children with ADHD and these are important techniques to guide behaviour. Biological parents may also have a history of ADHD and have similar negative school experiences, which may not be helpful as they are uncertain how best to approach the problem. Hence it is important that parents/carers and teachers share ideas and use the Home School Diary as a written communication tool. Children's worries may stem from problems at home. When this seems to be the case teachers may need to meet with parents/carers to advocate for the child and/or provide support to the family. Stressors may include difficulty completing homework due to the environment, unrealistic expectations of the child's ability and/or non-school related problems such as change in family situation and/or dynamics.

This section presents strategies that teachers can apply to support the child to reduce and/or cope with periods of anxiety and worry. It is important to be realistic about what can be achieved. It can be just as helpful to learn strategies to cope better with a child's behaviour as to learn strategies to improve the behaviour itself. In this section, we discuss the need for realistic expectations as well as the behavioural strategies that teachers can apply to help the child to face anxiety-provoking situations, control feelings of restlessness and apply breathing and relaxation techniques. Cognitive techniques are also discussed to support the child to apply a solution-focused problem-solving approach and use self-talk and positive self-statements to help them at times of stress.

Teachers and schools will already have structures in place to support many of the interventions introduced in the Young–Smith Programme. It will be useful to link up parents/carers and teachers to encourage an integrated strategy and share success. It is important to troubleshoot any obstacles and/or difficulties that arise by thinking of ways to adapt the techniques or strategies so they are successful in helping the child. Methods to motivate success and other topics that are generic to working with teachers and schools are described in Chapter 2. Supplementary information that specifically relates to the delivery of the anxiety session(s) is outlined in this chapter.

Realistic Expectations

Teachers are likely to have a good understanding about a child's relative strengths and weaknesses and the extent to which they compare developmentally with the rest of the class. Parents/carers may not share the same perspective and can have unrealistic expectations of the child's abilities and potential to achieve. Teachers therefore play an important role in supporting a child to reach their potential and helping parents/carers to adjust their expectations to better suit the child's social, cognitive and behavioural profile. It is, however, important that teachers recognize 'acting out' behaviours that aim to mask underlying difficulties and anxieties, such as: aimless running around, chattering and distracting others, pretending to feel sick or tired, asking permission to leave the classroom or devaluing the work by saying it is boring, stupid or already known. Younger children may present more obstinately and expressly refuse to engage, saying, 'I don't want to', 'I won't do that' or 'I don't like it.' Asking yourself, 'If I understood this to be a sign of anxiety rather than oppositional/challenging behaviour, how might my management approach differ?' can be a helpful way to consider the child's presentation in a different way.

Facing not Avoiding (Graded Hierarchy)

Teachers can work with the child to develop a graded hierarchy to support them to face up to school-related anxiety-provoking situations in small and manageable steps. This technique is described in the previous parent/carer section. For school-related anxieties, peers can support the child to face anxiety-provoking situations; peers are also good role models.

Restlessness

The anxious child in the classroom may also be the restless and active child. So, for a child with ADHD, this is 'double trouble'. If children seem more fidgety or active than usual, the teacher should consider whether this stems from underlying worries or anxieties. Some children run around as a coping strategy to manage discomfort, others use activity as a means of avoidance when they feel overwhelmed. The key here is to recognize there may be an underlying problem and identify appropriate strategies. In this case it may be helpful to include some strategies presented in Chapter 5 on hyperactivity.

Breathing and Relaxation

The breathing and relaxation techniques introduced in the parent/carer section may also be delivered by teachers for school-related anxieties. For younger children, they can be learned as a class activity during rest periods. It is preferable, however, for these techniques to be applied both at home and at school, where either parents/carers or teachers can prompt the child to apply them if the child becomes overactive or complains about physiological symptoms associated with anxiety.

Problem-solving

Anxiety may stem from poor problem-solving and decision-making skills. When this seems to be the case, consider including appropriate strategies that are outlined in Chapter 11.

Self-talk

Teachers can support children to develop positive self-talk and use positive self-statements (friendly thoughts). Developing a self-talk repertoire can be helpful to induce and maintain emotional control and/or to motivate functional behaviour. We suggest you discuss some examples of self-talk (both positive and negative) and their influence on the anxiety state by considering the differential impact these will have on the behaviour of the child. For example, 'I didn't make the football team but I'm going to practise so I will next time' compared to 'I'm not trying again, they don't want me so why should I bother.' It is easy for children with ADHD to lose track of positive thoughts when they feel anxious as lots of negative thoughts flood their mind. Encourage teachers to model positive self-talk and statements in front of the child. They should also prompt the child to use these techniques when the child appears anxious. Self-talk can be reinforced by reassurance and positive statements by others.

What Can We Do As Teachers?

Table 7.2 outlines a suggested approach for teachers, including a list of strategies that can be implemented at school. To maximize the effect of strategies, it is helpful to discuss them with the child's parents/carers so that similar or complementary strategies are implemented at both home and school

Table 7.2 School strategies for anxiety.

Realistic expectations
- Consider both strengths and weaknesses of the child.
- Set targets that the child is able to achieve so that they experience success.
- Support parents/carers to develop realistic expectations.
- Consider whether the child masks underlying problems with 'acting out' behaviours.

Facing not avoiding
- Support the child to face anxiety-provoking situations by devising a graded hierarchy of steps together with the child.
- Rate each step and place in a sequential order (lowest to highest).
- Work through each step and suggest techniques that will help them to remain calm and achieve the step.
- Involve peers as role models and/or to support the child to face anxiety-provoking situations.
- Give praise and rewards for effort and achievement.

Restlessness
- Remember that anxiety may increase restlessness and some strategies from Chapter 5 might also help.

Breathing and relaxation
- Identify a 'safe place' in school where the child can retreat if feeling upset or anxious.
- Breathing and relaxation techniques could be introduced as a class activity during rest periods.
- Communicate these with parents/carers so they can be practised at home.
- Prompt the child to use the techniques when feeling anxious, restless or overexcited.

Problem-solving
- Help the child solve problems that they are feeling stressed or worried about. See strategies in Chapter 11.

Self-talk
- Think up together some positive self-talk (friendly thoughts) and self-statements the child can apply to help manage feelings of anxiety.
- Model positive self-talk and self-statements in front of the child.
- Prompt the child to use them when feeling anxious.

Staff collaboration
- Ensure that all staff know and understand what strategies are being used and why.

(wherever possible). Lots of teachers and parents/carers find that using a 'Home School Diary' is an efficient way to share information (see Chapter 2).

We suggest that teachers read Chapter 2, which provides important background information about the delivery of the Young–Smith Programme. It is unlikely that teachers will have time to go through specific worksheets with children, although if parents/carers are unable to do this it would be helpful to make arrangements with the Special Educational Needs Coordinator. Guidance on how to do this is found in the 'CBT Interventions' section in each chapter. The worksheets introducing Buzz and his family are outlined in Chapter 3. All the materials (worksheets and Home Missions Record Form) are available for download from the companion website, www.wiley.com/go/young/helpingadhd. For older children (i.e., 12 years-plus), one may dispense with the Buzz worksheets if necessary and instead introduce the child directly to the topic, and, using the discussion prompts on the worksheets, apply this to the child's experience and discuss suggested strategies. Set Home Missions and support the child to complete them. Don't forget to give frequent feedback and praise. If a Star Chart is used (see Chapter 2) then this should be put in the 'Home School Diary' so parents/carers can also review it on a regular basis.

References

Bowen, R., Chavira, D. A., Bailey, K., Stein, M. T., & Stein, M. B. (2008). Nature of anxiety comorbid with attention deficit hyperactivity disorder in children from a pediatric primary care setting. *Psychiatry Research, 157*(1–3), 201–209.

Chorpita, B. F., Yim, L., Moffitt, C., Umemoto L. A., & Francis, S. E. (2000). Assessment of symptoms of DSM-IV anxiety and depression in children: A revised child anxiety and depression scale. *Behaviour Research and Therapy, 38*(8), 835–855.

Ferrin, M., & Vance, A. (2014). Differential effects of anxiety and depressive symptoms on working memory components in children and adolescents with ADHD combined type and ADHD inattentive type. *European Child & Adolescent Psychiatry, 23*(12), 1161–1173.

Goodman, R. (1997). The strengths and difficulties questionnaire: A research note. *Journal of Child Psychology and Psychiatry and Allied Disciplines, 38*(5), 581–586.

Jensen, P. S., Hinshaw, S. P., Kraemer, H. C., Lenora, N., Newcorn, J. H., Abikoff, H. B., et al. (2001). ADHD comorbidity findings from the MTA study: Comparing comorbid subgroups. *Journal of the American Academy of Child and Adolescent Psychiatry, 40*(2), 147–158.

Pliszka, S. R. (1998). Comorbidity of attention-deficit/hyperactivity disorder with psychiatric disorder: An overview. *Journal of Clinical Psychiatry, 59*(Suppl 7), 50–58.

Sexias, M., Weiss, M., & Müller, U. (2012). Systematic review of national and international guidelines on attention deficit hyperactivity disorder. *Journal of Psychopharmacology, 26*(6), 753–765.

Spence, S. H. (1998). *A measure of anxiety symptoms among children. Behaviour Research and Therapy, 36*(5), 545–566.

8

Frustration and Anger

Children with ADHD are particularly susceptible to feelings of frustration and anger, and often have temperamental outbursts due to lower capacity for self-regulation. These children are often hypersensitive and reactive; hence feelings of anger may quickly flare up. This may present as a 'flash in the pan' and they calm down equally quickly; however, other times it may take them longer to calm down. It is important to bear in mind that anger is a natural emotion that occurs for everyone to varying degrees and at different times. Anger is an adaptive emotion that serves to alert people to the threat of danger and prepare the body to respond. In a 'life or death' survival situation, it is appropriate to fight. However, responding that way just because you can't get your own way is inappropriate.

Aside from their problems with self-regulation, children with ADHD are hampered by the additional problem of struggling to inhibit the impulse to act out their feelings of frustration and anger. Emotional impulsivity is characterized by impatience, low tolerance of frustration, quickness to anger and excitability (Barkley & Fischer, 2010). Due to their impulsive responding, children with ADHD are less likely to stop and think of the consequences of their behaviour (for both themselves and for others) or stop and think of a better solution. This means that they not only struggle with feelings that are causing them distress, but also with behaviours that are likely to escalate the situation and exacerbate their feelings of distress. Furthermore, speaking out of turn, saying hurtful things to the people they love and/or hitting out at others may damage relationships. The person who may be the most harmed, however, is the child, who becomes stigmatized, rejected and isolated.

This chapter will examine frustration, anger and related behaviours in children with ADHD, and the impact this can have on their functioning in different areas of life. The assessment of anger and challenging behaviours will be discussed, followed by interventions and strategies for children and the adults around them using cognitive behavioural models.

Helping Children with ADHD: A CBT Guide for Practitioners, Parents and Teachers,
First Edition. Susan Young and Jade Smith.
© 2017 John Wiley & Sons Ltd. Published 2017 by John Wiley & Sons Ltd.
Companion website: www.wiley.com/go/young/helpingadhd

Presentation

Children with ADHD frequently get into trouble for temperamental, and sometimes violent, outbursts. Often this occurs because they act on their frustrations impulsively, or because they over-react to criticisms and/or the perceived aggression of others. A child's anger or challenging behaviour, however, may not be associated with one sole incident but result from a gradual build-up of frustration over a period of time. Each criticism, reprimand and piece of negative feedback cranks up feelings of stress, distress, irritation and frustration, and this may continue to build-up over time until the child appears to 'snap' over what may appear to be a minor trigger. The trigger may relate, for example, to a reward being postponed, such as not going to the park because it is raining. From the perspective of the parent/carer the weather is out of their control, but from the perspective of the child not receiving something they have eagerly awaited may be the 'last straw', resulting in a major temper tantrum.

Children may also get easily frustrated with themselves, especially when they are trying their best but their best just isn't good enough. They may be acutely aware that they are at the bottom of their English class, that their brother or sister is the 'star' of the family or that parents/carers are disappointed in them. Some children will pretend that they don't care, whilst others over-compensate by engaging in attention-seeking 'silly' behaviours.

Behavioural Functioning

Anger outbursts often lead to bad behaviour or acting out. Aggressive, hurtful or destructive behaviours may be observed, with the child lashing out at people or damaging property; sometimes they direct their anger inwardly through self-harming activities, such as head banging, biting and/or scratching. Whether externally directed or self-directed, acting out behaviours are unhelpful since the focus may become the (negative) behaviours and the feelings driving them may not be acknowledged. Furthermore, these behaviours are challenging to manage and very distressing for the people around the child. It is important to bear in mind that violent behaviours may lead to the risk that someone (self or others) may be injured. Whilst damage to property is upsetting, it is unlikely to cause serious injury.

There can be numerous reasons why a child may either act out his/her frustrations or frustrations increase to such a level that they are unhelpful. One relates to impulsive responding. Managing emotions requires the inhibition of responses; if the child has a high level of impulsivity they are less likely to be able to control their emotional response and instead act out on their feelings. Typical impulsive expressions of emotion include throwing items, answering back to parents/carers and teachers, shouting out hurtful comments like calling someone a bad name, hitting out or pushing other children. Often the child feels remorseful once they have calmed down, however the damage has been done. These behaviours are most likely to be triggered when the child feels stressed, and they are often perceived as having a low tolerance to feelings of frustration. What the child needs is strategies to better control their emotions and their behaviours.

For some children, the presentation is more complicated as they develop Oppositional Defiance Disorder (ODD). ODD is a diagnostic term for a pattern of behaviours including refusal to comply, disobedience, blaming others for mistakes, frequent arguing and loss of temper; 40 % of children with ADHD will develop ODD (Jensen et al., 2001). It is also more common in boys (approximately three boys for every two girls), which may relate to gender roles and behaviours rather than a genetic difference. It can be tricky to work out which behaviours relate to ADHD and which relate to ODD. For example, parents/carers report that children with ADHD don't listen to them, don't do as they are told, and don't learn from mistakes. However, there is a big difference between the child who 'can't' and the child who 'won't'. ADHD symptoms may mean the child is unable to focus, listen and follow instructions. ODD symptoms may mean that the child is refusing to focus, listen and follow instructions. Either way, parents/carers and teachers may be left feeling helpless, irritated and frustrated. They may feel that their authority is being challenged or disrespected. However, getting drawn into an authoritarian dyadic interaction will be unhelpful and may result in a breakdown of the relationship and an increase in challenging behaviours.

Academic Functioning

The school environment can be a source of frustration for children with ADHD who are trying to keep up, get things right, cope with making mistakes and cope with feeling overwhelmed. Boredom can be a painful experience and lead to undesirable emotions and behaviours, including frustration and anger. Angry ruminations are likely to take over and preoccupy the child's thinking, leaving them unable to focus on the task at hand. Furthermore, angry thoughts will fuel more angry thoughts and increase the likelihood of escalation into a behavioural outburst.

When children act out their feelings of frustration in class, this may present difficulties and challenge even the most experienced of teachers. Furthermore, these behaviours may distract other children, or, at worst, disrupt the whole class. In such cases this will lead to a loss of structure in the classroom and teachers may struggle to maintain control. This may represent a welcome diversion for the child, who gains a 'break' from having to sustain concentration on a task and/or control their behaviour. Psychologists call this 'secondary gain' and this needs to be avoided by watching out for warning signs that the child is feeling stressed and frustrated and may start to act out. In the school setting, acting out behaviours may include being the class clown, with the child moving off task and engaging in silly behaviours for the entertainment of others. The ADHD child may perceive this as a way to make friends as well as a way to avoid academic work.

Interpersonal Functioning

When it comes to making and managing friendships there are numerous skills or 'rules' of friendship that we endorse; these include good manners, listening skills, loyalty, consideration for others, collaboration, compromise, reciprocity and empathy. We think about what we are going to say and do, especially if this will impact on others in some way, as we endeavour to present ourselves as likeable people whose friendship has value so that people want to get to know us and spend time with us. For some children this process happens naturally, but others really have to work on it. ADHD makes it more difficult for children to make and manage friendships. They may have negative reputations, leading to peers (and their parents/carers) being wary of them. Others make friends but have difficulty sustaining them. This is particularly the case when a child is perceived as being emotionally reactive and prone to unpredictable temperamental outbursts. Children with ADHD are often upset after the event when they have calmed down and realize that what they have said or done has upset someone else. They often feel guilty and try to 'undo' it with apologies. Others cover up their feelings by pretending that they don't care; this may protect them from feeling guilty (which is not a pleasant emotion) since if you don't feel remorse then you don't feel guilt.

Similarly, family relationships may also be tested when there are frequent arguments and aggressive behaviours at home. Relationships in the family are likely to be strained if there is a culture of blame within the family – the child with ADHD can't help being the way they are. They may also get blamed by others for things that they have not done because they are the easy scapegoat. Siblings may feel jealous of the attention that they receive because they need extra help and monitoring. They may also resent it if they are expected to watch out for their sibling all the time.

Coping

Most children with ADHD will not have acquired positive strategies to help them control their feelings of anger. Instead, they may have learned how anger can function for them (e.g., getting what they want, being perceived as 'macho'). Children are quick to learn what behaviours gain the best results and then repeat them; hence a child may be more aggressive or angry if they learn that this helps them in some way. For example, it may be that fighting keeps bullies away when teachers aren't present, fighting brings respect, they get to stay up later at bedtime to avoid conflict or they may get their favourite sweets in a shop to avoid a public tantrum. This reinforces the behaviour and may even escalate it.

The people around children with ADHD may find their volatile temperament and level of unpredictability challenging to manage, especially when they act out. Parents/carers and teachers may feel frustration themselves if the child repeatedly engages in behaviours that are the target of their advice and interventions. This means that the child may be perceived as deliberately not following the rules, which in turn may be interpreted as being oppositional rather than unable. One needs to be mindful that a vicious cycle of frustration may arise between the child and the adult. One also wants to avoid bad behaviour becoming a self-fulfilling prophecy that has developed from the expectations of both parties. Parents/carers and teachers need to control and not be controlled; they will only achieve this by adopting a consistent approach and supporting the child to learn and apply appropriate strategies to control strong emotions.

Assessment

International guidance on the assessment and treatment of ADHD recommends that a comprehensive assessment procedure is carried out by trained and qualified healthcare practitioners in order to assess ADHD (Sexias, Weiss & Müller, 2012). This often includes a multi-method assessment, involving psychometric questionnaires, a clinical interview and observation of the child to assess their difficulties and behaviour in different contexts and settings. It is preferable to obtain multiple perspectives from different people involved in the child's care (including that of the child if possible), often requiring multi-agency liaison. To develop a care plan with appropriate interventions that are likely to succeed it is important to fully understand the nature and complexity of the child's difficulties across their development, including historic, environmental and psychosocial factors, the child's strengths and weaknesses and the support that they currently receive. In doing this, it is important to be mindful of any comorbid and social problems experienced by the child but also within the family.

Measures

A commonly used measure is the Strengths and Difficulties Questionnaire (SDQ; Goodman, 1997) for age two upwards, assessing conduct problems and prosocial behaviour. This is rated by parents/carers and teachers based on observation and knowledge of the child. The ratings are then compared against norms for the child's age and gender. This measure provides a baseline, which can then be repeated throughout the intervention. The Child Behaviour Checklist (CBC) of the Achenbach System of Empirically Based Assessment (ASEBA; Achenbach & Rescorla, 2001) is for six year olds and over. Amongst other areas, it measures parents/carers and teachers ratings of angry and oppositional behaviour. The Conners' Rating Scales 3rd Edition (Conners, 2008) for age six and over also gives an outcome on parents/carers or teachers ratings of oppositional behaviour. Measures also have child self-report versions available. An adult should support children completing self-reported questionnaires: children with ADHD may misread questions, miss out answers, respond impulsively and/or miscommunicate the rating. However, it is essential that responses are not influenced by leading questions. Children who struggle with reading should always have items read out to them. As for many measures, ratings may be subject to bias and must be interpreted cautiously by a trained practitioner.

Clinical Interview

An assessment should include interviews with both the child and their parents/carers in order to better understand the presenting problem. A range of areas to cover and possible questions include:

> 'Are there specific times or circumstances that seem to trigger anger outbursts?' 'What situations cause the child to feel frustrated or angry or to shout/hit out?' 'Does this happen with some people and not others?' 'Who?' 'Why do you think that is?' 'How distressing is it both for the child and the people around him/her? (Rate on a 5-point scale with 0 = not at all distressing and 5 = extremely distressing.)' 'What does the child do to manage feelings of frustration and anger?' 'How does the child usually behave in the situation?' 'How do others respond?' 'What do others do? (This can include friends, parents/carers, teachers and siblings.)' 'What helps the child with ADHD to stay cool and calm?' 'When did they face a frustrating situation and work out a way through it?' 'Who is best at helping them when they face these situations?'

It is important to determine whether adults think ahead to predict whether a situation will arise, and what plans they make to avoid confrontation. It is also important to identify whether the response of others escalates the situation, or calms it down. Are parents/carers consistent in their management of the problem, or is the child getting 'mixed messages'? What is the impact on the child at home, school and when out? What do they hope will be different?

During the interview, identify specific situations that are likely to trigger strong emotions. For example, not getting his/her own way, feeling left out, being reprimanded, feeling overwhelmed and confused about school work, not understanding instructions and feeling stupid. The problem may be triggered at specific times, such as when feeling tired or under pressure. It may also be triggered by interactions with specific people if the child perceives they are not liked or tolerated. Is the behaviour functional in any way, enabling the child to get what they want? This is very important, as a desired outcome will reinforce the behaviour and increase the likelihood that it will be repeated in the future. By the end of the interview, the clinician should have a 'picture' of when the child is likely to feel angry and distressed, how this may be associated with their ADHD symptoms' severity and presentation, how it is understood in the family and school, and the current coping strategies which may improve or maintain it.

Thoughts

Typically, anger is aroused by not getting what you want and/or by a perception that someone is being confrontational towards you. Angry feelings are increased by negative thinking and/or the expectation of a negative response from others. Thoughts such as, 'That's not fair', 'They deserve punishment', 'People don't like me' and 'I hate them all', increase feelings of frustration and anger. Children with ADHD frequently receive negative feedback at school and at home; many children also have interpersonal problems and low self-esteem. This means that feelings of anger and resentment may be quick to surface, and negative thinking will increase the likelihood they will act out their feelings of anger.

Feelings and Physiology

Children (especially younger children) are still acquiring language to express their feelings and it is helpful to have a list at hand for naming their feelings: angry, frustrated, irritable, annoyed, wound-up and rage are commonly used by children. They may notice physiological symptoms, such as feeling tense or shaky, tunnel vision, heart racing, rapid breathing or a headache. You should encourage children to use creative and individual ways of expressing their feelings in metaphors and drawings.

Remember that children can find the experience of these symptoms to be as distressing as the thoughts or situation. However, it is unlikely that children will make links between thoughts, feelings and behaviours, and this is not necessary for successful intervention. For younger children, the intervention is more likely to focus on behaviours, whereas older children might apply cognitive interventions and may be helped by learning that thoughts, feelings and behaviours are related to the anger and actually serve to escalate the feeling of anger, which in turn increases the likelihood they will act out their anger in some way.

Anger increases arousal, but so might other emotions, such as social anxiety. It is therefore important to bear in mind that other factors may contribute to the presentation. In such cases the therapist could draw on interventions presented in other chapters (depending on the presentation).

Behaviours

The most common behaviour problems are likely to involve the child lashing out in some way. This may be verbal, such as the child calling out or shouting nasty and hurtful things, or physical aggression, such as hitting, kicking, punching or throwing items. The child may also damage property in a temper by ripping up photographs, smashing items or punching a hole in a door. For children who are engaging in serious, risky and/or reckless behaviours, it is essential to consider the potential risk to self or others, and whether there may be an increased risk that they will be harmed by others who feel unable to cope with the presenting behaviour.

The problem for children with ADHD is that their anger may flare up so quickly that they are caught unawares and are unable to 'put on the brakes'. This means they do not stop and think of the consequences of their behaviours, although if they did, maybe they would find a better way to cope with their feelings of distress. Once the child has calmed down they usually feel regret, remorse and guilt over their behaviour; once the 'red mist' has cleared they recognize that they have caused distress to someone they like or love.

It is important that the therapist explores anger-provoking situations and the methods that the child (and those around the child) use to cope with feelings of distress and anger. In particular, it is important to identify positive and helpful strategies that have been used in the past. What helps the child stay cool and calm? When did the child face an anger-provoking situation and it worked out okay? Who is best at helping the child when they need to face a worrying situation? What approach does that person take?

Creative Methods

When children feel emotional, they might find it hard to express their feelings in words. In such cases we suggest the therapist draws a large 'anger bag' on a piece of paper and discusses with the child their understanding of anger. What different words does the child know? Have they heard of anger? What does it mean to them? What are the things that make the child feel angry inside? Do they know someone else who gets angry? What can they tell you about that person and their anger? Ask the child, with your help, to fill the bag with their anger; this may be in words or drawings and pictures that capture what anger means to them. This may include how the child notices it in their body, situations when it happens and what goes through their mind. To maintain some balance, the conversation should include how they cope with their angry feelings, who helps them, and when and under what circumstances they feel relaxed, calm and happy.

Behaviour Diary

A Behaviour Diary is an assessment of the antecedents to behaviours, the behaviour itself and the consequences of behaviours. This is recorded in a chart, also known as an 'ABC chart', that can be given to parents/carers and/or teachers to monitor behaviour. The chart will provide insight about the type of behaviour, its triggers and when it is most likely to present. Over time it can show how patterns emerge that may explain the causes of the behaviour.

Table 8.1 Example of a completed Behaviour Diary for anger and frustration.

Day/Time	Antecedent (What was happening just before the behaviour? Who was there? What happened earlier in the day that might be relevant?)	Behaviour (What did you observe? Describe the duration and severity.)	Consequence (What happened next? What was the result?)
Monday 8 a.m.	Joe was getting ready for school. He couldn't find his pencil case.	He searched his bedroom but when he couldn't find it he accused his brother of taking it. Joe went into his room and shouted at him. I shouted at Joe because of his behaviour.	I went to look for the pencil case and found it on the floor by his bed. Joe had missed it. Joe apologized but his brother was very upset and didn't speak to him on the way to school. We were all late getting to school.
Sunday 9 p.m.	I warned Joe that he had to go to bed after the TV programme had ended (in 10 minutes). He didn't reply but carried on watching television. After the programme ended I told Joe to go to bed.	Joe said he wanted to stay up for longer. He said that it wasn't fair as he had not heard me give the 10-minute warning. We had an argument over it and he threw some books across the room.	I gave Joe another 10 minutes because I wasn't certain that he had been listening when I gave the warning.

Table 8.1 shows a Behaviour Diary completed by the mother of a boy named Joe. In the first example, Joe was probably feeling frustrated because he could not find his pencil case. What probably made it worse was that there was some time pressure because they had to leave the house to get to school on time. As time passed, the pressure would have become greater, with Joe becoming increasingly upset and panicky. Joe didn't search his room very well for the pencil case but instead shouted at his brother as he assumed he had taken it. He probably shouted because he needed to vent his feelings of frustration and distress.

Joe felt sorry about this later when his Mum found the pencil case, but his behaviour had caused a lot of upset at home. There were several consequences to the argument. Joe's brother would not speak to him on the way to school, and they both arrived late due to the delay. Even though it wasn't his brother's fault, he may also have got into trouble for being late. It may also have meant that Joe's Mum was late for wherever she had to be. In the second example, Joe is watching television and claims that he had not heard a 10-minute warning for bedtime. It is possible that he did not hear his Mum give the warning; it is also possible that he did hear the warning but knows that if he pretends that he didn't, he will be able to delay bedtime. Joe and his Mum get into an argument and he ecomes so angry that he throws some books across the room. This leads his Mum to give in and he gets to stay up longer.

The purpose of a Behaviour Diary is to record several episodes over time, from which a pattern may emerge. For example, if the behaviours seem to be associated with the pressure of time then an intervention needs to take that into account and think of strategies to avoid this by being better prepared. In the second example, one can see how the behaviour has been reinforced by Joe getting what he wants. This increases the likelihood that he will behave this way again in the future when he wants something. It is important to identify reinforcement of this nature and set strategies to help Joe's Mum prevent this from happening (e.g., by ensuring that she has Joe's attention when she gives the 10-minute warning, by making up a '10-minute warning' sign on paper that looks like a road sign that she can hold up in front of him when giving it). These strategies involve preventing the likelihood that Joe will become distressed and angry in the first place, but that is not always possible. Joe also needs to learn strategies to control his feelings of anger and prevent angry outbursts that may have negative consequences.

CBT Interventions for Frustration and Anger

If the therapist is treating younger children and/or the worksheets are being used as a basis for treatment, the first session should always commence with Worksheets 1, 2 and 3 to introduce the child to Buzz and his family (Worksheet 1), introduce positive self-talk (Worksheet 2) and identify a reward system (Worksheet 3). The reward and self-talk strategies are applied in the session, at home and/or at school. See Chapter 3 for a suggested outline of how to plan and conduct the introductory session. All the Worksheets are available on the companion website, www.wiley.com/go/young/helpingadhd.

The first aim of the interventions and Worksheets in the frustration and anger session(s) is to introduce children to the concept of anger, teach them how to recognize it in their bodies, and help them to understand the situations that may cause it and the consequences of them acting out on their feelings of anger.

A further aim is to help them understand the relationship between ADHD and anger, and acquire cognitive and behavioural skills to manage it. The therapist will achieve this by setting an agenda, reviewing Home Missions completed between sessions, working through new worksheets (or just the strategies for older children) and setting new Home Missions. If required, a mid-session break can be offered halfway through the session; this may be particularly important for younger children. Chapter 2 provides generic information on the structure and content of sessions (irrespective of topic); supplementary information is included within this chapter that specifically relates to the delivery of the frustration and anger session(s).

Agenda

At the beginning of the session, show the child the written agenda (see Figure 8.1) that you have prepared prior to the session and go through it, verbally linking the themes and worksheets that you will introduce during the session. For the frustration and anger module, introduce Worksheets 13 and 14 by saying,

> Today we are learning about a time when Buzz had extra homework to do – reading at home. After that, we will have a short break and you can colour in the worksheet using these crayons. Then we will read about what happened when Buzz made a birthday present for his Mum.

Agenda

Folder Review

Buzz reads a Book [Worksheet 13]

Break

Buzz makes a Birthday Present [Worksheet 14]

Breathing Exercise (optional)

Home Missions

Figure 8.1 Example agenda for frustration and anger session(s).

Folder Review

When reviewing the folder with the child, aside from checking whether the Home Missions are completed, take the opportunity to revise important information and/or concepts, as this will support the child to consolidate the learning points and/or newly acquired skills. Ensure that you make time to look at the illustrations, colourings, paintings, magazine cuttings and/or photographs that the child has added to the folder. Discuss them and try to relate these to discussions about Buzz and his family and/or topics or strategies that have been covered. Aside from acting as a revision prompt, this will also act as a reward system for the child. Praise should be given verbally, but you can also reward by adding stickers, handwritten notes or smiley faces. If Home Missions were set then you should review their Home Missions Record Form for comments and feedback from parents/carers and discuss this with the child.

Worksheet 13 Buzz reads a Book

Worksheet Description

To download this worksheet, please visit the companion website

Buzz is behind with some reading in school. His teacher has set him extra reading to do with his Mum for homework. He is the only one in class who was given extra homework and he feels that it isn't fair. At home, Buzz and his Mum read the book together. The book is about a race between a slug and a hare. As he reads out loud, Buzz's Mum corrects him a lot. Buzz feels annoyed and he loses interest in the story. He doesn't care about the story any more, and he throws the book across the room.

Worksheet Prompts

Buzz is feeling annoyed, how else might he be feeling?
What has led to Buzz feeling that way?
What does your body do when you feel frustrated or angry?
Draw a picture of yourself and label what happens in your body when you feel angry.
Can you tell me about a time when you have felt like Buzz?
What do you do to keep calm when you feel this way?
What can other people do to help you when you feel this way?
What could Buzz have done to stop himself from throwing the book across the room?
What can Buzz do to calm himself down and keep calm?
Write down a COOL CALM phrase to say to yourself if you feel annoyed.

Worksheet 13 is about anger management and aims to help children consider how feeling stressed and under pressure may lower their frustration and anger tolerance threshold. It provides children with an opportunity to talk about how they respond emotionally when faced with tasks that they find difficult, thus increasing self-reflection and self-awareness. The exercise draws on challenges that children with ADHD may face, such as being in trouble at school, falling behind with work, feeling resentment for having additional homework set, feeling monitored and singled out and receiving repeated negative feedback. Through discussion, the child is led to consider functional anger-management strategies, including methods to help prevent them from acting out on their feelings of anger.

In the story, Buzz first started to feel upset and annoyed when his teacher set him extra homework. He doesn't feel that it was fair as he is the only one in the class who got extra homework. He may have felt frustrated with himself before that because he was behind with his reading, and having extra homework will have escalated his feelings. When doing the extra reading at home, Buzz is struggling to get it right and his Mum repeatedly corrects him. This escalates Buzz's feelings even more and he doesn't want to read the story any more. He feels so angry inside that he throws the book across the room. Read the Stimulus Sheet to the child, or, if they wish, they can read it with you. Check that the child has understood the story and answer any questions they might have. Encourage the child to tell you about times when they feel they have been singled out and treated unfairly.

In the story Buzz becomes increasingly upset and frustrated. Start by asking the child, 'How is Buzz feeling?' Discuss how he starts with feelings of frustration, followed by feeling annoyed and then angry. Ask the child, 'What is the difference between feeling frustrated and feeling angry?' and summarize the answer, 'Frustration is not as strong as anger. It's when you feel just a little bit angry, it sometimes happens when you struggle to do something.' Encourage the child to think about how Buzz's feelings became stronger and to consider what may have contributed to their accumulation (e.g., negative feedback from others and how it made him feel inside).

It is important to help the child identify physiological symptoms of anger. Children with ADHD may feel that they suddenly switch into an anger outburst without warning, but if they can learn to identify early warning signals in their body they will have the opportunity to intervene in the anger process and choose a different way to behave. Ask the child, 'How do you feel in your body when you feel frustrated?' Ask, 'What about when you feel angry, is it the same?' For anger, the child might say that they feel their body tenses up, their heart starts to pound, they feel sweaty or their face gets hot. Then ask them, 'What comes first?' For younger children, it might be helpful to draw a gingerbread man and ask them to show you which parts of the body change when they feel frustrated. Repeat the exercise for when they feel angry. Give hints to prompt the child to reflect on these changes like 'some people notice they feel tense or their breathing gets faster', and ask them to draw a picture to illustrate what happens in their body when they feel angry.

Next, help the child reflect on a time they might have felt like Buzz. It might be a similar experience when they felt frustrated about something and this escalated into an angry outburst. Listen to their story. Prompt them to recall what they were thinking and feeling at that time. Move on to talking about what they already do to help themselves stay calm and control their temper. Children are likely to have varied levels of skills in this area and some may say, 'I don't know' whilst others may already have strategies. You can prompt them with suggestions such as, 'Did you get someone to help you?' 'Did you leave the situation?' 'Did you take some deep breaths?' 'Maybe you told yourself that you can get through this?' Ask the child to consider what other people did that was helpful. You can also ask what might have been helpful (even if it wasn't done at the time) and prompt the child to consider other options, 'Would it help if your teacher had spoken to you on your own?' 'Would it help to be able to have time out of the room for five minutes?'

Returning to the story about Buzz, work together with the child and make a list on the Task Sheet of the things Buzz can do to help in this situation. For example, he could tell himself that the teacher isn't singling him out but trying to help him. Likewise, he could tell himself that his Mum is trying to help him. He could have decided on a special reward that he would receive once he had finished reading the story. He could ask for a break and/or take deep breaths to relax. He could use positive self-talk (friendly thoughts) by telling himself, 'I don't have to get upset, I just have to read the story' or 'It will be okay, I can do this.' Then decide on the best COOL CALM self-talk statement that Buzz could have used and write this down on the Task Sheet. Next, revise the list of strategies generated for Buzz and circle ideas that might help the child when they experience feelings of frustration and anger. Add any new ideas they may come up with.

Give praise for the child's effort in the session. If you choose to set Home Missions based on this Worksheet we suggest asking the child to do the following:

1) Decorate the Worksheet by colouring in the pictures and/or add to them with pictures on the theme of the story. These could be photographs or pictures in magazines or comics.
2) Talk to your parents/carers and/or teacher about times when you feel frustrated or angry. You could talk to your parent/carer about what happens in your body (and show them your drawing on the Task Sheet).
3) Tell your parents/carers and/or teacher about the COOL CALM statement you are going to try out. They should know about this plan so they can prompt you to use it and/or give praise when they notice you are using it.
4) In addition to the COOL CALM statement, use one of the other strategies that you came up with for Buzz and report back next time on how it went. Share the strategy with parents/carers and teachers to help you to implement the ideas.

If Home Missions are set, remind parents/carers to complete the Home Missions Record Form and to place this is the folder for review at the next session.

Mid-session Break

This should be provided at an appropriate point in the session as outlined in Chapter 2.

Worksheet 14 Buzz makes a Birthday Present

Worksheet Description

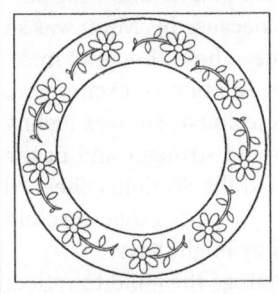

Buzz's favourite class at school is art. His teacher says he is good at art. He likes to do paintings and he likes to make things, especially with modelling clay. Buzz made a special plate for his Mum's birthday. It took him a long time to get it right. He painted flowers on it in her favourite colour. Buzz's Mum loved her present. She put it on the table at home where everyone could see it, but Buzz's older brother knocked it off the table by accident and it smashed to pieces. Buzz was very upset with his brother. He thinks that his brother did it on purpose. Buzz and his brother got into an argument and then Buzz felt so angry that he started a fight.

To download this worksheet, please visit the companion website

Worksheet Prompts

Why did Buzz get so angry with his brother?
What led to Buzz feeling that way?
What was Buzz thinking?
What happens in your body when you feel angry?
Have you ever hit out at anyone or broken anything when you felt angry?
What do you do to keep calm when you feel this way?
What can other people do to help you when you feel this way?
What could Buzz have done to stop himself fighting with his brother?
Together let's write out ideas of all the things Buzz can do to keep CALM and COOL if he notices he is feeling wound up.
Now let's look at the things you thought would help Buzz and circle the ones that might also help you.

Worksheet 14 focuses on the build up to physical aggression. It prompts the child to consider times when they have engaged (or felt like engaging) in physical aggression themselves (e.g., lashing out at others, kicking, punching, hitting out). Through discussion, the child is helped to identify an early warning signal that will cue that they may be about to lose control. This is achieved by discussing the physiological changes in the body that are commonly associated with anger (e.g., hot face, increased heart rate and tense stomach) and linking these feelings with negative thoughts and behaviour. Recognition of these warning signals affords the opportunity to apply anger control strategies and prevent aggressive behaviour.

In the story, Buzz is upset that his brother has broken his Mum's present. His anger has been fuelled because it took him a lot of care and time to make the present. Buzz was excited about making his Mum a plate and he felt proud of the plate (especially when she placed it where everyone would see it). Although his brother knocked it over by accident, Buzz suspects that he did it on purpose. Buzz might believe that his brother was jealous because his Mum was so pleased with him and that she had displayed the plate. These thoughts make Buzz feel even angrier. Thus, Buzz was feeling a lot of emotions – excitement, anticipation, pride, love, distress, anger and perhaps jealousy. He was feeling overwhelmed by his emotions, which grew stronger and stronger and in the end he hit out and began to fight with his brother. Read the Stimulus Sheet to the child, or, if the child wishes, they can read it with you. Check that the child has understood the story and answer any questions they might have.

When working through the Discussion Sheet, encourage the child to reflect more deeply on why Buzz felt angry, beyond 'Because his brother broke the plate.' You can ask, 'Why might Buzz have thought his brother broke the plate on purpose?', 'What else was Buzz feeling?' and 'Do you think Buzz put a lot of care and time into making the present?' Whilst it may have seemed that Buzz 'snapped' when the plate got broken and burst into a temper, there is likely to have been a build-up. Encourage the child to think about this by asking the child about what happened during the argument, what each child might have said, what each child might have been thinking and how each child was feeling. Buzz's brother, for example, may have been feeling upset that he had broken the plate, and that he had upset Buzz and his Mum on her birthday. He may feel guilty. He may feel that he is being unfairly blamed and in turn this could have led to him also feeling angry. Encourage the child to consider that there was a build-up of anger that 'ping-ponged' between the boys, and escalated each time. The difference between them was that Buzz could not control his feelings but his brother could.

Revise the physiological symptoms of frustration and anger that were discussed in Worksheet 13. Consider whether any additional body symptoms can be added for this more extreme form of anger (that resulted in physical aggression). The aim is to demonstrate that there is an increased and more intense physiology present. Amend the gingerbread man (if this was used). Liken the build-up of thoughts and feelings to a grumbling volcano, each thought making the lava heat up and rise until there is a big eruption and it all spills out. Talk about how this releases energy and tension, but the lava is scalding hot and spills over everywhere causing damage in its path. Tell the child to imagine that they are a wizard with special skills who can talk to the lava and make it cool down and stop grumbling. What would they say?

Help the child reflect on a time they might have felt angry like Buzz. It might be a similar experience when they felt so angry about something that they hit out. Ask, 'Have you ever hit out at anyone or broken anything when you have felt angry?' You may need to reassure the child that they will not be in trouble with you if they say they have. You can say, 'Sometimes people do things when they are angry without really thinking about the outcome. They might regret what they have done later.' If the child has never engaged in physical acts of aggression, then ask about a time when they felt like lashing out physically. Importantly, ask them what stopped them from doing this. Listen to their story and draw on helpful strategies that they already use (discussed in Worksheet 13). Prompt them to recall what they were thinking and feeling at that time.

Remind the child, 'Everyone gets angry at times but we have to learn to do something about it without hurting others.' Direct the child to think about their own early warning signal. In Worksheet 13 the child thought about the order of physiological symptoms and identified what they thought came first. Check this out with the child to see if they still think that is the first signal. If it is not, then change it to something different. Teach the child that when they feel this way (e.g., hot in the face, or beginning to speak more loudly) this should trigger them to intervene in the anger process. This is the signal they must look out for.

Return to the story about Buzz and work together with the child to think of the things Buzz can do to help in his situation. For example, he could walk away, count to three, take deep breaths, use positive self-talk or find his Mum. Point out that if Buzz walks away from the situation he could give himself some time alone to calm down. He could also use breathing and relaxation techniques (see Chapter 7). Go back to the early warning signal and decide what would be the quickest and most effective intervention at that stage (for Buzz). It is very important that the therapist forms an explicit relationship between SIGNAL and INTERVENTION. For example, this might be FEEL HOT = WALK AWAY (a behavioural intervention with the child leaving the anger-provoking scene) or FEEL TENSE = STOP (a cognitive intervention with the child saying to themselves '*stop*'). Next, direct the child to think of COOL CALM self-talk statements that Buzz could use and write down ideas for how Buzz can keep CALM and COOL if he notices he is feeling wound up. Finally, revise the list of strategies generated for Buzz and circle ideas for the child to try.

Give praise for the child's effort in the session. If you choose to set Home Missions based on this Worksheet we suggest asking the child to do the following:

1) Decorate the Worksheet by colouring in the pictures and thought bubbles, and/or add to them with pictures on the theme of the story. These could be photographs or pictures in magazines or comics.
2) Talk to your parents/carers and/or teacher about what happens when you feel very angry. Choose one warning signal that lets you know the anger is building up. This should be shared with your parents/carers and school.

3) Talk to your parents/carers and/or teacher about times when you have felt very angry. Tell them what happens in your body (show them the bodily response drawing if this has been done and revised). Tell them about your early warning signal that has been identified that will trigger an intervention.
4) Tell your parents/carers and/or teacher about the SIGNAL = INTERVENTION plan. Describe the intervention you have selected. This may include a COOL CALM statement you are going to try out or taking a break. Parents/carers and teachers should know about this plan so they can prompt you to use it and/or give praise when they notice you are using it.
5) In addition, use one of the other strategies that you came up with for Buzz and report back next time on how it went. Share the strategy with your parents/carers and teachers.

If Home Missions are set, remind parents/carers to complete the Home Missions Record Form and to place this is the folder for review at the next session.

Feedback and Rewards

At the end of the session, appropriate rewards identified from the Worksheet 3 Reward Task should be applied (e.g., the child should engage in positive self-talk). See Chapter 2 for more information about feedback and rewards.

Working with Parents/Carers

This section presents strategies that parents/carers can apply to support the child to reduce and/or cope with feelings of frustration and anger. It is important to be realistic about what can be achieved. It can be just as helpful to learn strategies to cope better with a child's behaviour as to learn strategies to improve the behaviour itself.

Parents/carers may need to recognize their own feelings of frustration and anger and how these are communicated to the child. Children can learn how to manage their feelings from observation, so it is important that parents/carers manage their own feelings effectively and role-model successful strategies of self-control. When children feel that unreasonable demands are being put on them and they are criticized, blamed and/or made to feel that they are a failure, they are more likely to act out negative feelings of resentment, frustration and anger through oppositional and/or challenging behaviour. In turn, a reciprocal and negative cycle may develop between parents/carers and the child, with parents/carers feeling frustrated, stressed and angry themselves, and having less control over what they say and do. Figure 8.2 represents this negative cycle and can be used to help parents/carers reflect on their own thoughts, feelings and behaviours when children display challenging behaviours. Parents/carers should be invited to consider how, with repetitive cycles, feelings become more intense and both parties feel less in control. If this can be recognized and understood, parents/carers have the opportunity to break the cycle by adopting a new and/or different approach.

Parent/carers' Behaviour:
Increase Voice
Make more demands of the child
Criticize the child

Child becomes increasingly frustrated, angry and challenging

Parent/carers' Thoughts:
"My child is trying to test me"

Parent/carers' Feelings:
Annoyed
Fed up
Upset
Stressed

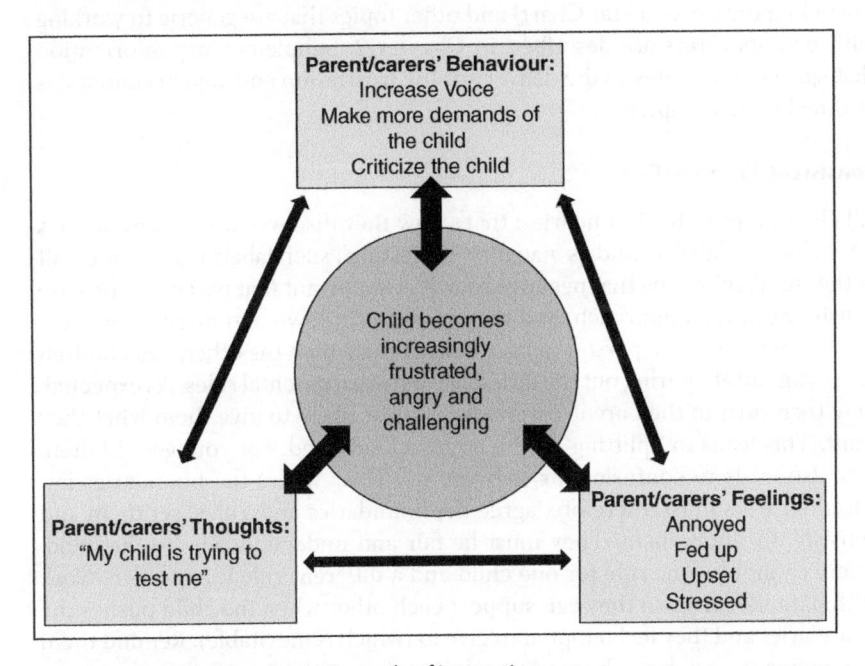

Figure 8.2 Reciprocal and negative cycle of interaction.

In this section we discuss the need for parents/carers to agree boundaries and rules, and adopt a consistent approach to managing anger outbursts. Parents/carers are guided to identify anger triggers and warning signals when a child is approaching the 'red zone', and advice is given about how to avoid escalation. Behavioural strategies are outlined that support the child to face frustrating and anger-provoking situations, and help parents/carers to manage their child's anger outbursts, including withdrawal and relaxation techniques. Cognitive techniques are also discussed, including dealing with negative thinking, using self-talk and positive self-statements, and visualization techniques to induce a sense of security and calm. When working with parents/carers, the therapist should introduce suggested techniques and strategies; practise and rehearse them in role-plays during the sessions if appropriate (without the child present). In future sessions, parents/carers should report back to the therapist about how they managed with the techniques at home. It is important to troubleshoot any obstacles and/or difficulties that arise by thinking of ways to adapt the techniques or strategies so they are successful in helping the child.

A key strategy to change behaviour and improve cognitive skills is to find motivators to promote success. Children with ADHD tend to respond better to immediate rewards as they have difficulty with delayed gratification for longer-term rewards (even if these are bigger and better). Methods to motivate success (including the use of a Star Chart) and other topics that are generic to working with parents/carers are described in Chapter 2. Supplementary information that specifically relates to the delivery of the frustration and anger session(s) is outlined in this chapter.

Consistent, Firm and Fair

All children push the boundaries; that's how they discover where they are. It's not helpful to label a child as 'naughty' or 'testing'; such labels may even result in the child embracing that negative role. It is important that parents/carers are consistent in their approach, and they need to sit down and discuss this. It is very common for one person to be a 'softer touch' than the other, and children are very good at figuring out the difference between parental rules. As expected, they then turn to the parent/carer who is most likely to give them what they want. This leads to 'splitting' in the approach adopted. For younger children, this also leads to confusion, as they are not clear where the boundaries lay. Parents/carers must, therefore, agree the boundaries and 'rules', set them and consistently apply them. They must be fair and understandable to the child. There cannot be one rule for one child and a different rule for another. Work with parents/carers so they can support each other when the child pushes the boundaries and they feel tempted to give in (which is inevitable). Remind them that giving in may be a short-term solution, but in the longer-term it sets up difficulties as the child learns what behaviours circumvent the rules. In turn, the next time the child wants something they repeat the behaviour.

Identify Triggers

There are times and situations that are likely to 'press the buttons' for both the child and the parents/carers. If you can identify these in advance, you can intervene and avoid a situation getting out of control. Because children with ADHD commonly have more difficulty with emotion regulation, they have a low reactivity threshold so they may react to smaller triggers and take longer to return to a calm state. Discuss with parents/carers the times and situations that often lead to an angry outburst from the child; they usually know exactly what these are but it is helpful to explicitly list them. Parents/carers should be directed to think about what situations are likely to lead the child to feel stressed, pressured or overwhelmed. Situations that trigger frustration are typically times when the child perceives themselves as unable to keep up or to reach the standards or expectations of others, and/or feels they have to juggle lots of competing demands. Problems may arise across domains, for example, at school, at home doing chores and homework or in managing interpersonal relationships. Situations that trigger anger usually involve confrontation, such as sibling disagreements or being told to do something that the child doesn't want to do (e.g., it may be deemed as boring or aversive by the child). The trigger may also relate to how the child is feeling, for example feeling tired, hungry, worried and/or anxious.

Behaviour Diary

In order to identify specific situations that trigger angry outbursts, ask parents/carers to complete a Behaviour Diary (described earlier in this chapter) to monitor behaviour. Discuss the information recorded in the diary with parents/carers to gain further insight and understanding about the type of behaviour, its triggers and when it is most likely to present. Over time patterns emerge that may explain the causes of some behaviours. This can be helpful to determine which interventions may be best introduced to address the problem.

Identify Warning Signals

Support parents/carers to identify specific indicators that can act as a warning that their child's level of arousal is approaching the 'red zone'. Break down interactions by asking:

1) The 'orange zone': at what point did you notice that the child was starting to feel annoyed or stressed? How did you know that? (Prompt: what the child said or did, how the child appeared to them, body symptoms)
2) The 'red zone': at what point did you notice that the child was really struggling, feeling very angry or overwhelmed? How did you know that? (Prompt: what the child said or did, how the child appeared to them, body symptoms)

It is also helpful to have a discussion about what interventions have been helpful and unhelpful to diffuse a situation. It is just as important to learn what doesn't work.

Avoid Escalation

When in a confrontational situation, there is always some form of escalation. 'It takes two to tango', which means that both parties have the opportunity to attend to internal and/or external signals that the child is approaching the 'red zone'. It only takes one person to change their reaction or behaviour to break the reciprocal negative cycle. Internal signals may relate to feeling hot or flushed, or noticing that you have raised your voice or have moved uncomfortably close to someone. External signals may relate to noticing these things in the other person. There are times when a person appears to suddenly erupt; this usually occurs when a person suppresses their angry feelings. However, the escalation still exists, as inside there has been a gradual wind-up; in such cases it is important for the person to attend to internal signals. Once you recognize a person is approaching the 'red zone', there are several things that can be done to avoid a situation from escalating further:

- Focus on speaking in a calm and steady voice
- Check that both people are listening to each other – is the child paying attention and is the parent/carer really listening to the child?
- Take time out to calm down and decide on the next step (ensure the child is safe and supervised)
- Stop saying hurtful things in the moment.

Body Sensations and Anger

There is a physiological response to feelings of anger, particularly when you are in a confrontational situation. Your heart starts to race and you feel hot and flushed. You have 'tunnel vision', with the other person and your emotions being the focus of your attention. Also, if someone acts in an aggressive and confrontational way towards you, you are likely to respond in the same way. For example, if someone shouts at you, you shout back. If someone hits out at you, you may want to hit back. It is important to recognize this relationship, as if you intervene in the process and take steps to calm down you will get less caught up in a reciprocal negative cycle. It is sometimes noted that when children are frustrated and angry their symptoms of restlessness and hyperactivity increase. In many respects this is a functional strategy to reduce feeling stressed and distressed, much in the same way as an adult will use physical exercise to help them gain a sense of calm, control and cognitive rationalization. The difference is that an adult will purposefully apply this strategy, if they find it helpful, but children do not, they just react. However, purposefully channelling restlessness, noticing that a child is becoming frustrated and stressed and/or the introduction of some form of physical exercise may be helpful.

Withdrawal

Sometimes it's best to remove a child from a situation if it is becoming unmanageable or too overwhelming. This gives space for both parents/carers and child to control their feelings, rationalize the situation and think of a different way to handle it. However, it is important to note that there is a difference between avoiding a situation because you can't face it (which may be a dysfunctional behaviour – see Chapter 7) and taking time out in order to aid the reflective process and think of a more positive way to manage it.

Address Negative Thinking

Help parents/carers to notice and deal with their own negative thinking. Negative thoughts about a child may be linked with expectations (especially if these are unrealistic), misunderstandings of behaviour, beliefs about the child's intentions and/or their own experiences. Negative thinking may also relate to the parent's/carer's mental state and has been strongly associated with feelings of depression and anxiety. You can help parents/carers to identify negative thinking by asking, 'What was going through your mind in that situation with your child?' In addition, explore the impact of negative thinking by asking, 'If you thought of the behaviour as your child being unable rather than refusing to do it, how would that change what you were thinking and feeling?' or by asking, 'What would you say if it was someone else in this situation?' 'What advice would you give?'

Self-talk

Parents/carers can support their children to develop positive self-talk and use positive self-statements. Self-talk (friendly thoughts) that will help with angry feelings include, 'Keep cool' and 'Stay calm'. Children should also be encouraged to make positive self-statements and self-instructions such as, 'It's not worth it. Walk away.' Encourage parents/carers to model positive self-talk and self-statements in front of the child and to consider ways to develop their own positive self-talk and self-statements. They should also prompt the child to use the techniques if they notice warning signals that the child is approaching the 'red zone'. Self-talk can be reinforced by reassurance and positive statements by others.

Problem-solving

Feelings of frustration and anger may arise in response to a child not knowing how to effectively cope with a situation and/or resolve a problem. It may be that the child has difficulty with asserting to others what it is that they need or want. If a child struggles with being assertive, they may find it difficult to deal with demands made by peers, for example. The child may also not admit to others that they are struggling. This means that the child's feelings are channelled into anger, which in turn interferes with good decision-making. This is particularly true for children with ADHD who already have difficulties with problem-solving, decision-making and following through with solutions. When this problem seems to present, consider including appropriate strategies outlined in Chapter 11 (Problem-solving).

Visualization

Talk to parents/carers about the ways they encourage the child to visualize images that induce a sense of security, safety and calm. This involves generating a relaxing image and prompting the child to use this image when they feel upset and/or stressed. For children, the image may relate to lying in bed with their mother stroking their hair or cuddling a favourite toy. The technique can be rehearsed in sessions with parents/carers by asking them to envisage their own soothing image (for example, they are sitting on a quiet beach feeling the warmth of the sun). Direct them to enhance this image with the soothing sounds they can hear, ask what they can see, what they can smell and what they can feel at their fingertips.

Breathing and Relaxation

Breathing and relaxation techniques may also help a child maintain a sense of control. A typical breathing and relaxation exercise is included in the psychoeducational booklet 'So I have ADHD', which can be downloaded from the Psychology Services Website (www.psychology-services.uk.com/resources). Parents/carers should practise the techniques with their child to help them gain control of physiological symptoms. Remind parents/carers that the more children practise these techniques, the more natural they will become. We suggest that good times to practise include before bed, when travelling and before or after school. Parents/carers should also prompt the child to apply these techniques if the child is complaining about physiological symptoms that are associated with frustration and anger.

What Can We Do As Parents/Carers?

Table 8.2 outlines a suggested approach, including a list of strategies that can be implemented at home. To maximize the effect of strategies it is helpful to discuss these with your child's teacher so they may be implemented at both home and school (wherever possible). Lots of parents/carers and teachers find that using a 'Home School Diary' is an efficient way to share information (see Chapter 2).

Aside from reading the current chapter, we suggest that parents/carers read Chapter 2, which provides important background information about the delivery of the Young–Smith Programme. For younger children, we suggest that parents/carers set aside some time to sit down with the child (around 45–60 minutes) and work through the Worksheets recommended for each topic. Guidance is found in the 'CBT Interventions' section within each chapter on how to do this. The worksheets introducing Buzz and his family are outlined in Chapter 3. All the materials (worksheets and Home Missions Record Form) are available for download from the companion website www.wiley.com/go/young/helpingadhd. For older children (i.e., 12 years-plus), you can dispense with the Buzz Worksheets if necessary and instead introduce the child directly to the topic, and, using the discussion prompts on the Worksheets, apply this to the child's experience and discuss suggested strategies. Set Home Missions and support the child to complete them. Don't forget to give frequent feedback and praise. Make a Star Chart (see Chapter 2), put it in a prominent place and start to use it on a daily basis.

Table 8.2 Home strategies for frustration and anger.

Be consistent, firm and fair
- Agree boundaries and rules with both parents/carers.
- Develop a consistent approach to deal with challenging behaviour.

Identify triggers
- Think ahead of situations where your child may become over-aroused.
- Make a plan of how to avoid a problem developing and/or how to manage it.

Identify warning signals
- Identify specific indicators that act as a warning that your child is approaching the 'red zone'.

Avoid escalation
- Speak to your child in a calm and steady voice.
- Check you are both listening to each other.
- Stop saying hurtful things in the moment.
- Change focus by engaging in physical exercise.

Withdrawal
- As a parent/carer, take time out to help you stay calm.
- If needed, remove your child to a calm space.

Self-talk
- Together, think up some positive self-talk statements (friendly thoughts) and self-instructions your child can apply to help manage feelings of frustration and anger.
- Prompt your child to use them when feeling frustrated or angry.

Visualization
- Practise visualization techniques using calming images.
- Prompt your child to apply the techniques when feeling upset and aroused.

Problem-solving
- Help your child solve problems that are causing them to feel stressed or worried about. See strategies in Chapter 11.

Breathing and relaxation
- Practice breathing and relaxation techniques together.
- Prompt your child to use them when feeling aroused.

Role model
- Be a role model to your child by using strategies yourself.
- Do this out loud so your child can observe and learn what you do.

Working with Teachers and Schools

Anger is a normal emotional state that is experienced by everyone. It is dysfunctional, however, when we become intensely angry over small things, when it leads a person to behave in a provocative and/or confrontational way, and when we lack appropriate methods to control powerful emotions. Giving up at the first hurdle is an unhelpful way of dealing with feelings of frustration. Behaving in an aggressive manner (both verbally and physically) towards people and/or damaging property are ineffective ways to deal with feelings of anger.

Children with ADHD commonly have more difficulty with emotional regulation, meaning that they have difficulty controlling their emotional state. They may appear to over-react to small triggers and take longer to return to a calm state. Because of their ADHD symptoms, children often struggle with some schoolwork. They may feel confused and overwhelmed. This makes problem-solving less efficient and can lead to frustration, especially in the classroom. They are also often aware that their peers are able to more quickly grasp a concept, which makes them conclude that they are 'stupid'. Children will tend to focus on this aspect of their performance, rather than what they do well; they may also feel shame if they perceive themselves as different in a negative way and this can lead to defensiveness.

The physiological signs of stress, frustration and anger may increase the symptoms of restlessness and hyperactivity and, in turn, this may make the child with ADHD harder to manage in the classroom. Similarly, when children behave in an aggressive and confrontational way towards peers and/or teachers it can cause disruption in the classroom as well as distress to the person on the receiving end. Many teachers feel confident about how to deal with this type of behaviour, but it is still distressing for them and in such cases it is important they gain support by talking things through with a colleague.

The reciprocal and negative cycle of interaction outlined in Figure 8.2 and described in the parents/carers section of this chapter may also apply to child–teacher relationships. This relationship is important as children may perform better and achieve more with a teacher they like than with a teacher they feel they don't get along with so well. Teachers are professionals and it is unlikely that they allow personal feelings about a child to interfere with their performance and role. However, teachers are also human, with good days and bad days, and it can be difficult sometimes to avoid getting caught up in a reciprocal and negative cycle of interaction. If children are very prone to anger outbursts this may be intolerable as well as inappropriate in the classroom setting. Teachers may not only have to manage children who are oppositional and challenging towards them, but also children who are aggressive and confrontational towards other children. The skill is to recognize that there is trouble brewing and cut it off before the 'red zone' is reached.

This section presents strategies that teachers can apply to support the child to control feelings of frustration and anger. It is important to be realistic about what can be achieved. It can be just as helpful to learn strategies to cope better with a child's behaviour as to learn strategies to improve the behaviour itself. In this section we discuss methods to identify anger triggers and warning signals that a child is approaching the 'red zone', and advice is given about how to avoid escalation. Behavioural strategies are outlined to support the child to face frustrating and anger-provoking situations, including peer mentoring, withdrawal and relaxation techniques. Cognitive techniques are also discussed to deal with negative thinking, support the child to apply a solution-focused problem-solving approach and use self-talk and positive self-statements to help them at times of stress and to induce a sense of calm and control.

Teachers and schools will already have structures in place to support many of the interventions introduced in the Young–Smith Programme. It will be useful to link up parents/carers and teachers to encourage an integrated strategy and share success. It is important to troubleshoot any obstacles and/or difficulties that arise by thinking of ways to adapt the techniques or strategies so they are successful in helping the child. Methods to motivate success and other topics that are generic to working with teachers and schools are described in Chapter 2. Supplementary information that specifically relates to the delivery of the frustration and anger session(s) is outlined in this chapter.

Identify Triggers

If teachers can identify specific tasks or situations when the child feels particularly challenged (and hence frustrated), then teachers have the opportunity to predict that a problem may arise and plan how to deal with it. Discuss with teachers the times and situations that have led to the child acting out in frustration or irritability. Consider with the teacher whether these then build up and result in an angry outburst, or whether this is precipitated by different times and situations. Does the child have any strategies that they apply themselves? Are these effective, ineffective or do they actually make things worse?

Situations that trigger frustration and irritability usually involve struggling with academic concepts or perceiving an obstacle, whereas situations that trigger angry outbursts are often interpersonal in nature. This may not relate solely to interpersonal conflict, but also to feelings of shame and/or embarrassment, so consider what may be going on internally for the child as opposed to merely focusing on behaviour. If the triggers involve interpersonal problems and/or social situations at school, it may be helpful to include some of the strategies in Chapter 9 on social skills and relationships. Once a list has been generated, discuss with teachers what interventions can be introduced to avoid a problem developing. Teachers should also be encouraged to use and analyse Behaviour Diaries for this purpose. However, it is very important to review behaviours at a time when the child is ready to do so and when teachers have the time to listen carefully rather than making hasty judgements.

Identify Warning Signals

Using the same techniques as for parents/carers, described earlier in this chapter, support teachers to identify specific indicators that can act as a warning that the child's level of arousal is approaching the 'red zone'.

Avoid Escalation

In the school setting, teachers are most likely to apply techniques to avoid a situation escalating out of control when heated arguments flare up between peers. Once the teacher recognizes a child is approaching the 'red zone' and/or notices a child is engaging in provocative behaviour (such as name calling, making threats), the teacher may intervene to prevent this from escalating further by:

- Redirecting the focus of the argument by speaking to the children in a firm but calm and steady voice.
- Sending one or both children to a 'Time Out' area for a period of time to cool down.
- Talking to the children separately about what has upset them and helping them find a way to resolve the problem.

It is common for teachers to remove the child from a situation that is growing in intensity and becoming unmanageable. This can help to give space for the child to calm down and provides an opportunity to re-frame the situation and plan a solution.

Address Negative Thinking

In some cases it may be helpful to consider whether a reciprocal and negative cycle of interaction has arisen (see Figure 8.2 in parents/carers section) and discuss how negative thinking may be influencing the teacher–child relationship. It is important that a teacher does not feel blamed or criticized in any way, the discussion is an acknowledgement that teaching can be challenging and sometimes situations of conflict arise which may lead to the development of unhelpful beliefs. Negative thoughts about the child with ADHD may be associated with unrealistic expectations, poor self-efficacy, misunderstandings or beliefs about the child's intentions and/or myths about ADHD. You can help teachers to explore negative thinking by asking, 'What was going through your mind in that situation with the child?' In addition, explore the impact of negative thinking by asking, 'If you thought of the behaviour as a signal that the child was feeling overwhelmed rather than being deliberately oppositional, how would that change your perception?' 'How would that change how you deal with the problem?' Alternatively you could ask, 'What would you say to a colleague in this situation?' 'What advice would you give?'

Self-talk

Teachers can support children to develop positive self-talk (friendly thoughts) and use positive self-statements. Self-talk that will help with feelings of frustration and anger in the school setting is similar to that proposed for use at home (see parents/carers section in this chapter for examples). It is advantageous for the same self-talk repertoire to be developed that can be used in both home and school settings. Teachers should also prompt the child to use these techniques if they notice warning signals that the child is approaching the 'red zone'. Self-talk can be reinforced by reassurance and positive statements by others.

Peer Role Models

Children with ADHD may not fully attend to instructions, have difficulty organizing their work and/or struggle with some academic concepts. They become irritated and frustrated when they don't know what to do and/or can't get it right. In some cases, this may be resolved by pairing the child with an appropriate peer role model (or applying a similar format for group activities). It's important that children are instructed to collaboratively engage to complete the task (rather than one doing all the work and the other observing).

Problem-solving

Frustration and anger may stem from poor problem-solving and poor decision-making skills. When this seems to be the case, consider including appropriate strategies that are outlined in Chapter 11.

Breathing and Relaxation

The breathing and relaxation techniques introduced in the parents/carers section of this chapter may also be delivered by teachers. It is preferable, however, for these techniques to be applied both at home and at school, where either parents/carers or teachers can prompt the child to apply them if the child becomes over-aroused.

Teacher Control

When managing crises, it is crucial for teaching staff to have self-awareness of their own emotions and/or behaviours that are being communicated to the child. It is important that they do not convey anger or distress but calm control.

What Can We Do As Teachers?

Table 8.3 outlines a suggested approach for teachers, including a list of strategies that can be implemented at school. To maximize the effect of strategies, it is helpful to discuss them with the child's parents/carers so that similar or

Table 8.3 School strategies for frustration and anger.

Identify triggers
- Think ahead of situations that may arise when a child may become over-aroused.
- Make a plan of how to avoid a problem developing and/or how to manage it.

Identify warning signals
- Identify specific indicators that act as a warning that the child is approaching the 'red zone'.

Avoid escalation
- Identify teachers/assistants to provide support to the child who are skilled at working with the child in a non-judgemental way, and ensure that all staff know and understand what strategies are being used and why.
- Support the child to gain recognition of their own feelings and escalating arousal levels.
- Identify a 'secret signal' (often non-verbal) to communicate to the child that they are losing self-control.
- Ensure that all strategies used are 'owned' by the child and that they know they are designed to support rather than control them.
- Redirect the focus of the argument by speaking to the child in a firm but calm and steady voice.
- Send the child to a 'Time Out' area for a period of time to cool down.
- Talk to the child separately about what has upset them and help them find a way to resolve the problem.

Self-talk
- Together, think up some positive self-talk statements (friendly thoughts) and self-instructions the child can apply to help manage feelings of frustration and anger. Share these with parents/carers.
- Prompt the child to use them when feeling frustrated or angry.

Peer role models
- For specific tasks, pair the child with an appropriate peer role model.
- Emphasize the need for them to collaborate to complete the task.

Problem-solving
- Support the child to resolve problems that are causing them to feel stressed or worried. See strategies in Chapter 11.

Breathing and relaxation
- Practise breathing and relaxation techniques together.
- Prompt the child to use them when feeling aroused.
- Identify a 'safe space' within the school where the child can retreat when feeling upset, frustrated or angry.

Rehearsal
- Rehearse these strategies at times when the child is calm and does not require them.

complementary strategies arethey may be implemented at both home and school (wherever possible). Both teachers and parents/carers find that using a 'Home School Diary' is an efficient way to share information (see Chapter 2).

We suggest that teachers read Chapter 2, which provides important background information about the delivery of the Young–Smith Programme. It is unlikely that teachers will have time to go through specific worksheets with children, although if parents/carers are unable to do this it would be helpful to make arrangements with the Special Educational Needs Coordinator. Guidance on how to do this is found in the 'CBT Interventions' section in each chapter. The worksheets introducing Buzz and his family are outlined in Chapter 3. All the materials (worksheets and Home Missions Record Form) are available for download from the companion website, www.wiley.com/go/young/helpingadhd. For older children (i.e., 12 years-plus), one may dispense with the Buzz worksheets if necessary and instead introduce the child directly to the topic, and, using the discussion prompts on the worksheets, apply this to the child's experience and discuss suggested strategies. Set Home Missions and support the child to complete them. Don't forget to give frequent feedback and praise. If a Star Chart is used (see Chapter 2) then this could be put in the 'Home School Diary' where parents/carers can also review it on a regular basis.

References

Achenbach, T. M., & Rescorla, L. A. (2001). *Manual for the ASEBA school-age forms & profiles*. Burlington, VT: University of Vermont, Research Center for Children, Youth and Families.

Barkley, R. A., & Fischer, M. (2010). The unique contribution of emotional impulsiveness to impairment in major life activities in hyperactive children as adults. *Journal of the American Academy of Child & Adolescent Psychiatry, 49*(5), 503–513.

Conners, C. K. (2008). *Conners 3rd edition*. Toronto: Multi-Health Systems.

Goodman, R. (1997). The strengths and difficulties questionnaire: A research note. *Journal of Child Psychology and Psychiatry and Allied Disciplines, 38*(5), 581–586.

Jensen, P. S., Hinshaw, S. P., Kraemer, H. C., Lenora, N., Newcorn, J. H., Abikoff, H. B., et al. (2001). ADHD comorbidity findings from the MTA study: Comparing comorbid subgroups. *Journal of the American Academy of Child and Adolescent Psychiatry, 40*(2), 147–158.

Sexias, M., Weiss, M., & Müller, U. (2012). Systematic review of national and international guidelines on attention deficit hyperactivity disorder. *Journal of Psychopharmacology, 26*(6), 753–765.

9

Social Skills and Relationships

In our society we strive for social recognition and acceptance. The childhood years are important formative years for social development, when children test the boundaries and learn social rules and values. All children will vary in their social interaction, how many friends they want to have around them, how they value friendships and relationships and how they view themselves when relating to others. For children with ADHD, the key difference is that they find making and maintaining friendships more difficult, and ADHD may impact on how they adhere to social rules. Children may compensate by stating they have lots of friends, but on closer inspection they have a high number of superficial friendships, for example they may cite their whole class as being their friends. Friendship may also be founded on neighbourhood proximity and/or family relationships. For example, their friends might be the next-door neighbour and/or children of their mother's friends. Often it is not until the adolescent years when children begin to select their own friendship circles that interpersonal problems fully come to the fore. The evaluation of their popularity and social performance (evaluated by both themselves and others, the latter often being the perceived response of others) will influence their self-esteem.

Social problems also impact on family relationships. Sibling relationships can be confrontational and competitive. Siblings may also feel angry about what they perceive to be attention-seeking behaviour by their ADHD brother or sister, and/or feel envious of the (additional) attention they receive. For those children who are persistently hyperactive, impulsive and/or emotionally labile, their behaviour may take a particular toll on family, sibling and teacher relationships, as they are perceived as difficult and challenging to manage. If they are perceived to be uncooperative and confrontational, this can become an obstacle to the maintenance of functional and adaptive relationships.

This module will examine social skills and relationships in children with ADHD and the impact this can have on their social functioning in different areas of life. The assessment of social skills will be discussed, followed

Helping Children with ADHD: A CBT Guide for Practitioners, Parents and Teachers,
First Edition. Susan Young and Jade Smith.
© 2017 John Wiley & Sons Ltd. Published 2017 by John Wiley & Sons Ltd.
Companion website: www.wiley.com/go/young/helpingadhd

by interventions and strategies for children and the adults around them using cognitive behavioural models.

Presentation

Over time children with ADHD are likely to experience repeated exposure to social and/or interpersonal situations that have gone wrong and resulted in negative consequences. Younger children with ADHD often lack self-awareness and do not understand how their own behaviours have influenced the interaction. Older children may have some self-awareness that they get things wrong, but are at a loss to know what to do about it. Irrespective of whether there is self-awareness or not, the child may feel socially isolated and unhappy. This may become a negative cycle and self-fulfilling prophecy (as seen in Figure 9.1) that leads to the development of social anxiety. To cope with social anxiety, children may avoid social situations, which in the long run will continue the anxiety (see Chapter 7 for information and interventions for anxiety).

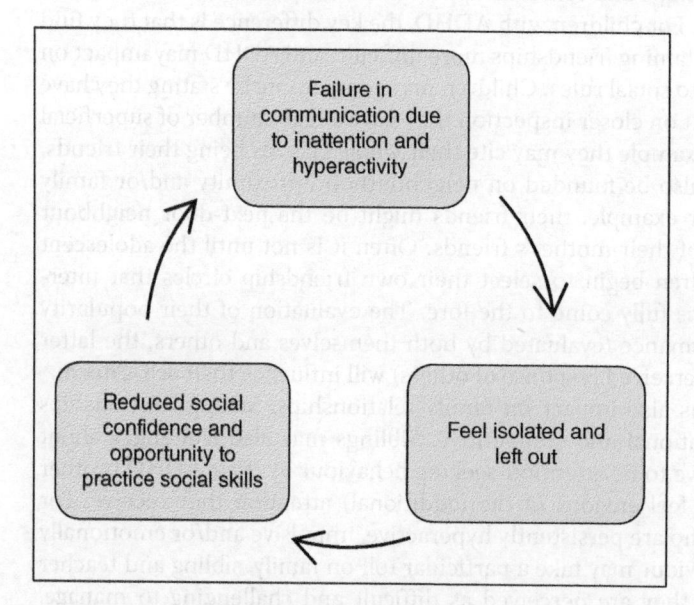

Figure 9.1 The negative social interaction cycle.

There are a number of characteristics that may influence the outcome of social exchanges, and these relate to the child's behaviour, social skills and styles of communication. Often, the child is not referred with a specific request for help with social skills, but the presenting problem relates to bullying, being bullied, managing conflict, withdrawal and/or social isolation.

Behavioural Functioning

Reports suggest that up to 15 % of children with ADHD have experienced bullying, though this may vary across cultures (Chou, Liu, Yang, Yen & Hu, 2014). This usually occurs when a child is perceived as 'different' in some way to their peers and/or vulnerable, isolated or unable to stand up for themselves. Of course the figures don't include children who don't speak out about such experiences. Figures may also be higher when a comorbid Autism Spectrum Condition is present. Children with ADHD may be bullied if they are perceived to be slower, unpredictable, attention-seeking, aggressive or spiteful. Children are very astute at realizing who is the easiest target to wind up, cause to over-react and get into trouble. Even with low level bullying, such as name-calling, children with ADHD may react impulsively and become the victim of jokes and ridicule.

Alternatively, children with ADHD may over-compensate by developing strategies to accommodate friendships and create a sense of popularity or belonging. This may include ingratiating themselves to 'in-groups' by being eager to please and, in an effort to fit in, doing things they are asked to do without question. Older children may try to gain friendships through sexual promiscuity. These behaviours allow others to take advantage of them. On the other hand, children with ADHD may also be seen by others as being the bully, especially when there have been multiple situations when the child has reacted in negative or hurtful ways towards others.

Poor impulse control enhances the likelihood that children with ADHD will react badly in a social situation. If a child with ADHD feels a negative emotion during a social interaction, such as blame, confusion or hurt, they are more likely to jump to conclusions regarding the meaning or intention of others and act upon these feelings. This impulsive responding means that they do not stop and think to clarify the situation or consider alternative possibilities and options to make sense of and/or resolve the situation. Maladaptive responses can lead to conflict and further social difficulties, with skills in negotiating, questioning and having an internal debate becoming lost.

Academic Functioning

Keeping up in a classroom can be difficult for children with ADHD, and this can then be problematic for teaching staff. It is essential that there is a positive relationship between pupils and their teacher in order to aid learning and provide a safe environment. Cognitive and behavioural problems may become more marked for children with ADHD if they are worried about being disliked.

The promotion of social skills is an intrinsic part of the school curriculum. Teachers should watch out for difficulties and problem areas that may develop in peer interactions, and intervene as appropriate. In addition, children may be quick to notice any differences between them, and in some instances this may lead to bullying. This may be overt bullying or less obvious, with the ADHD child being left out of activities, such as being the last to be selected to participate in a team, being excluded from lunch groups or having no one to sit next to on the school bus. Social factors may also obstruct children with ADHD from optimizing their opportunity to learn in the academic environment. Chatting to peers, distracting peers and focusing on peer activities and friendships when they should be focusing on a task will all impact on their learning. It is important that teachers are aware of the ways that ADHD may impact on communication and adapt class work as necessary with repetition, visual aids and clarification.

Interpersonal Functioning

Attention is an important component for developing skills in remembering, listening and following information. As a result, the style of communication adopted by children with ADHD can often seem one-sided. Children with ADHD often present with the following impairments in their communication style:

- A fast pace of speech and frequent changes of topic, which can be difficult to follow;
- Speaking too loudly and an inability to adapt volume to the environment, which can seem boisterous or aggressive;
- Talking too much with limited pauses for others to speak;
- Not turn-taking, which limits conversation;
- Interrupting when others are speaking;
- Irrelevant or 'loose' topics which can seem difficult to follow;
- Not acknowledging what others have said or noticing questions.

Due to their attention problems, children with ADHD frequently have moments when they miss information presented verbally. They are easily distracted by their own thoughts and by external stimuli; in the social context this means that they may not hear what people say or not hear all of what has been said (just parts of it), and they may quickly forget it afterwards. This is especially noticeable when the child is being given instructions to follow, as they often don't know what to do or how to proceed because they have missed key information. They can also find it difficult to follow conversations and hold in mind what is being said whilst considering their own thoughts; as a result, the train of conversation seems odd or jumbled with loose associations or rapidly changing topics. Their communication may be perceived as disingenuous, uncaring or, in some cases, oppositional.

ADHD is also an obstacle to the efficient processing of non-verbal behaviour in social situations. Non-verbal behaviour includes all aspects of communication that does not involve the spoken word, such as gestures, facial expressions, eye contact, adherence to personal space, volume, pitch and tone of voice, and body posture.

When engaging in conversation, a person must achieve two things; they must note what is being said and the manner in which this is being communicated. This requires a person to switch attention between verbal and non-verbal signals of communication, and children with ADHD may struggle with these competing tasks, especially when the non-verbal signal is subtle. Non-verbal behaviour often clarifies intent and meaning, and if non-verbal cues are missed this can lead to misinterpretations and misunderstandings. Impulsive responding may also contribute to the misinterpretation of social communications.

Coping

There are several ways children with ADHD may cope with social challenges. They may respond by seeking the company of much younger children, who are more accepting of differences in communication style, or much older children (or even young adults) who are likely to be more tolerant. They may overcompensate for feelings of social inadequacy by becoming the 'life and soul of the party' and expending great effort to entertain others (e.g., being the joker, playing the fool). Of greater concern is when they seek to ingratiate themselves to others for social acceptance by complying with requests to engage in anti-social behaviours (e.g., theft, joyriding, firesetting). Being more competent at discerning social cues, their 'friends' are quick to escape the notice of others, however children with ADHD are more likely to be found out and/or apprehended. As they grow older, girls, in particular, may be sexually promiscuous in an attempt to gain friends. They are at risk of contracting sexually transmitted diseases and infections, and of teenage pregnancy.

Assessment

International guidance on the assessment and treatment of ADHD recommends that a comprehensive assessment procedure is carried out by trained and qualified healthcare practitioners in order to assess ADHD (Sexias, Weiss & Müller, 2012). This often includes a multi-method assessment, involving psychometric questionnaires, a clinical interview, and observation of the child to assess difficulties and behaviour in different contexts and settings. It is preferable to obtain multiple perspectives from different people involved in the child's care (including that of the child if possible), often requiring multi-agency liaison. To develop a care plan with appropriate interventions that are likely to succeed it is important to fully understand the nature and complexity of the child's difficulties across their development, including historic, environmental and psychosocial factors, the child's strengths and weaknesses, and the support that they currently receive. In doing this, it is important to be mindful of any comorbid and social problems experienced by the child but also within the family.

Measures

The most commonly used assessment of social skills for children is the Strengths and Difficulties Questionnaire (SDQ; Goodman, 1997), used by parents/carers and teachers for children aged two years or above. The Revised Children's Anxiety and Depression Scale (RCADS; Chorpita, Yim, Moffitt, Umemoto & Francis, 2000) for age six and upwards is also helpful as this measures social anxiety and has both parent/carer and child versions. The ratings are then compared against norms for the child's age and gender. They provide a baseline of functioning, which can be repeated to assess the child's progress. An adult should provide support to children completing self-report questionnaires: children with ADHD may misread questions, miss out answers, respond impulsively and/or miscommunicate the rating. However, it is essential that responses are not influenced by leading questions. Children who struggle with reading should always have items read out to them. As for many measures, ratings may be subject to bias and must be interpreted cautiously by a trained practitioner.

Table 9.1 Social skills questionnaire.

	Not at all	Somewhat	Very much
The child seems to understand it is important to take turns in conversations and can do this.			
The child gets into conflicts at school every week.			
The child shares with others.			
The child interrupts others in conversations.			
The child is popular with peers.			
The child listens to what others say.			
The child has difficulty taking turns in conversation.			
The child asks other people about their interests and activities.			
The child speaks too fast or too loud.			
The child wanders off topic.			

In addition, the social skills questionnaire in Table 9.1 can be used to help clarify targets for treatment. When completing the questionnaire, it is important to enquire about factors that might impact or mediate the child's functioning. This can be achieved by asking, 'What makes it easier? What makes it harder?' and prompting the respondent to think about both the influence of the situation as well as the influence of different people. This information can also be obtained by asking the parent/carer to monitor performance using a Behaviour Diary (described later).

Clinical Interview

An assessment should include interviews with both the child and the parents/carers in order to better understand the presenting problem. By the end of the interviews, the clinician should have a 'picture' of the child's strengths and needs in the area and what currently helps or doesn't help.

With parents/carers, a range of areas to cover and possible questions include:

> 'When did you first notice their social difficulties?' 'What happened?' 'Do you know what triggered it?' 'How was it resolved?' 'Does the child do that elsewhere?' 'How do others respond when there are disagreements?' 'Is the child better in 1:1 situations?' 'Does it happen with everyone (school friends, family members, adults)?' 'What do you expect?' 'What is the impact on the child at home, school and/or elsewhere?' 'What do you hope for?'

It is important to determine whether adults think ahead to predict whether a situation will arise and what plans they make. It is especially helpful to identify specific situations that may be improved by planning or goal-setting, for example listening to instructions, following instructions or being in situations when the child wants to make a good impression and/or must adhere to rules. If you can predict when problems are likely to occur, you can prepare for them by rehearsing and practising appropriate responses.

Thoughts

Depending on the child's age and level of maturity, it may be difficult to interview them about their thoughts and beliefs regarding their social skills and interactions. Social skills require some reflection and self-awareness in order to understand the self in relation to others, and to evaluate one's behaviour in a social situation and change it as necessary. Often children experience social situations as fleeting and forgotten; it can be difficult for the child to hold interactions and events in mind and in order, whilst considering alternatives. The result of this can be the child jumps to conclusions about what social situations mean, thinking of what first pops into mind, and sometimes this leads them to misinterpret the intentions of others.

In the case of social anxiety, children may experience thoughts about being embarrassed, standing out or being singled out. These may be experienced as thoughts such as 'Everyone will laugh at me'. They may also visualize an image of being in a situation when they have forgotten what to do and imagine what might happen and how others will react. If children are unable to communicate negative thinking, they should be encouraged to access them by drawings.

Feelings and Physiology

Children may cope by defending themselves against difficult feelings and denying they would like friends, or claiming that a situation is someone else's fault. Underneath this, they may feel sad, lonely, disappointed and rejected. It may be difficult for them to articulate these feelings, so 'give' them a language by suggesting words and/or by suggesting they use pictures or drawings. Sometimes, children are more able to identify characters on TV or in books who have similar experiences before relating it to themselves, and the Buzz worksheets can aid with this. Physiological responses are commonly associated with social anxiety (see Chapter 7) and include blushing, having butterflies in the tummy, feeling sick and/or developing a headache.

Behaviour

When assessing social skills, there are key behavioural factors to watch out for, including whether the child finds themselves in frequent conflict, and whether they are at risk of peer rejection. When there is confrontational or aggressive behaviour, the therapist should assess when and where this is most likely to happen, who else is present and how things usually end up (e.g., the consequences of the behaviour). It is important to identify what triggers the behaviour (e.g., being in situations when the child has to make new friends, being in large groups or social gatherings) and what skills they have to manage their feelings, resolve disagreements and avoid interpersonal conflict (see Chapter 8). It can be helpful to gain objective information about the child's social skills and behaviour, such as asking, 'When was the last birthday party or sleepover you went to?' rather than relying on self-reported social skills.

Creative Methods

Children who have difficulty articulating their thoughts and feelings can be encouraged to explore these through drawings. A technique that is helpful for assessing social relationships is the 'Draw a World' task. The therapist asks the child to draw a world (this could be a city or an island or planet). Everyone the child knows is in this world and the child is asked to draw the people who are important to them and who they get along with. The child then draws a vehicle (spaceship, boat, car) that can transport people both into and out of the world. The child is asked to draw the people they do not get along with and would like to leave the world. If they would like more people in their world, they can draw those people on their way to the world; the child can explain why they would like them there and what he/she likes about the new people (these people need not necessarily be people the child already knows, but can be people who represent characteristics that they value). Use the drawing as a basis for discussion with the child; ask them to explain what makes a good/bad friend and what makes keeping friends difficult.

Behaviour Diary

A Behaviour Diary will be useful to assess whether there are patterns in the child's social behaviours and help target treatment. Parents/carers and/or teachers are asked to record situations where the child displays socially inappropriate skills, noting the antecedents and consequences of the behaviour. Behaviour Diaries are also known as 'ABC charts'. It is important to consider how parents/carers and/or teachers respond to the behaviour.

Table 9.2 Example of a completed Behaviour Diary for social skills.

Day/time	Antecedent (What was happening just before the behaviour? Who was there? What happened earlier in the day that might be relevant?)	Behaviour (What did you observe? Describe the duration and severity.)	Consequence (What happened next? What was the result?)
Sunday afternoon	Joe was playing at home with a school friend.	Joe and his friend wanted to do different things. Joe's friend said that his idea was boring, so they had an argument.	Joe started to shout and he pushed his friend on the sofa. Joe's friend got upset and decided to go home.

Table 9.2 shows a Behaviour Diary completed by the mother of a child called Joe. The example gives just one episode, but the purpose of a Behaviour Diary is to record several episodes over time, from which a pattern may emerge. For example, it may, with more recordings, indicate that Joe lacks the debating and compromising skills that would help him to avoid arguments in social situations.

CBT Interventions for Social Skills

If the therapist is treating younger children and/or the worksheets are being used as a basis for treatment, the first session should always commence with Worksheets 1, 2 and 3 to introduce the child to Buzz and his family (Worksheet 1), introduce positive self-talk (Worksheet 2) and identify a reward system (Worksheet 3). The reward and self-talk strategies are applied in the session, at home and/or at school. See Chapter 3 for a suggested outline of how to plan and conduct the introductory session. All the worksheets are available on the companion website www.wiley.com/go/young/helpingadhd.

The aims of the interventions and worksheets in the social skills session(s) are to introduce children to the concept of social skills, including conversation and conflict resolution strategies, and help them develop their ability to reflect and understand their own experiences. The therapist will achieve this by setting an agenda, reviewing Home Missions done between sessions, working through new worksheets (or just the strategies for older children) and setting new Home Missions. If required, a mid-session break can be offered halfway through the session; this may be particularly important for younger children. Chapter 2 provides generic information on the structure and content of sessions (irrespective of topic); supplementary information is included within this chapter that specifically relates to the delivery of the social skills session(s).

Agenda

At the beginning of the session, show the child the written agenda (see Figure 9.2) that you have prepared prior to the session and go through it, verbally linking the themes and Worksheets that you will introduce during the session. For the social skills module, introduce Worksheets 15 and 16 by saying:

> Today we are going to read a story about Buzz. He is talking to his friends about a great movie they all saw. After that, we will have a short break and you can colour in the worksheet using these crayons. After the break we are going to look at another worksheet and read about what happens when Buzz goes to the park.

Agenda

Folder Review

Buzz goes to the Movies [Worksheet 15]

Break

Buzz goes to the Park [Worksheet 16]

Home Missions

Figure 9.2 Example agenda for social skills session(s).

Folder Review

When reviewing the folder with the child, aside from checking whether the Home Missions are completed, take the opportunity to revise important information and/or concepts, as this will help the child to consolidate the learning points and/or newly acquired skills. Ensure that you make time to look at the illustrations, colourings, paintings, magazine cuttings and/or photographs that the child has added to the folder. Discuss them and try to relate these to discussions about Buzz and his family and/or topics or strategies that have been covered. Aside from acting as a revision prompt, this will also act as a reward system for the child. Praise should be given verbally, but you can also reward by adding stickers, handwritten notes or smiley faces. If Home Missions were set then you should review the Home Missions Record Form for comments and feedback from parents/carers and discuss this with the child. See Chapter 2 for more information about the folder review and Home Missions.

Worksheet 15 Buzz goes to the Movies

Worksheet Description

To download this worksheet, please visit the companion website

It's break time and Buzz is in the school playground with a group of friends. Everyone is talking about the blockbuster movie that they saw at the cinema last weekend. The movie was fantastic. It had dinosaurs and sea monsters in it, and aliens from outer space! It was so exciting that Buzz dropped his popcorn all over the floor! Everyone is talking about their favourite parts of the movie but Buzz can't wait to tell his story about the popcorn. He interrupts and shouts over his friends. One of the girls starts crying. Buzz feels upset too, as all he wanted to do was tell his story.

Worksheet Prompts

What happened here? What caused the problem?
Why was the girl crying?
Do you think Buzz did something wrong?
What did Buzz's friends think about his behaviour?
Tell me what it's like for you being in a group of people.
Do you ever find it hard to listen, remember and take turns?
Together let's write out ideas of things that Buzz can do to help him listen and take turns.
Now let's look at the things you thought would help Buzz and circle the ones that might also help you.

Worksheet 15 is a conversation skills exercise that focuses on the need to adhere to rules of conversation (e.g., to listen and take turns to speak). Additionally, the child is invited to consider the impact of their behaviour on others and how this may be perceived as aggressive and cause distress.

The exercise moves on to identify methods to develop better listening and turn-taking skills.

Begin by reading the Stimulus Sheet aloud to the child, or, if they wish, they can read it with you. Check they have understood the narrative. If they have a story in mind that has happened to them, tell them there will be a chance to talk about this next (and praise them for waiting). The child may also want to talk about a movie they have seen recently. Remember to bring them back to the task after you have listened to their story. This is an opportunity to model turn-taking and listening (and you can draw on this later). Start the discussion points by asking the child what they think happened and what caused the problem. If necessary, prompt the child to consider whether Buzz was impatient, had poor listening skills and/or didn't take turns in the conversation. More specifically, ask why the child thinks the girl in the story started to cry and discuss their ideas. You may need to summarize, 'There are lots of reasons, but we might guess that she felt upset when Buzz interrupted her turn. Maybe she thought he wasn't interested or she was upset that she didn't have the chance to finish.' Talk about the child's understanding of whether Buzz did 'something wrong'. This is a grey area since Buzz did not intend to upset anyone; however, the impulsivity and urge to speak led to upset for him and the girl. Find out if the child has a sense of what the other children in the story may think.

Next, ask about the child's own experience of being in groups. This could include friends, family, school and so on. Carefully listen to the child's story and ask questions. Help them to reflect on whether they find it hard to listen or take turns. You may need to reassure the child that they will not be in trouble with you if they say they have found it hard. You can say, 'It's very common for people to not always listen or forget to ask about other people and take turns, we all do it sometimes.' These problems may not only present in a group setting; you may have noticed a time during the sessions where the child has displayed these behaviours that you can reflect on with the child. Remember to summarize what you have noticed, for example, 'Sometimes you find it difficult to listen to others if you are not interested in what they say, sometimes you interrupt when you want to say something.'

Move on to consider aspects of non-verbal communication. Ask, 'How often do you know what other people are thinking or feeling?' It may be easier for the child to connect with their own experience and they may reflect on how their own family or friends react in situations with them, for example how they know that their dad is pleased or angry with them. Direct the child to think about tone of voice and body language. Then relate this to how people may interpret Buzz's behaviour. Point out that Buzz may have communicated an emotion that he didn't intend!

Using the Task Sheet, move on to think about the strategies Buzz has to help him listen and take turns. Encourage the child to circle the ideas that may also help them. One way to practice turn-taking is to get a plastic ball and roll it towards each other across a table in turns. The rule is that you are only allowed to speak when you are holding the ball! Then do it without the ball until the child has mastered the skill.

Give the child praise for their effort in the session. If you choose to set Home Missions based on this worksheet we suggest asking the child to do the following:

1) Decorate the worksheet by colouring in the pictures and thought bubbles, and/or add to them with pictures on the theme of the story. These could be photographs or pictures in magazines or comics.
2) Practise taking turns when talking to people – remember to think of the ball!
3) Choose a time to watch a TV programme with your parent/carer that has people in it. Pay attention to things like the tone of their voice or body posture. Together make a list of things you spot that help you work out what people are thinking and feeling. Try it also with the sound muted.

If Home Missions are set, remind parents/carers to complete the Home Missions Record Form and to place it in the folder for review at the next session.

Mid-session Break

This should be provided at an appropriate point in the session as outlined in Chapter 2.

Worksheet 16 Buzz goes to the Park

Worksheet Description

Buzz is at the park. He's got no one to play with and he feels sad. Yesterday he upset all his friends at the park because he kicked their football into someone's back garden. Buzz told his friends that it wasn't his fault. The other children are upset because no one is at home so they can't get the ball back. This means they can't play football. Buzz is sitting on a bench all on his own watching the others play on the swings. He feels lonely and wants to be friends again.

To download this worksheet, please visit the companion website

Worksheet Prompts

Buzz is feeling lonely today at the park. Why did his friends fall out with him?
Draw a picture of you and the people you like.
Why do you like them?

(Continued)

> **Worksheet 16 (Continued)**
>
> What makes a good friend?
> How do you try to be a good friend?
> Have you ever fallen out with friends? What did you do to make up? Did it work?
> If you were Buzz, what would you do to make friends again?
> Together let's write ideas of all the things Buzz can do to make up with his friends.
> Now let's look at the things you thought would help Buzz and circle the ones that might also help you.

Worksheet 16 is a social skills exercise that focuses on the values of friendship and maintaining friendships. This worksheet aims to help children reflect on their own social skills and friendships, especially when friendship difficulties arise, and how they are managed. In this exercise the child will develop interpersonal relationship skills, including functional methods of resolving interpersonal conflict.

Start the task by reading the Stimulus Sheet to the child, or, if they wish, they can read it with you. Check that the child has understood and listened. You should check that they understand that the incident happened yesterday and that this has affected how Buzz feels at the park today, and summarize their understanding. Move on to working through the Discussion Sheet.

Begin by asking the child why they think Buzz's friends fell out with him. Guide the child to reflect on what happened and how Buzz's friends felt. The child may have ideas about whether the friends' actions were fair or not, and you can explore this further. Shift the focus to the child's own relationships by asking them to draw a picture on the Task Sheet of the people they like. Let the child know it doesn't have to be the best drawing and they can always finish it at home. Older children may prefer to write the names rather than draw. Talk about what qualities make a good/bad friend. You can ask open questions as prompts such as, 'What do you do together?' 'How do you have fun?' 'How do you look after each other?' 'What would *they* be like as a person?' The child's understanding of what makes a good friend will depend on their age and ability as well as experience of relationships, and focusing on the positive aspects whilst acknowledging any negative aspects will help this process remain balanced. The child's concept of friendship will vary from shared interests and spending time together to more personal values like being reliable and trustworthy. You can help them with learning new vocabulary in this area if needed by reflecting back their statements, 'I understand that you like it when you can tell a friend about your computer game, you like a friend who listens to you.' Summarize the child's ideas in a balanced way, for example, 'So for you, a good friend is someone you can talk to, spend time with and doesn't say mean things about you to other people. That sounds like a good friend. You don't like it if they steal things, which would upset you.' Move on to asking the child to explore how they try to be a good friend. It may help to ask the child to think of situations they themselves displayed friendship qualities (e.g., playing outside, helping someone, a time in the classroom, being interested in what they are doing).

The next discussion points are about repairing friendships. Link the experience of Buzz with the child's own experience. Begin by asking the child if they have ever fallen out with a friend. Ask the child to share their experiences. Help them focus on whether they acted to repair the relationship by asking, 'What happened?' 'How did it turn out?' It may be that there was no resolution, in which case ask if in hindsight, the child wishes they had done something different to mend the friendship. Finally, move back to Buzz's situation and ask the child to consider what Buzz could do in his situation to make friends again. Record the child's ideas on the Task Sheet, and ask them to circle the ones they could also try out themselves.

Give the child praise for his/her effort in the session. If you choose to set Home Missions based on this Worksheet we suggest asking the child to do the following:

1) Decorate the Worksheet by colouring in the pictures and thought bubbles, and/or add to them with pictures on the theme of the story. These could be photographs or pictures in magazines or comics.
2) Choose one of the ideas discussed for how to make up after an argument. Try it out next time you fall out with someone.
3) What makes a good friend? Identify some things you would look for in a new friend. Keep an eye out to see if you spot a possible new friend at school or elsewhere.

If Home Missions are set, remind parents/carers to complete the Home Missions Record Form and to place it in the folder for review at the next session.

Feedback and Rewards

At the end of the session, appropriate rewards identified from the Worksheet 3 Reward Task should be applied (e.g., the child should engage in positive self-talk). See Chapter 2 for more information about feedback and rewards.

Working with Parents/Carers

This section presents strategies that parents/carers can apply to support the child to develop social skills. We discuss the need for parents/carers to model positive and skilled behaviour and ensure that children have the opportunity to practise newly acquired social skills. It is important to be realistic about what can be achieved. It can be just as helpful to learn strategies to cope better with a child's behaviour as to learn strategies to improve the behaviour itself. We suggest that parents/carers engage in specific techniques to support the child's acquisition of positive social skills, including role-play and rehearsal, and observe and comment on positive social skills demonstrated by the child and others. Often children only receive feedback regarding negative interactions, and it is important to notice and praise positive social skills. We discuss methods to manage stress and interpersonal conflict, and specify how parents/carers can teach children to be assertive in communicating their needs and desires appropriately. Cognitive techniques are discussed in terms of planning and using a solution-focused problem-solving approach.

When working with parents/carers, the therapist should introduce suggested techniques and strategies; practise and rehearse them in role-play during the sessions if appropriate (without the child present). In future sessions, parents/carers should report back to the therapist how they managed with the techniques at home. It is important to troubleshoot any obstacles and/or difficulties that arise by thinking of ways to adapt the techniques or strategies so they are successful in helping the child.

A key strategy to change behaviour and improve cognitive skills is to find motivators to promote success. Children with ADHD tend to respond better to immediate rewards as they have difficulty with delayed gratification for longer-term rewards (even if these are bigger and better). Methods to motivate success (including the use of a Star Chart) and other topics that are generic to working with parents/carers are described in Chapter 2. Supplementary information that specifically relates to the delivery of the social skills session(s) is outlined in this chapter.

Behaviour Diary

In order to identify specific situations in which the child is impaired by their social skills, ask parents/carers to complete a Behaviour Diary (described earlier in this chapter) to monitor behaviour. Discuss the information recorded in the diary with parents/carers to gain further insight and understanding about the type of behaviour, its triggers and when it is most likely to present. Over time it can be seen how patterns emerge that may explain the causes of some behaviours. This can be helpful to determine which interventions may be best introduced to address the problem.

Role Model

Children learn from parents/carers and often copy their behaviour. It is important, therefore, to remind parents/carers that they are role models for the child and to be mindful to display positive social skills. It may be helpful to reinforce these behaviours after a social event by talking to the child about the event and how they managed some of the interactions (both positive and negative). For example, the parent/carer could draw attention to things they did, such as summarizing information, reflecting thoughts and ideas back to the person they were talking to, asking questions and showing curiosity. They should also point out what they did not do (even if they felt like it), such as shout, show irritability or interrupt others.

Opportunity

Talk to parents/carers about ways they can provide their child with the opportunity to practise social skills. This requires interaction with others. Some families often spend time with other people and some do not. It is important for children to learn how to interact with a range of people, including those outside of school or family (for example, youth clubs, church activities, sports clubs, neighbourhood friends, family friends). Identify whether parents/carers have underlying anxieties about how their child will interact, and especially whether they feel the need to protect their child from negative experiences. Sometimes this has arisen from a negative cycle in the past, when the child with ADHD has become overly excitable, boisterous and more difficult to manage in a new situation and/or with novel stimuli. This has ended up with the child being reprimanded, possibly ostracized by others and even in tears. Everyone feels stressed and it leads to the belief that it is easier to avoid these situations arising in the first place. However, avoidance is a dysfunctional strategy as it limits the opportunity for the child to learn to behave appropriately and rehearse newly acquired social skills. Encourage parents/carers to face up to challenging situations rather than avoid them (see Chapter 7 for more information and guidance on this topic).

Role-Play and Rehearsal

Parents/carers can support their child by preparing for anticipated situations through role-play and rehearsal. For example, if a child is anxious about raising a topic of concern they have with someone, they can rehearse the scene with their parent/carer. It is helpful to switch roles in the role-play in order for the child to gain a perspective from both sides of the interaction. The role-play should be repeated many times in order to hone skills and build confidence. Parents/carers can rehearse turn-taking with the child by rolling a ball across a table (as previously described for Worksheet 15). This technique can also help the child learn skills to keep a conversation going (e.g., by asking questions). In addition, card games can be beneficial for rehearsing turn-taking rules. Card games that progress to higher levels of difficulty are especially useful as they can develop a child's ability to cope with losing and introduce the idea of deliberately losing to help another player.

Notice Positive Social Skills and Give Praise

Encourage parents/carers to be attentive and praise their child when they notice good social skills (e.g., listening, turn-taking, acts of consideration). This will positively reinforce the behaviour as well as improve the child's confidence.

Notice the Behaviour of Others

Parents/carers can point out good social skills that they observe in others. It is better to do this with television characters rather than with people that the child knows in order to avoid the development of a negative dynamic; the child might feel resentful and/or envious of praise being given to someone else perceived to be 'better' or more skilled than them.

Managing Stress and Interpersonal Conflict

Sometimes, dealing with a child with ADHD is frustrating and stressful (see Chapter 8 for techniques to help with feelings of frustration and anger). The therapist should watch out for signs of stress in parents/carers and advise them to look after themselves and not let things get on top of them. Parents/carers can also help their child to do the same. It is important to foster a sense of collaboration (between parent/carer and child) as opposed to being at war with each other. To avoid negative reciprocal interactions, encourage parents/carers to be consistent and calm but firm when communicating with the child. If things become heated or the person starts to feel stressed and emotional, take 'time out' of the situation, walk away, use techniques to help calm down and think rationally about what to do/say next. If parents/carers recognize that their own behaviour has contributed to an escalation of the situation, they should say they are sorry to the child and explain why they are apologizing. This also models the technique to the child and teaches them to stop and think, calm down, rationalize the problem, think of the consequences of the interaction and deal with it appropriately. By acquiring and practising these techniques themselves, parents/carers can support the child to apply them in a similar way.

Assertiveness

Assertiveness is the balance between being passive (not effectively communicating what you want) and being aggressive (putting your point across too strongly or too negatively). Children with ADHD may feel upset and frustrated if they feel unable to assert their desires and needs. Parents/carers can support their child to develop assertiveness skills by explicitly telling them to speak clearly and calmly, state what they want, and why they want it. Then advise them to wait and listen to what the other person has to say. If the child still feels the same way, encourage them to reiterate the point (calmly and without raising their voice) and expand on the explanation for why they want it (or think it is the best idea).

The child must be prepared to compromise, so each person meets halfway. It may be necessary to give a gentle reminder that sometimes you do not get what you want, and you have to 'agree to disagree'. By engaging the child in a debating stance, even if they do not get the desired outcome, they should feel they have been listened to and heard, had their feelings considered and they should have some understanding of the rationale behind the outcome.

What Can We Do As Parents/Carers?

Table 9.3 outlines a suggested approach, including a list of strategies that can be implemented at home. To maximize the effect of strategies, it is helpful to discuss them with your child's teacher so they can be implemented at both

Table 9.3 Home strategies for social skills.

Role model
- Be a role model to your child by using strategies yourself.
- Reflect back and explicitly discuss these with your child.

Opportunity
- Make opportunities for your child to practise their social skills.

Role-play and rehearsal
- Working together, discuss and prepare for anticipated challenging situations.
- Practise communication skills using role-play. Switch roles with your child.
- Roll a ball across a table to teach turn-taking skills and how to keep the momentum of a conversation.
- Play card games to practise turn-taking and develop the ability to cope with losing.

Notice positive social skills and give praise
- Notice and praise positive skills when the child demonstrates them.
- Watch television together and comment on positive social skills demonstrated by a television character.

Managing stress and conflict
- Take 'time out' and walk away from the situation if you need to.
- Use techniques to calm down (e.g., breathing exercises and self-talk statements) and rationalize the situation (see strategies in Chapters 7 and 8).
- Apologize if your own response has contributed to an escalation of the problem.
- Prompt your child to apply these skills.

Assertiveness
- Speaking clearly and calmly, state what you want and why you want it.
- Wait and listen to what the other person says.
- Take turns to debate.
- Be prepared to compromise.
- Be prepared to not get what you want – agree to disagree.

home and school (wherever possible). Lots of parents/carers and teachers find that using a 'Home School Diary' is an efficient way to share information (see Chapter 2).

We suggest that parents/carers read Chapter 2, which provides important background information about the delivery of the Young–Smith Programme. For younger children, we suggest that parents/carers set aside some time to sit down with the child (around 45–60 minutes) and work through the worksheets recommended for each topic. Guidance on how to do this is found in the 'CBT Interventions' section in each chapter. The worksheets introducing Buzz and his family are outlined in Chapter 3. All the materials (Worksheets and Home Missions Record Form) are available to download from the companion website www.wiley.com/go/young/helpingadhd. For older children (i.e., 12 yearsplus), you can dispense with the Buzz worksheets if necessary and instead introduce the child directly to the topic, and, using the discussion prompts on the worksheets, apply this to the child's experience and discuss suggested strategies. Set Home Missions and support the child to complete them. Don't forget to give frequent feedback and praise. Make a Star Chart (see Chapter 2), put it in a prominent place and start to use it on a daily basis.

Working with Teachers and Schools

The school environment provides the opportunity for the child to interact with adults and peers and both older and younger children. The child will be engaged in work and play involving a broad range of topics and social contexts that are not experienced outside of school. Teachers are likely to already be helping children to develop their skills in listening, turn-taking, understanding others and solving disagreements. Sometimes Special Educational Needs Coordinators run social skills groups; these may take a general approach or they may include sessions that focus on specific social skills, highlighting different ones in turn.

This section presents strategies that teachers can apply to support the child to better develop social skills. It is important to be realistic about what can be achieved. It can be just as helpful to learn strategies to cope better with a child's behaviour as to learn strategies to improve the behaviour itself. In this section we discuss behavioural strategies that can be applied, such as setting up signals to prompt prosocial behaviour and engaging in role-play and rehearsal. Often, children only receive feedback regarding negative interactions and it is important to notice and praise positive social skills. Cognitive techniques are also discussed, such as explicitly drawing attention to the micro-techniques teachers use to communicate effectively. We discuss methods to manage stress and interpersonal conflict, and specify how teachers can help the child to be assertive in communicating their needs and desires appropriately. We give advice about preparing the child for new social situations and key points of transition as the child progresses at school.

Teachers and schools will already have structures in place to support many of the interventions introduced in the Young–Smith Programme. It will be useful to link up parents/carers and teachers to encourage an integrated strategy and share success. It is important to troubleshoot any obstacles and/or difficulties that arise by thinking of ways to adapt the techniques or strategies so they are successful in helping the child. Methods to motivate success and other topics that are generic to working with teachers and schools are described in Chapter 2. Supplementary information that specifically relates to the delivery of the social skills session(s) is outlined in this chapter.

Role-Model

Hopefully, teachers are already modelling prosocial skills. However, what the child with ADHD needs is an explicit link to be made between behaviour and interaction. Teachers can provide that bridge by naming the skills they use when providing feedback to the child. For example, 'When you told me your story I made eye contact with you and nodded to show you that I was listening', and 'When you were talking, I was being patient. I waited for you to finish what you wanted to say before I took my turn to speak.'

Prompts

Teachers can set up signals that can be used to prompt the child to engage in a behaviour, such as touching their ear if the child is not listening, touching their lips if the child is talking too much or moving a hand downwards to indicate the child needs to calm down. If the child learns to respond to these signals, then it will prevent the child from feeling overly criticized in front of peers and will foster a sense of supportive collaboration with the teacher (the child will feel the teacher is helping rather than criticizing).

Role-Play and Rehearsal

Teachers can support the child to prepare for anticipated situations through role-play and rehearsal activities, as described in the previous section for parents/carers.

Notice Positive Social Skills and Give Praise

Encourage teachers to be attentive and praise the child when they notice good social skills (e.g., listening, turn-taking, acts of consideration). This will positively reinforce the behaviour as well as improving the child's confidence.

Managing Stress and Interpersonal Conflict

The therapist should watch out for indications that a teacher is feeling stressed and frustrated with the child with ADHD, as this won't help the relationship between them. This can easily happen because children with ADHD can be demanding on time and patience, especially when they are disruptive in class. Teachers, like everyone, have good days and bad days, and sometimes they are better able to cope than others. If you notice that a teacher is feeling stressed then run through the strategies outlined in the parents/carers section for managing stress and interpersonal conflict.

With respect to supporting the child to manage interpersonal conflict, teachers are in a better position than parents/carers to observe these types of conflict, as in the school setting children must get along with all types of peers, some they like a lot and some less so. Methods to de-escalate the situation by walking away, stopping and thinking, calming down (e.g., using self-talk and/or breathing techniques), rationalizing the problem and/or getting help from a teacher are useful strategies to reinforce. To move on and prevent resentment building up, it is important that children learn to both give and accept an apology. This can be difficult for children who are stubborn and highly resistant to backing down. Teachers can help here by explaining to the child that giving an apology can make everyone feel better and help to move past the problem. It is also important to feel that an apology has been acknowledged and accepted. If the child with ADHD does not appear to 'listen' to an apology, they may appear insincere and uncaring.

Bullying

A child being bullied or bullying others is not acceptable in any situation. In line with the school policy, teachers must immediately address bullying behaviour.

Assertiveness

Sometimes, problems arise because the child is unable to appropriately assert their needs and desires. The child may go off at a tangent, shout or mumble. Teachers can support the child becoming more assertive by reinforcing the technique described in the previous section for parents/carers.

New Social Situations

The school environment changes over time. There are structural and qualitative changes both within class and within the school community as the child moves from junior/infant school, to middle school and then to senior school. As the child progresses through these stages, the expectations of teachers change and the child will need to take on greater responsibility for their behaviour and schoolwork. School activities and subjects change, together with the methods of teaching. The class teacher will change each year and children will be taught by an increasing number of teachers; peer friendships change, with children leaving the school and new children joining.

It is important that children with ADHD are provided with support during key transitions because they may struggle more than their non-ADHD peers with structural change and loss of peer networks. Feelings of uncertainty and anxiety may increase the likelihood that they will act out (see Chapter 7). It will be helpful for a pastoral teacher or Special Educational Needs Coordinator to talk to the child to help prepare them for the next stage in school life and the expectations this will bring. Similarly, if moving outside of the school environment (for example on school trips) the child may feel a mix of emotions leading them to feel labile and increase the possibility of them behaving in an unpredictable way. Prepare for this by specifying a clear code of conduct expected in the novel environment and give clear instructions (written if necessary).

What Can We Do As Teachers?

Table 9.4 outlines a suggested approach for teachers, including a list of strategies that can be implemented at school. To maximize the effect of strategies, it is helpful to discuss them with the child's parents/carers so that similar or complementary strategies are implemented at home and school (wherever possible). Both teachers and parents/carers find that using a 'Home School Diary' is an efficient way to share information (see Chapter 2).

We suggest that teachers read Chapter 2, which provides important background information about the delivery of the Young–Smith Programme. It is unlikely that teachers will have time to go through specific worksheets with children, although if parents/carers are unable to do this it would be helpful to make arrangements with the Special Educational Needs Coordinator. Guidance on how to do this is found in the 'CBT Interventions' section in each chapter. The worksheets introducing Buzz and his family are outlined in Chapter 3. All the materials (worksheets and Home Missions Record Form) are available to download from the companion website, www.wiley.com/go/young/helpingadhd. For older children (i.e., 12 years-plus), one may dispense with the Buzz worksheets if necessary and instead introduce the child directly to the topic, and, using the discussion prompts on the worksheets, apply this to the child's experience and discuss suggested strategies. Set Home Missions and support the child to complete them. Don't forget to give frequent feedback and praise. If a Star Chart is used (see Chapter 2) then this could be put in the 'Home School Diary' where parents/carers can also review it on a regular basis.

Table 9.4 School strategies for social skills.

Role-model
- When giving feedback to a child, explicitly name the strategies you use to communicate effectively (e.g., making eye contact, talking slower, turn-taking).

Prompts
- Set up signals to prompt an appropriate response or behaviour.

Role-play and rehearsal
- Working together, discuss and prepare for anticipated challenging situations.
- Practise communication skills using role-play. Switch roles with the child.
- Roll a ball across a table to teach turn-taking skills and how to keep the momentum of a conversation.
- Play card games to practise turn-taking and develop the ability to cope with losing.

Notice positive social skills and give praise
- Notice and praise positive skills when the child demonstrates them.

Managing stress and conflict
- Take 'time out' and walk away from the situation if you need to.
- Use techniques to calm down (e.g., breathing exercises and self-talk statements) and rationalize the situation (see strategies in Chapters 7 and 8).
- Teach the child to apply methods of de-escalation (e.g., walk away, stop and think, calm down, rationalize the problem, get help and advice).
- Discuss giving and receiving apologies (and role-play if necessary).
- Deal with issues of bullying as soon as you become aware of them.

Assertiveness
- Speaking clearly and calmly, state what you want and why you want it.
- Wait and listen to what the other person says.
- Take turns to debate.
- Be prepared to compromise.
- Be prepared to not get what you want – agree to disagree.

New social situations
- Talk to the child and prepare them for key transitions in school structure (e.g., moving up to middle school).
- Specify expectations of behaviour and supplement with a written code of conduct and instructions.

Staff collaboration
- Ensure that all staff know and understand what strategies are being used and why.

References

Chorpita, B. F., Yim, L., Moffitt, C., Umemoto L. A., & Francis, S. E. (2000). Assessment of symptoms of DSM-IV anxiety and depression in children: A Revised Child Anxiety and Depression Scale. *Behaviour Research and Therapy, 38*(8), 835–855.

Chou, W. J., Liu, T. L., Yang, P., Yen, C. F., & Hu, H. F. (2014). Bullying victimization and perpetration and their correlates in adolescents clinically diagnosed with ADHD. *Journal of Attention Disorders, Nov 2014*, doi: 10.1177/1087054714558874.

Goodman, R. (1997). The strengths and difficulties questionnaire: A research note. *Journal of Child Psychology and Psychiatry and Allied Disciplines, 38*(5), 581–586.

Sexias, M., Weiss, M., & Müller, U. (2012). Systematic review of national and international guidelines on attention deficit hyperactivity disorder. *Journal of Psychopharmacology, 26*(6), 753–765.

10

Setting Goals and Planning Ahead

Without the skills to plan and sequence information we are leaves in the wind, deprived of control and destined to chance or luck. Due to their cognitive and executive deficits, people with ADHD often need help to develop skills to set goals and plan how to achieve them. In their daily activities, children must work towards short-term goals, whether these are getting ready for school and leaving the house on time or preparing for a school quiz. This differs to the achievement of long-term goals, which may bring rewards such as getting good grades in exams or being selected for the school football team. Children with ADHD value immediate rewards because they find planning and waiting difficult, hence they avoid setting long-term goals as these often involve delayed gratification. Furthermore, planning ahead relies a lot on the ability to organize, which is also something that people with ADHD find difficult. These skills and abilities are called executive functions and include: skills in memory, flexible thinking, planning, directing behaviour, organizing and reasoning. As children develop and grow older their executive function skills improve from their past experience of applying these skills to achieve increasingly complex activities.

This chapter will, therefore, focus on the development of these skills. We consider the difficulties that children with ADHD have in this domain and how these difficulties impact on their functioning in different areas of life. The assessment of planning skills will be discussed, followed by interventions and strategies for children and the adults around them using cognitive behavioural models.

Presentation

The skills to set goals and make plans to achieve them need to be learned and honed in childhood because as they mature into adolescence and adulthood young people must increasingly set and make plans to achieve important goals

Helping Children with ADHD: A CBT Guide for Practitioners, Parents and Teachers,
First Edition. Susan Young and Jade Smith.
© 2017 John Wiley & Sons Ltd. Published 2017 by John Wiley & Sons Ltd.
Companion website: www.wiley.com/go/young/helpingadhd

in their life, such as academic and occupational success, financial stability, independence and social acceptance. This means that they must learn to set specific and realistic goals, break these down into steps, engage in goal-directed behaviour and organize, sequence and prioritize activities.

Behavioural Functioning

Working towards a goal requires motivation, sustained attention and the ability to tolerate delayed gratification. Children with ADHD, however, are hampered from engaging in this functional process for several reasons. Making a plan to complete a goal can be a difficult starting place for a child who is impulsive and may dive head-first into an activity or situation before thinking it through. On realizing this halfway through, children with ADHD are more likely to leave the task rather than try to correct the mistake. You may have seen a child who rushes in to write a story and then after a few sentences gives up when they realize that they have not thought through what will happen, or a child who starts building a toy and then, having not considered what should go first, becomes frustrated and leaves it unfinished. Staying on task, using mental effort, and getting through these times can be challenging for all children, but children with ADHD seem to need greater external reinforcement, such as rewards and motivation from adults.

Another problem that children with ADHD face is difficulty with time perception. This should not be mistaken for an inability to tell the time or choosing to ignore time boundaries. They find time to be a confusing and abstract concept and find it difficult to track and estimate time; yet the child must estimate how long it will take to achieve a goal and the steps they must take when working towards it, as this is part of the planning process. Good planning skills also require the development of skills in organization and prioritization. Children with ADHD may have good intentions to plan ahead but more immediate attractions interfere with them seeing this through. As a result, things like homework get left to the last minute (or are not done at all) and tools or materials that they need are frequently lost and/or forgotten. A consequence of poor organizational skills is that the child may appear oppositional as they are viewed as not doing things on time, not doing what they are told, and not having the right equipment for school. This can lead to children being reprimanded unnecessarily for perceived oppositional behaviour instead of receiving help for the real – and unrecognized – problem.

Academic Functioning

At school, children must increasingly take responsibility for planning and organizing their work. When children are at a young age, parents/carers and teachers do a lot for them, but as they grow older this should naturally reduce. In parallel, the structure of the school day becomes looser, affording greater opportunity for children to practise their planning and organization skills. However, children with ADHD may be behind their peers and their chronological age in terms of maturity – even those with higher cognitive ability – and this should be factored into expectations. Indeed, children with ADHD may stand out as the ones disadvantaged by not having the correct materials or equipment for class, whose homework was rushed or incomplete and who appear confused over where they have to be when or what they have to do when. If they get behind in their schoolwork, they may feel overwhelmed and distressed and act out these feelings inappropriately (e.g., with frustration or anger). Even higher-ability children with ADHD struggle with longer-term assignments. They are prone to procrastination and may require a higher level of structure in order to display their true potential.

Interpersonal Functioning

When it comes to interpersonal situations, other children and adults find it very frustrating when the child with ADHD forgets plans, arrives somewhere late or not at all, or is not prepared when they do get there, and the child is therefore perceived as unreliable. This can cause tension in relationships, leave people feeling confused and create hostility, especially if it is assumed that it is because the child is 'not trying' or 'doesn't care', when this may be quite untrue.

Coping

Children may start to avoid the types of situations described or overly rely on others to make plans and do things for them. As the child develops these skills there needs to be a corresponding adjustment in the amount of support they receive. Skills should be built up gradually as the child works towards having independence.

Assessment

International guidance on the assessment and treatment of ADHD recommends that a comprehensive assessment procedure is carried out by trained and qualified healthcare practitioners in order to assess ADHD (Sexias, Weiss & Müller, 2012). This often includes a multi-method assessment involving psychometric questionnaires, a clinical interview and observation of the child to assess their difficulties and behaviour in different contexts and settings. It is preferable to obtain multiple perspectives from different people involved in the child's care (including that of the child if possible), and often one that involves multi-agency liaison. To develop a care plan with appropriate interventions that are likely to succeed it is important to fully understand the nature and complexity of the child's difficulties across their development, including historic, environmental and psychosocial factors, the child's strengths and weaknesses and the support that they currently receive. In doing this, it is important to be mindful of any comorbid and social problems experienced by the child but also within the family.

Measures

The Conners' Rating Scales 3rd Edition, for age 6–18 years (Conners, 2008), and the Brief Rating Inventory of Executive Functioning (BRIEF; Gioia, Isquith, Guy, Kenworthy & Baron, 2001), for 5–18 years, are rating scales that include items of executive function, such as planning and organization. These compare the frequency of a child's perceived functioning with norms obtained from the general population for their age and gender. It is recommended that the perspectives of different people be obtained in order to gain a broad perspective of the child's functioning across different settings; for example, a parent/carer and teacher may complete the questionnaires for behaviour at home and school respectively. Both measures may also be self-rated by the young person (Conners' from age eight years and BRIEF from age 11 years); however, their use depends on the child's reading ability and level of insight. Ratings are also helpful to obtain a baseline assessment of perceived functioning, which is then repeated after intervention to evaluate efficacy at outcome. An adult should support children completing self-report questionnaires. Children with ADHD may misread questions, miss out answers, respond impulsively and/or miscommunicate the rating. However, it is essential that responses not be influenced by leading questions. Children who struggle with reading should always have items read out to them. As is the case for many measures, ratings may be subject to bias and must be interpreted cautiously by a trained practitioner.

As well as questionnaire-based assessments, there are a number of objective psychometric tests that measure skills related to planning and organization in children. Both the Behavioural Assessment of Dysexecutive Syndrome in Children (BADS-C; Emslie, Wilson, Burden, Nimmo-Smith & Wilson, 2003), for 7–16 years, and the Delis–Kaplan Executive Function System (DKEFS; Delis, Kaplan & Kramer, 2001), which can be used in people aged 8 years to adult, include sub-tests for planning ability. Whilst administering objective tests, it is important to observe and note how children approach these tasks.

Clinical Interview

To obtain richer and more descriptive information about the child, it is essential that rating scales and objective tests are supplemented with a semi-structured interview with those who know the child best. It is good practice for this to be done with multiple people who are involved in the child's life and to consider the different settings and contexts in which the child interacts. Parents/carers and teachers will be able to explain the struggles of the child across different settings and how these impact on the child's functioning and progress. Children may over-rate their own social competence, hence the therapist should include objective questions, for example, 'When was the last time he/she was invited to a birthday party/sleepover?'

The clinical interview should also explore whether expectations are appropriate to the child's level of development and overall cognitive ability. For example, a six-year-old child will not typically remember everything they need for school without any help and nor will they be able to make complex plans for the school day, but an 11-year-old will be making steps towards achieving these skills. If expectations appear to be unrealistic, parents/carers should be encouraged to adjust them to a more appropriate level. Bear in mind that children will not have the same priorities or perception of a situation as adults, nor will they have the same goals; children with ADHD are more likely to respond to the moment and not recognize the need to make plans. In fact, the greatest problem to be resolved may simply be that the child does not set and specify goals. The aim of the assessment is to identify key areas to prioritize, such as remembering to bring their pencil case to all lessons or writing down homework at the end of the lesson and telling their parent/carer when they get home. This will focus the targets for intervention and create realistic, achievable goals, rather than those that aim to improve a general concept such as 'getting organized for school'.

Children with ADHD have difficulty with delayed gratification and hence are averse to setting long-term goals. Discuss with parents/carers and teachers how the child responds to long-term goals; the long term may be perceived by the child to be the end of the week – a perception that may considerably differ to the parent/carer and teachers view! A child can get a sense of a year by relating this to annual events such as birthdays, Christmas or holidays. When developing skills over time and working towards longer-term achievements, the child will need to be supported to learn to break goals down into smaller and more immediate, achievable steps.

Thoughts

Negative thinking may interfere with the planning process, and these thoughts need to be identified in the assessment. Young children are unlikely to be able to work at this cognitive level, but older children may notice thoughts like, 'I'll do it later', 'I'll leave it until after X' or 'It's boring, I don't want to'. If the task is perceived as difficult, thoughts might be, 'I can't be bothered' or 'I don't want it anyway'. These thoughts lead to procrastination and prevent the child working to achieve a set task. Everyone will recognize these types of thoughts and these may be present for some tasks more than others, depending on the type of task, its duration or novelty. It is important to identify the tasks which the child most commonly struggles with, as these will become the targets of treatment.

In particular, look out for thoughts (or images) which decrease motivation; these may be especially apparent for long-term tasks which seem too distant to be achievable. When negative thoughts can be identified, treatment needs to focus on strategies to help the child set aside these thoughts whilst they specify a goal and set steps towards it. Breaking a goal down into smaller steps in this way teaches the child how to make a plan.

Feelings and Physiology

To understand what helps or hinders children's planning and organization skills, the therapist should consider any associated feelings or emotional states that may impact on behaviour. Feeling unmotivated, frustrated, apathetic, bored, uninspired or overly controlled may cause the child to give up, rebel and withdraw. More positive feelings, such as excitement, motivation and anticipation, may have a beneficial influence, especially if harnessed via good feedback.

Behaviour

During the interview, ascertain whether the responses of others reinforce a lack of effort. Ask, 'What does your mum do if you are not ready on time?' or 'What happens if you forget to pack something you need for school or sports?' The interview should aim to establish if there is a pattern of adults compensating for the child by doing things for them, as this reduces the opportunity for the child to develop skills. If this is the case, then this should be a target for intervention. Equally, it is important to ensure that expectations of what the child can or should be doing themselves are realistic and achievable.

CBT Interventions for Setting Goals and Planning Ahead

If the therapist is treating younger children and/or the worksheets are being used as a basis for treatment, the first session should always commence with Worksheets 1, 2 and 3 to introduce the child to Buzz and his family (Worksheet 1), introduce positive self-talk (Worksheet 2) and identify a reward system (Worksheet 3). The reward and self-talk strategies are applied in the session, at home and/or at school. See Chapter 3 for a suggested outline of how to plan and conduct the introductory session. All the Worksheets are available on the companion website www.wiley.com/go/young/helpingadhd.

The aim of the interventions and worksheets in the setting goals and planning ahead session(s) are to introduce children to the concepts of setting goals for the future and planning to achieve these goals. The therapist will achieve this by setting an agenda, reviewing Home Missions done between sessions in the folder, working through new worksheets (or just the strategies for older children) and setting new Home Missions. If required, a mid-session break can be offered halfway through the session; this may be particularly important for younger children. Chapter 2 provides generic information on the structure and content of sessions (irrespective of topic); supplementary information is included in this chapter that specifically relates to the delivery of the goals and planning session(s).

Agenda

At the beginning of the session, show the child the written agenda (see Figure 10.1) that you have prepared prior to the session and go through it, verbally linking the themes and worksheets that you will introduce during the session. For the goals and planning module, introduce Worksheets 17 and 18 by saying:

> A circus has come to town and Buzz has been to see it. We will read the story and hear about the amazing things he sees. Buzz wants to learn how to juggle. He will need to make a plan to help him learn this skill. After that, we will have a short break and you can colour in the worksheet using these crayons. After the break we are going to find out what Buzz can do to prepare for his birthday party.

Agenda

Folder Review

Buzz goes to the Circus [Worksheet 17]

Break

Buzz and his Birthday Party [Worksheet 18]

Home Missions

Figure 10.1 Example agenda for goals and planning session(s).

Folder Review

When reviewing the folder with the child, aside from checking whether the Home Missions are completed, take the opportunity to revise important information and/or concepts, as this will help the child to consolidate the learning points and/or newly acquired skills. Ensure that you make time to look at the illustrations, colourings, paintings, magazine cuttings and/or photographs that the child has added to the folder. Discuss them and try to relate these to discussions about Buzz and his family and/or topics or strategies that have been covered. Aside from acting as a revision prompt, this will also act as a reward system for the child. Praise should be given verbally but you can also reward by adding stickers, handwritten notes or smiley faces. If Home Missions were set then you should review the Home Missions Record Form for comments and feedback from parents/carers and discuss this with the child.

Worksheet 17 Buzz Goes to the Circus

Worksheet Description

A circus has come to town. Buzz's Mum took him to see the show and he saw the circus acts juggling with five balls; some even did it walking on a tightrope! It was wonderful and Buzz thought it was very clever. Buzz has decided that he wants to learn to juggle just like the circus acts. He gets five balls from the school gymnasium but he can't figure it out. All the balls keep dropping on the floor. He's getting tired and decides to give up.

To download this worksheet, please visit the companion website

Worksheet Prompts

Why do you think Buzz can't do the task?
What could Buzz do to make it easier?
What could Buzz say to himself to keep trying and not give up?
Together let's write out some positive, motivating statements that Buzz can use to keep trying.
Tell me about a time when you didn't give up on something difficult. What did you do?
If a task is too big, what can you do?
Together let's write out a list of the things that Buzz can do to help him learn a new skill.
Now let's look at the things you thought would help Buzz and circle the ones that might also help you.

Worksheet 17 aims to develop the child's skill in setting realistic goals, making plans to achieve them and persevering in order to reach targets. The exercise introduces the basic concept of skill development – this involves practice and patience! The scenario will help the child reflect on what they already know and apply this knowledge in a more systematic way in order to acquire new skills. The exercise ends with the child describing a time when they were successful in achieving a difficult task because they didn't give up and reflecting on how to manage big tasks.

Read the Stimulus Sheet out loud to the child or, if they wish, they can read it to you, and check they have understood the narrative. Summarize the story by saying, 'So Buzz went to the circus and saw lots of great things. Now he wants to learn to juggle and he started with five balls.' Ensure the child knows and understands the concept of juggling. Next, ask the child to consider why Buzz isn't able to do the task and what he can do to make it easier. Prompt the child to consider that new tasks or skills are usually acquired by commencing with something easy and, with lots of practice, gradually introducing more complexity. Discuss where Buzz went wrong and summarize, for example, 'Buzz was trying to use all the balls at once before he had practised. Juggling with five balls is very difficult and we think that's why he gave up. He got fed up with the balls falling on the floor. It would be easier to use one or two balls to start.' Move on to discuss what Buzz might say to himself to keep going and not give up, for example, 'I can do this if I keep trying' or 'Come on Buzz try again.' Identify and write down motivating statements on the Task Sheet. It is important to note the statements the child generates in his/her own words. You might also consider things that Buzz might do to support and motivate himself, such as learning to juggle with a friend and setting a date/time to demonstrate three-ball skills, four-ball skills and five-ball skills to his family.

Next, ask the child to think of a time they had to persevere and learn a new and difficult skill. This might be when they learned to ride a bicycle, for example. Encourage the child to think about the stages of skill acquisition, such as starting off with having stabilizers attached to the bicycle, removing the stabilizers and having the help of a parent/carer, practising in the back garden, cycling in the park and so on. Also consider what factors motivated the child to achieve the skills, including both what they did and what they said to themselves. Talk about what to do if a task seems too big or difficult. Ideas may include breaking the task into smaller chunks, having a break, asking someone for help or watching someone else do it first. Summarize these ideas to reinforce them, then relate them to Buzz's goal (to learn to juggle five balls) and write down on the Task Sheet all of the ideas the child has that could help Buzz learn this skill. Ensure that some generic steps are included; for example, ask a friend to learn with him, get help from a parent/carer, get information by doing an Internet search, make a practice schedule and set a deadline. Ask the child to circle the ones that might work for them when they set goals and make plans in the future.

Give praise for the child's effort in the session. If you choose to set Home Missions based on this worksheet we suggest asking the child to do the following:

1) Decorate the worksheet by colouring in the pictures and thought bubbles, and/or add to them with pictures on the theme of the story. These could be photographs or pictures in magazines or comics.

2) Set a goal for the week. Choose a new skill you want to learn and make a plan for what you will do to achieve it. Tell parents/carers or teachers about this. The skill could be to get ten balls in the net or to juggle! It could also be to get all your spellings correct in the weekly test.
3) Write out things you can do and/or say to yourself to help you persevere and achieve the goal. Let parents/carers or teachers know so they can prompt you.
4) Bring a photograph to the next session of you achieving the goal (e.g., a photograph standing next to a net and holding up the number of fingers for the number of goals scored, a photograph of them juggling balls or a photograph of the marked spelling test). Put it in your folder.

If Home Missions are set, remind parents/carers to complete the Home Missions Record Form and to place it in the folder for review at the next session.

Mid-session Break

This should be provided at an appropriate point in the session, as outlined in Chapter 2.

Worksheet 18 Buzz and his Birthday Party

Worksheet Description

To download this worksheet, please visit the companion website

It is Buzz's birthday next week and his Mum has said that he can have a party. How exciting! But guess what happens … his brother gets chickenpox and Mum has to look after him and doesn't have time to plan the party. She says that Buzz will have to help her. Oh dear, there is so much to do! Buzz has to invite his friends, plan the games they will play and decide what food and party decorations to buy. Buzz's Mum has told him to make a list of what needs to be done.

Worksheet Prompts

Can you help Buzz to plan what he needs to do for the party? What needs to be done?

Draw or write in each bubble some of the things that need to be done to achieve each of the party goals.

What do you think needs doing first? What can wait until the day of the birthday party?

What kind of things do you have to do each day? What might help you to plan, organize and remember all the things you have to do?

> **Worksheet 18 (Continued)**
>
> Together let's write out a list of things that Buzz can do to help him plan and organize the party.
> Now let's look at the things you thought would help Buzz and circle the ones that might also help you.

Worksheet 18 is a planning exercise that cues children to plan and organize an event. In this exercise the child is directed to specify goals, break them down into smaller steps and set priorities. The child is asked to do this in written form in order to learn the process. In future, the child should be encouraged to apply the skill in the same way (i.e., in writing), as this provides the child with a template to follow when working towards their goal.

Begin by reading the Stimulus Sheet out loud to the child, or, if the child wishes, they can read it to you. Check they have understood the narrative. Using the Task Sheet, help the child to think of what Buzz needs to do to plan the party. Start by identifying the goals (invite friends, plan games, choose food and decorations). Next, ask the child to draw or write in each bubble some of the things that need to be done to achieve each of the party goals. For example, for the 'invite friends' goal you might list tasks such as buy (or make) invitations, write the invitations and hand them out. Ask the child, 'What do you think needs doing first?' 'What can wait until the day of the birthday party?' Have a discussion about what order things need to be done in and number the bubbles accordingly. Buzz should invite his friends first because if he leaves that too late some of his friends may not be able to come!

The next stage is very important, as the therapist must communicate that the child has applied a planning process that involves: (1) setting goals, (2) breaking them down into smaller steps and (3) ordering the steps. You could use a 'stairs' metaphor by stating that a goal is at the top of the stairs and the child is standing at the bottom of the stairs. Each step takes them a bit closer to reaching the goal. Ask the child to think about what they have to do each day and how they remember to do it. Do they make a list or mind map? Where do they put it? For younger children, this may be too complex but you can ask, 'At home or school do you have lists of things to do?' 'Do people remind you what to do first?' 'What do your parents/carers or your teachers use to help them?' 'I bet they make notes and use a diary.' Talk to the child about how parents/carers or teachers might use a diary to set and plan goals, such as making plans for what they must do in the week. Then, returning to Buzz's story, make a list on the Task Sheet of what he can do to plan the party. Ensure that some generic steps are included, such as setting goals and/or tasks, making a list, ordering the tasks and putting what to do and when in a week planner or diary. Finally, ask the child to circle the things that they could try to help them to develop their own planning and organizing skills.

Give praise for the child's effort in the session. If you choose to set Home Missions based on this worksheet we suggest asking the child to do the following:

1) Decorate the worksheet by colouring in the pictures and thought bubbles, and/or add to them with pictures on the theme of the story. These could be photographs or pictures in magazines or comics.
2) Talk to your parents/carers about planning and organizing an event at home. This could be preparing for something happening at school or a weekend activity. It doesn't have to be complex and could be making your favourite chocolate brownies! You must write down the goal, the steps (in order) and put them into a day or week planner, or a diary.
3) Bring the plan you followed to the next session and put it in your folder. Also bring a photograph to the next session of you achieving the goal, for example a photograph of your family eating the chocolate brownies! Put it in your folder.

If Home Missions are set, remind parents/carers to complete the Home Missions Record Form and to place it in the folder for review at the next session.

Feedback and Rewards

At the end of the session, appropriate rewards identified from the Worksheet 3 Reward Task should be applied (e.g., the child should engage in positive self-talk). See Chapter 2 for more information about feedback and rewards.

Working with Parents/Carers

This section presents strategies that parents/carers can apply to support the child to develop skills for setting goals and making plans. It is important to be realistic about what can be achieved. It can be just as helpful to learn strategies to cope better with a child's behaviour as to learn strategies to improve the behaviour itself. In this section we discuss the need for parents/carers to learn and apply a planning process themselves. Usually adults already have these skills and apply the process automatically, but it is important to point out the actual stepped process, as parents/carers need to be aware of this to communicate it to the child. We also discuss how parents/carers can support the child with verbal and visual prompts and the introduction of external techniques, such as alarms, diaries, calendars, lists and routines. When working with parents/carers, the therapist should introduce suggested techniques and strategies; practise and rehearse them in role-plays during the sessions if appropriate (without the child present). In future sessions, parents/carers should report back to the therapist how they managed with the techniques at home. It is important to troubleshoot any obstacles and/or difficulties that arise by thinking of ways to adapt the techniques or strategies so they are successful in helping the child.

A key strategy to change behaviour and improve cognitive skills is to find motivators to promote success. Children with ADHD tend to respond better to immediate rewards, as they have difficulty with delayed gratification for longer-term rewards (even if these are bigger and better). Methods to motivate success (including the use of a Star Chart) and other topics that are generic to working with parents/carers are described in Chapter 2. Supplementary information that specifically relates to the delivery of the goals and planning session(s) are outlined in this chapter.

Teach the Planning Process

Outline the fundamental planning process to parents/carers. They must support their child to apply this process in order to reinforce at home the skills learned in sessions. This involves four core steps: (1) set goals – they should discuss things to do with the child and help them to identify and set goals; (2) break down goals into smaller steps – list them; (3) order the steps – rewrite the steps in a graduated order as for the stairs metaphor described in the section about Worksheet 18; and (4) write out what to do and when in a planner, calendar or diary.

Verbal Prompts

Parents/carers can prompt their child, who may have forgotten or become distracted from the task, by asking, 'What comes next?' or 'What do you need to do next?' If parents/carers remember to do this, it may prevent confrontational exchanges over what should have been done and what has not been done. When children lose track of plans, parents/carers should prompt them to refer to the written plan and point out the order, 'So you have done *A*, *B* and *C*. *D* comes next.'

Alarm Prompts

Children may become side-tracked from achieving their steps/goals because they lose track of time or incorrectly estimate how long it will take to achieve steps. Parents/carers should watch out for this problem and help the child to better estimate time and structure for the activity. In addition, parents/carers should encourage the child to use alarms on mobile phones, tablets or computers (or a cooking alarm or egg timer!) to prompt the child to remember to do a task and/or help with the child's time management. Depending on what is used, this may not prompt specifically what to do but will give a reminder that something needs to be done.

Calendars/Diaries

Pin a calendar on the wall where the child can't miss it (e.g., on their bedroom wall, by a desk where they do their homework, in the bathroom or on the fridge door) and support the child in their writing on it what they have to do (including steps towards goals). If a diary is already in use (such as a Home School Diary) then use it! Encourage parents/carers to encourage the child to add his/her own notes and comments. Parents/carers and the child must get into a routine of checking and using the diary on a regular basis.

Visual Symbols

Use pictures and symbols in diaries/calendars rather than words to depict routines and tasks. When used to prompt steps or stages in a planned task, these can aid children to develop a sense of sequence and help them remember where they are up to and what they still have to do. It is motivating to include a picture of the end goal; this is often done in recipe books, which usually display a picture of the completed dish as well as giving a list of ingredients and outlining the cooking process. Some cookery books include several photographs of the cooking process. Parents/carers can find symbols and pictures on the Internet, or be extra creative and take photographs. Parents/carers should explain to the child that each picture shows a different part of the routine to help him/her plan ahead.

Lists

Lots of people use lists to remind themselves of things to do. Lists should be on show somewhere that's easy to refer to and should not be overwhelming in the number of things to do. For example, parents/carers can encourage children to write down what they need in their school bag and tick it off when complete; lists for homework can also be useful. Parents/carers can role-model the technique themselves in their own daily activities. Remind parents/carers to praise the use of these techniques.

Routines

Discuss with parents/carers how having routines can help children with planning ahead as they are able to learn what is next. Talk about the types of routines that are already practised at home, such as morning, bedtime, homework and chore routines. Discuss methods for successful implementation of routines. It is essential that everyone plays their part, and agrees with and sticks to the same routine.

Rewards and Self-praise

Parents/carers can encourage their child to reinforce achievement of goals by praising him/herself with rewards or positive self-talk. This is especially important when the child has delayed immediate gratification in order to achieve a long-term goal.

What Can We Do As Parents/Carers?

Table 10.1 outlines a suggested approach, including a list of strategies that can be implemented at home. To maximize the effect of strategies, it is helpful to discuss them with your child's teacher so they can be implemented at both

Table 10.1 Home strategies for setting goals and planning ahead.

Teach the planning process
- Set goals.
- Break down goals into smaller steps.
- Order the steps and put them into a list.
- Write out tasks in a planner, diary or calendar.
- Write out the process so your child can use it as a template in future.

Verbal prompts
- If your child loses track, prompt by asking 'What comes next?'
- Reiterate the process and state where the child has got to.

Alarm prompts
- Encourage your child to set alarms and reminders on mobile phones, tablets or computers.

Calendars/diaries
- Pin a calendar where your child will see it – use it to note goals and steps.
- Use a Home School Diary (or another diary) to note goals, steps and lists. Place them in a timeline.

Visual symbols
- Use pictures and symbols in calendars/diaries to depict tasks, steps and routines.
- Add a picture of the end goal your child is working towards.

Routines
- Agree a routine with the whole family and ensure everyone knows their part in the routine.

Rewards and self-praise
- Ensure you give extra reward/praise to acknowledge when your child achieves a longer-term goal.
- Encourage your child to give themselves praise and to share their achievements with others.

home and school (wherever possible). Lots of parents/carers and teachers find that using a 'Home School Diary' is an efficient way to share information (see Chapter 2).

We suggest that parents/carers read Chapter 2, which provides important background information about the delivery of the Young–Smith Programme. For younger children, we suggest that parents/carers set aside some time to sit down with the child (around 45–60 minutes) and work through the Worksheets recommended for each topic. Guidance is found in the 'CBT Interventions' section in each chapter on how to do this. The Worksheets introducing Buzz and his family are outlined in Chapter 3. All the materials (worksheets and Home Missions Record Form) are available to download from the companion website www.wiley.com/go/young/helpingadhd. For older children (i.e., 12 years-plus), you can dispense with the Buzz Worksheets if necessary and instead introduce the child directly to the topic, and, using the discussion prompts on the Worksheets, apply this to the child's experience and discuss suggested strategies. Set Home Missions and support the child to complete them. Don't forget to give frequent feedback and praise. Make a Star Chart (see Chapter 2), put it in a prominent place and start to use it on a daily basis.

Working with Teachers and Schools

The school environment is the place where children will most commonly be expected to set and work towards goals, both short-term and long-term. Indeed, this is explicit in the school curriculum, and as young children pass through the school system there is a corresponding expectation that they will learn to plan, organize and monitor their own work. For children with ADHD to succeed, they often need longer-term goals broken down into concrete, smaller, perhaps daily, targets to maintain motivation. This section presents strategies that teachers can apply to support the child to develop these skills. It is important to be realistic about what can be achieved. It can be just as helpful to learn strategies to support the child as to learn strategies to improve the behaviour itself. In this section we discuss the need for teachers to specify and reinforce the planning process, and to communicate the actual process to the child. We also discuss how teachers can support the child with verbal and visual prompts and apply external techniques such as alarms, diaries, calendars and lists. Teachers probably use these already and the aim is for teachers to get the child to use these techniques themselves.

Teachers and schools will already have structures in place to support many of the interventions introduced in the Young–Smith Programme. It will be useful to link up parents/carers and teachers to encourage an integrated strategy and share success. It is important to troubleshoot any obstacles and/or difficulties that arise by thinking of ways to adapt the techniques or strategies so they are successful in helping the child. Methods to motivate success and other topics that are generic to working with teachers and schools are described in Chapter 2. Supplementary information that specifically relates to the delivery of the goals and planning session(s) is outlined in this chapter.

Teach the Planning Process

Outline the fundamental planning process to teachers. They must support the child to apply this process and reinforce the skills at school. This involves four core steps: (1) set goals – they should discuss with the child what tasks he/she needs to do and help the child to identify and set goals; (2) break down goals into smaller steps – list them; (3) order the steps – rewrite the steps in a graduated order as for the stairs metaphor described in the section about Worksheet 18; and (4) write out what to do and when in a planner, calendar or diary. When setting academic tasks, teachers should explicitly state the steps as well as the goal and for longer-term assignments check that the work has actually been completed at each step.

Verbal Prompts

Perhaps the most obvious and accessible way to aid planning and organization is the verbal prompt, as described in the parent/carer section of this chapter. Teachers often use this strategy in class. Review this with the teacher and check what seems to work best, and identify whether there are any gaps or specific areas of need.

Alarms Prompts

Discuss the use of alarm prompts as described in the parent/carer section of this chapter. An example of this is the school bell!

Calendars/Diaries

Use calendars or diaries to remember dates and look ahead. If a Home School Diary is in place, encourage the child to write in the diary themselves. If not, it is helpful to start a Home School Diary, although younger children will need more help and supervision at home and school to do this. Teachers can model the use of a calendar by having a 'class calendar' that is used to record school events and daily schedules.

Visual Symbols

Use the same techniques as for parents/carers described earlier in this chapter. Teachers may already use visual symbols in classrooms (e.g., with pictures on walls and notice boards), but children may need to be introduced to a more individualized approach.

Lists

Discuss the use of list prompts as described in the parent/carer section of this chapter.

Rewards and Self-praise

Discuss these techniques as described in the parent/carer section of this chapter.

What Can We Do As Teachers?

Table 10.2 outlines a suggested approach for teachers, including a list of strategies that can be implemented at school. To maximize the effect of strategies, it is helpful to discuss these with the child's parents/carers so that similar or

Table 10.2 School strategies for setting goals and planning ahead.

Teach the planning process
- Set goals.
- Break down goals into smaller steps.
- Order the steps and put them into a list.
- Write out tasks in a planner, diary or calendar.
- Write out the process and place it in the Home School Diary so the child can use it as a template for future work.

Verbal prompts
- If the child loses track, prompt by asking 'What comes next?'
- Reiterate the process and state where the child has got to in it.

Alarm prompts
- Encourage the child to set alarms and reminders on mobile phones, tablets or computers.

Calendars/diaries
- Pin a calendar where the child will see it – use it to note goals and steps.
- Use a Home School Diary (or another diary) to note goals, steps and lists. Place them in a timeline.

Visual symbols
- Use pictures and symbols in calendars/diaries to depict tasks, steps and routines.
- Add a picture of the end goal the child is working towards.

Rewards and self-praise
- Ensure you give extra reward/praise to acknowledge when the child achieves a longer-term goal.
- Encourage the child to give themselves praise and to share their achievements with others.

Staff collaboration
- Ensure that all staff know and understand what strategies are being used and why.

complementary strategies are implemented at both home and school (wherever possible). Both teachers and parents/carers find that using a 'Home School Diary' is an efficient way to share information (see Chapter 2).

We suggest that teachers read Chapter 2, which provides important background information about the delivery of the Young–Smith Programme. It is unlikely that teachers will have time to go through specific Worksheets with children, although if parents/carers are unable to do this it would be helpful to make arrangements with the Special Educational Needs Coordinator. Guidance on how to do this is found in the 'CBT Interventions' section in each chapter. The worksheets introducing Buzz and his family are outlined in Chapter 3. All the materials (worksheets and Home Missions Record Form) are available to download from the companion website www.wiley.com/go/young/helpingadhd. For older children (i.e., 12 years-plus), one may dispense with the Buzz worksheets if necessary and instead introduce the child directly to the topic, and, using the discussion prompts on the Worksheets, apply this to the child's experience and discuss suggested strategies. Set Home Missions and support the child to complete them. Don't forget to give frequent feedback and praise. If a Star Chart is used (see Chapter 2) then this could be put in the 'Home School Diary' where parents/carers can also review it on a regular basis.

References

Conners, C. K. (2008). *Conners* 3rd edition. Toronto: Multi-Health Systems.

Delis, D. C., Kaplan, E., & Kramer, J. H. (2001). *Delis–Kaplan Executive Function System (D-KEFS)*. San Antonio, TX: The Psychological Corporation.

Emslie, H., Wilson, F. C., Burden, V., Nimmo-Smith, I., & Wilson, B. A. (2003). *The behavioural assessment of dysexecutive syndrome in children*. London: Harcourt Assessment.

Gioia, G. A., Isquith, P. K., Guy, S. C., & Kenworthy, L. (2000). *Behavior Rating Inventory of Executive Function (BRIEF)*. Odessa, FL: Psychological Assessment Resources.

Sexias, M., Weiss, M., & Müller, U. (2012). Systematic review of national and international guidelines on attention deficit hyperactivity disorder. *Journal of Psychopharmacology, 26*(6), 753–765.

11
Problem-solving

As children grow up they encounter new problems every day. They experience academic challenges and social dilemmas. As they grow older they increasingly make their own decisions and choices. Children must learn to solve problems and make good choices if they are to avoid making mistakes during the pathway to adulthood.

Cognitive development is implicated in efficient problem-solving, as brain maturation is required to develop these skills. Indeed, problem-solving draws on a mixture of executive functioning skills, such as attention, memory, organization, planning, flexible thinking, sequencing and inhibition of responses. These higher-ability skills are often slower to develop in children with ADHD. Hence, children with ADHD may be hindered in their problem-solving abilities compared to their peers. They may also give-up too easily, especially if they sense that they are going to fail. The irony lies in the fact that their 'problem' is that they do not engage in a problem-solving process that requires them to first recognize and define the problem and generate multiple solutions, and then consider the best option (see Table 11.1). Flexible thinking and an ability to resist the urge to act on the first idea that comes to mind is needed to do this. The problem is further complicated by adults intervening and stepping in to assist when they note that a child is struggling to resolve a problem. This is well-intentioned and sometimes necessary in the moment (especially if there are concerns around safety), but in the long run it does not support an autonomous learning process. In order to develop a sense of self-efficacy and an internal locus of control, it is better to prompt the child to engage in a problem-solving process so they themselves can figure out what to do. In turn, this will lead the child to feel confident in their ability to tackle the challenges they will inevitably face.

This chapter will look at problem-solving skills in children with ADHD and the impact that deficits in these skills can have in their functioning in different areas of life. The assessment of problem-solving skills will be discussed,

Helping Children with ADHD: A CBT Guide for Practitioners, Parents and Teachers,
First Edition. Susan Young and Jade Smith.
© 2017 John Wiley & Sons Ltd. Published 2017 by John Wiley & Sons Ltd.
Companion website: www.wiley.com/go/young/helpingadhd

followed by interventions and strategies for children and the adults around them using cognitive behavioural models.

Presentation

In parallel with the expectations of others, it is important to bear in mind that a child's ability to solve problems evolves over time. Their autonomy and confidence to solve problems will considerably change between the ages of 6 and 11 years, but of course the journey will continue into adulthood and beyond as they increasingly rely on their own judgements and take responsibility for the decisions that they make.

Behavioural Functioning

How children face problems depends on many factors, including their cognitive ability, past experience and the level of organized and effective support available to them. The challenges that they face will also vary; some challenges will have dangerous consequences to the self, others or property if mismanaged. Some children will have had many opportunities to face new situations surrounded by supportive adults who help them to learn how to manage. This involves a process of scaffolding whereby the child has been supported step-by-step to think through and take action to solve a problem or develop a skill at a rate that both moves them beyond their current comfort zone (whilst also being achievable) until they can consistently manage it themselves. Other children may have fewer opportunities to face new experiences and/or inadequate support from adults. They may be anxious in new situations and feel overwhelmed cognitively and/or emotionally, and may be uncertain about how to access support. The development of positive problem-solving skills requires a flexible thinking style to generate new ideas. The child must inhibit any reactive emotional and/or impulsive response (such as hitting or kicking out).

Academic Functioning

Problem-solving is an integral part of both the school curriculum and extracurricular activities. Children learn an explicit problem-solving process for some academic work (e.g., solving maths problems, developing techniques to write a story) but this is not transferrable to other school situations. In school, children are expected to follow rules, and cooperative behaviour is expected, as is the art of compromise. It is in these areas that children with ADHD are likely to have most difficulty; they may be told *what* to do but the actual rationale or process is not always communicated.

The most common problems that present for children with ADHD in school relate to feeling misunderstood, being perceived by others as lacking in effort

Table 11.1 The problem-solving process.

---

1. **Recognize a problem:** inattention may lead a child to miss external or internal cues that a problem is arising, such as noticing early warning signals in tone of voice, facial expressions or anxious thoughts.
2. **Define the problem:** once a potential indicator that a problem may be arising has been recognized, the child needs to think carefully about what may be the cause. Is it something they have done or said? Is it something they have not done that they should do?
3. **Generate multiple solutions:** the child should brainstorm as many solutions as possible. Some will be better than others, but that doesn't matter. Generating solutions needs good memory skills to hold ideas in mind, so it is best to write them down by making a list of potential solutions.
4. **Consider the best option:** the child must inhibit the urge to act on the first solution that comes to mind, as it may not be the best solution. The child needs to generate lots of possible solutions and then decide which is the best. To do this, they must consider the advantages and disadvantages of each solution, and the potential consequences.
5. **Take action:** once the child has considered all the options carefully, they should select the best solution and act on it calmly and rationally. If this involves a long process of several steps, it is important that they see it through to fruition (so the whole of the selected solution is implemented rather than half of it).
6. **Evaluation:** the child should review the outcome and consider whether they were successful in achieving their goal. If not, they should return to their list of potential solutions to consider whether another might be better.

(perceived as 'won't' rather than 'can't'), not wanting to admit they do not understand for fear of being labelled 'stupid', having a lack of control over their impulse to act on an idea, being teased or bullied and/or being taken advantage of by peers. This is complicated by their tendency to be emotionally reactive and respond to perceived challenges or insults with anger. This impacts on their ability to resolve problems positively, for example, by making it less likely that they will engage in a functioning problem-solving process to consider how best to respond and/or resolve a problem, but instead lash out with aggression.

Interpersonal Functioning

Social situations require on-going problem-solving in the form of working out what someone means and how to respond. This is a constant, simultaneous flow of information exchange, which creates an interaction. The dilemmas that arise for children with ADHD often relate to how to make friends with someone, how best to apologize, how to manage competing friendships, how to respond to criticism or provocation and whether to involve an adult (and how best to do this). The methods that a child will use to resolve interpersonal problems will depend on their perception of what is expected, what they believe others might think of them, their skills and their self-confidence.

Coping

Children with ADHD may lack self-efficacy by feeling that they are no good at solving problems, feeling that they don't know how to resolve the problem or that even if they try they will mess it up. This attitude will influence their motivation to engage in a problem-solving process. Children who feel that problems are unmanageable, just happen to them and/or are outside of their control, are more likely to apply a strategy of avoidance. Ignoring the problem or pretending that it doesn't exist is unhelpful as the problem may escalate, with small problems becoming big problems that are harder to resolve. If problems are allowed to build up, children are more likely to feel distressed, overwhelmed and less able to cope and engage in a functional problem-solving process.

Assessment

International guidance on the assessment and treatment of ADHD recommends that a comprehensive assessment procedure is carried out by trained and qualified healthcare practitioners in order to assess ADHD (Sexias, Weiss & Müller, 2012). This often includes a multi-method assessment involving psychometric questionnaires, a clinical interview and observation of the child to assess difficulties and behaviour in different contexts and settings. It is preferable to obtain multiple perspectives from different people involved in the child's care (including that of the child if possible), often requiring multi-agency liaison. To develop a care plan with appropriate interventions that are likely to succeed it is important to fully understand the nature and complexity of the child's difficulties across their development, including historic, environmental and psychosocial factors, the child's strengths and weaknesses and the support that they currently receive. In doing this, it is important to be mindful of any comorbid and social problems experienced by the child but also within the family.

Measures

The Brief Rating Inventory of Executive Functioning for 5–18 years (BRIEF; Gioia, Isquith, Guy, Kenworthy & Baron, 2001) and the Delis–Kaplan Executive Function System (DKEFS; Delis, Kaplan & Kramer, 2001) are both rating scales that assess executive functioning skills, including problem-solving skills. An adult should support children completing self-reported questionnaires: children with ADHD may misread questions, miss out answers, respond impulsively and/or miscommunicate the rating. However, it is essential that responses are not influenced by leading questions. Children who struggle with reading should always have items read out to them. As is the case for many measures, ratings may be subject to bias and must be interpreted cautiously by a trained practitioner.

Table 11.2 provides a scale that can be used to assess whether the child applies any of the problem-solving stages outlined in Figure 11.2. The scale should be completed for the frequency the child engages in the problem-solving stages without being prompted or supported by others. It can be repeated to assess whether they are able to achieve the stages with support. The scale aims to provide a discussion point, so it is important to identify context and situational differences that may be present by asking for specific examples. The scale will help the therapist to identify target areas for treatment.

Table 11.2 Assessment of problem-solving skills.

	Never	Sometimes	Often	Always
The child can recognize that a problem is developing.				
The child is able to define the problem.				
The child will generate lots of ideas for how to resolve a problem.				
The child considers the advantages and disadvantages of each idea.				
The child considers the potential consequences of each idea.				
The child will carry out the chosen solution through to the end.				
The child can consider whether the solution was successful or not.				

Clinical Interview

Discuss with the child and those around them what happens when they are faced with a problem, who helps and what helps. Younger children will rely on adults to help them more than older children will, so it is important to determine who is already helping the child on a daily basis, the context of this support, the specific strategies used and who implements them. It is just as important to ascertain strategies that have been applied in the past that have not been helpful. Not everyone will see a problem in the same way. It can be useful to table the problems faced, who sees things in what way and their priority (using ratings of 0–10). For example, for a child who is overly active in class, their teacher may see the child's behaviour as the problem. Parents/carers may see a lack of effective support as the problem. The child may not see this as a problem at all and/or think that the class topic is the problem as it is boring.

Whilst problems can be resolved rationally and pragmatically, those who do not engage in a skilled problem-solving process may respond to them in an emotionally reactive way. This is normal, but it may distort and/or escalate the problem. It is important to assess the child's emotional reaction to problems by determining their level of anxiety, frustration, distress and so on. If they feel overwhelmed then they are more likely to engage in immediate, maladaptive solutions. Children may respond and collaborate better if the word 'challenge' is used rather than 'problem', and for younger children it may be helpful to apply a traffic light system to rate a problem/challenge (see Figure 11.1).

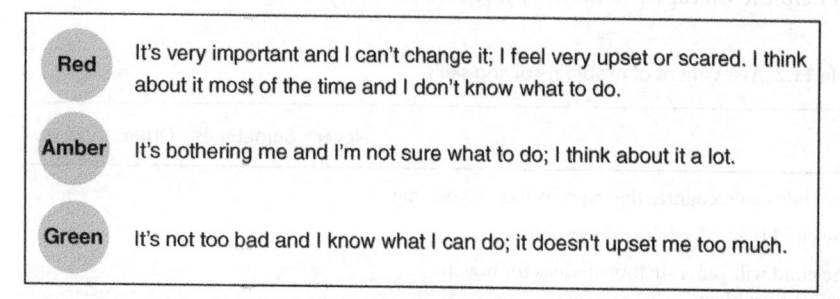

Red — It's very important and I can't change it; I feel very upset or scared. I think about it most of the time and I don't know what to do.

Amber — It's bothering me and I'm not sure what to do; I think about it a lot.

Green — It's not too bad and I know what I can do; it doesn't upset me too much.

Figure 11.1 Traffic light system of problem severity.

In the assessment, try to establish the sticking point in the problem-solving process. Table 11.2 will help to start this discussion when it is applied to recent circumstances. Look out for repetitive themes of maladaptive solutions or avoidance. A child may resolve problems by avoiding them in the hope that the problem will go away. It can be helpful just to talk to someone about worries and concerns, rather than bottling them up inside. If a child ignores a small task because they don't know what to do, it often becomes a bigger task, which is even harder. They ignore it again and it grows again; the cycle repeats over and over and becomes a vicious cycle of avoidance. Other children may have good ideas on how to solve problems but become distracted and go off-task when following them through. Breaking tasks down and recording a problem-solving style in this way will help identify patterns in the child's approach to problem-solving. Parents/carers and teachers may also apply a specific problem-solving style and sometimes this may be entrenched and rigid. Praise functional strategies and make dysfunctional strategies a target for intervention.

Acting out a chosen solution will often involve a level of self-confidence; hence the interview should also assess the child's self-confidence and self-efficacy. If a child lacks confidence, some good solutions may not be perceived to be a solution at all. When discussing solutions that have been considered in the past, ask the child to rate their confidence in taking these actions. This will indicate whether raising self-esteem and developing self-confidence needs to be included as a target of treatment (see Chapter 12).

Thoughts

During the assessment you should try to identify any thoughts or images that go through the child's mind that may impact on effective problem-solving, for example, 'You thought about doing X, why did you decide to do that? What made you decide not to do X?' Older children will be better at recognizing and reporting their thoughts. Look out for negative and unhelpful thoughts that may increase avoidance, such as 'There's no point', 'I can't do it' or 'I don't know how'. Younger children may find it easier to express their thoughts as images, such as 'How did you imagine it would turn out?' Negative thinking may indicate anxiety or low self-esteem (see Chapters 7 and 12).

Feelings and Physiology

It is important to assess the emotional impact on the child and those around them that these problems or challenges are having. Stress, upset, frustration and apathy are common feelings. Children may say 'I don't care' or 'I don't like it', depending on their age and vocabulary. Other indicators may be more visible, such as crying, avoidant behaviour, changes in breathing and facial expressions.

Behaviours

In the clinical interview you should look for, and highlight, strategies that are helping or hindering the child in problem-solving. Behaviours which may help include trying and having a go, breaking down the problem, seeking support, doing what helped in the past and/or attempting to imitate others' behaviour (the latter of course being functional behaviours!). Less helpful behaviours are likely to include doing the first thing that comes to mind, leaving it for someone else to solve the problem, ignoring the problem and responding aggressively.

It may be helpful to supplement the assessment by asking for a Behaviour Diary to be completed to record how often the child presents with a problem, their response to having the problem (behavioural and emotional), their approach to managing it, the specific techniques applied and the outcome. Details about how to record and analyse this information can be found in Chapter 6.

CBT Interventions For Problem-Solving

If the therapist is treating younger children and/or the worksheets are being used as a basis for treatment, the first session should always commence with Worksheets 1, 2 and 3 to introduce the child to Buzz and his family (Worksheet 1), introduce positive self-talk (Worksheet 2) and identify a reward system

(Worksheet 3). The reward and self-talk strategies are applied in the session, at home and/or at school. See Chapter 3 for a suggested outline of how to plan and conduct the introductory session. All the worksheets are available on the companion website resource page, www.wiley.com/go/young/helpingadhd.

The aims of the interventions and worksheets in the problem-solving session(s) is to teach children to apply a systematic process to resolve problems and develop helpful rather than maladaptive responses when faced with challenging situations. The therapist will achieve this by setting an agenda, reviewing Home Missions completed between sessions, working through new worksheets (or just the strategies for older children) and setting new Home Missions. If required, a mid-session break can be offered halfway through the session; this may be particularly important for younger children. Chapter 2 provides generic information on the structure and content of sessions (irrespective of topic); supplementary information is included within this chapter that specifically relates to the delivery of the problem-solving session(s).

Agenda

At the beginning of the session, show the child the written agenda (see Figure 11.2) that you have prepared prior to the session and go through it, verbally linking the themes and Worksheets that you will introduce during the session. For the problem-solving module, introduce Worksheets 19 and 20 by saying:

> Today we have a story about Buzz and his school project. He has to make a castle but he's been putting it off and now he is running out of time. After that, we will have a short break and you can colour in the Worksheet using these crayons. After the break we are going to think about a problem Buzz has with another boy who isn't nice to him. In fact, the boy is stealing his things. We are going to talk about what Buzz should do.

Agenda

Folder Review

Buzz makes a Castle [Worksheet 19]

Break

Buzz and the New Boy [Worksheet 20]

Home Missions

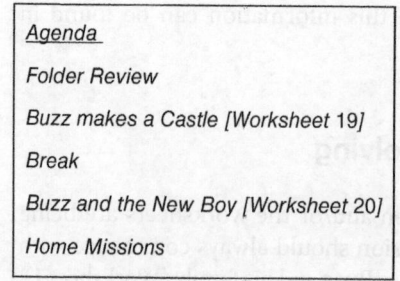

Figure 11.2 Example agenda for problem-solving session(s).

Folder Review

When reviewing the folder with the child, aside from checking whether the Home Missions are completed, take the opportunity to revise important information and/or concepts, as this will help the child to consolidate learning points and/or newly acquired skills. Ensure that you make time to look at the illustrations, colourings, paintings, magazine cuttings and/or photographs that the child has added to the folder. Discuss them and try to relate these to discussions about Buzz and his family and/or topics or strategies that have been covered. Aside from acting as a revision prompt, this will also act as a reward system for the child. Praise should be given verbally, but you can also reward by adding stickers, handwritten notes or smiley faces. If Home Missions were set then you should review the Home Missions Record Form for comments and feedback from parents/carers and discuss these with the child.

Worksheet 19 Buzz makes a Castle

Worksheet Description

Buzz has a school project. He must make a castle using things he finds at home. He has some ideas and he likes making things, but this is a big project and he is unsure where to start and what materials he should collect. Buzz has put off the task all week. The project is due in tomorrow and he still hasn't done it.

To download this worksheet, please visit the companion website

Worksheet Prompts

What is Buzz's problem exactly?
Is Buzz facing the problem or avoiding the problem?
What might happen in the end if Buzz doesn't do the project? How might Buzz feel about that?
What would you tell Buzz to do? What materials would you use to make the castle?
Have you ever avoided a problem?
Together let's write out some ideas of the things Buzz can do to help him make the castle and complete his project on time.
Now let's look at the things you thought would help Buzz and circle the ones that might also help you.

Worksheet 19 introduces the concept of maladaptive problem-solving strategies, in this case avoidance. The child will learn that avoidance is not a solution in the longer-term and identify helpful ways to prevent this from happening. It is important to direct the child to think about initial activities that may help them; these might include making a plan and writing a list of ideas about what they intend to do and when they will do it. The child might add to the activity list after talking to, or working with, other people (friends, parent/carer and siblings) to get help with the task. The exercise draws on children's ability to be creative and talk about how they would complete the task (e.g., using cereal boxes, egg boxes, cotton wool, paint, etc.) and to translate these ideas into a functional list to direct behaviour and achievements.

Read the Stimulus Sheet aloud to the child, or, if they wish, they can read it with you, and check they have understood the narrative. Allow the child to ask any questions and guide them to identify and define the problem by asking 'What is Buzz's problem exactly?' This is a core question that the child needs to learn to ask themselves when they are faced with a problem. The question helps the child to set aside feelings of stress and/or being overwhelmed and consider precisely what the difficulty is. This helps the child to recognize and define the problem. Talk through how Buzz feels about the task – it seems so big that he is not sure what to do or where to start. Help the child to consider whether Buzz is facing the problem or avoiding the problem and summarize, 'That's right, Buzz is avoiding the problem. He needs to make the castle but he keeps finding other things to do instead.' Move on to discuss the consequences of avoiding the problem, for example, Buzz might get in trouble at school or let others down. This might lead to him feeling upset, frustrated and/or disappointed in himself. Ask the child what they suggest Buzz could do to help himself. Discuss what materials Buzz could collect from home to make the castle.

Next, ask the child to consider whether they have ever avoided a problem themselves. This might be a similar situation at school, or one that is quite different. Did they engage in a different, perhaps more fun, activity instead? If they say no, you can normalize this by saying, 'Most people have avoided a problem at some time, have a think.' You may have to give the child prompts; delaying doing school homework is usually a good one! Ask the child to describe the situation, what happened and how it was resolved in the end.

Moving back to Buzz's problem, record ideas that would help Buzz complete the project on the Task Sheet, including ideas for materials. Point out that Buzz might have felt stuck, but they had lots of ideas, so perhaps talking to a friend might have helped Buzz (and been more fun!). It is very important that you record the process as well as the activity. Explain the 'process' to the child to be like a flight of stairs; the castle is at the top of the stairs and to reach the castle they must walk up each step. The steps are the process, or the journey, they take to reach the castle at the top.

The aim is for the child to carry forward generic strategies for resolving problems (see Table 11.1) that they can apply themselves to the different problems they face. Hence, aside from the suggestions for what Buzz should do in this specific situation, ensure the list includes generic strategies they can take forward, such as ask yourself what is the actual problem (define it), write out a list of things to do, ask someone for help (specify who), check with the teacher if they don't understand and get information from a book or the Internet. Invite the child to circle any strategies that they could apply to their own problems.

Give praise for the child's effort in the session. If you choose to set Home Missions based on this Worksheet we suggest asking the child to do the following:

1) Decorate the worksheet by colouring in the pictures and thought bubbles, and/or add to them with pictures on the theme of the story. These could be photographs or pictures in magazines or comics.
2) When faced with a problem in the week, try one of the strategies like asking for help or looking it up.
3) Ask someone you know, like a family member or friend, how they deal with situations when they don't know what to do.
4) Make a castle and write out the steps you took to achieve it!

If Home Missions are set, remind parents/carers to complete the Home Missions Record Form and to place it in the folder for review at the next session.

Mid-session Break

This should be provided at an appropriate point in the session as outlined in Chapter 2.

Worksheet 20 Buzz and the New Boy

Worksheet Description

To download this worksheet, please visit the companion website

Every Saturday Buzz has a special job to do. His Mum gives him some money to go to the shop and buy her favourite magazine, *Magic*. With the change he is allowed to buy himself a treat and he usually buys some sweets. There is a new boy in town who isn't very nice. For the past two weeks he has waited for Buzz to come out of the shop and taken his sweets. The boy is bigger than Buzz and Buzz is scared of him. Buzz doesn't know what to do.

Worksheet Prompts

What is Buzz's problem exactly?
How do you think Buzz feels? Why has he not told anyone?

(Continued)

> **Worksheet 20 (Continued)**
>
> Have you or someone you know ever had a problem like this? Has anyone ever upset you by calling you names or saying nasty things about you? What did you do? How did it end up?
>
> Together let's write out some ideas of things Buzz can do to help him solve the problem.
>
> Which one do you think is best for him and why?
>
> Now let's look at the things you thought would help Buzz and circle the ones that might also help you.

Worksheet 20 consolidates the systematic problem-solving process by taking the child through each stage of identifying and taking steps to resolve a problem. This involves encouraging the child to brainstorm lots of potential solutions, consideration of the advantages and disadvantages of each solution and their consequences, implementing the best solution and evaluating its effectiveness. The process involves a decisional balance exercise to help the child evaluate the best solution. For this exercise, it is important to emphasize the process as well as the specific solutions to Buzz's problem in order that the child acquires a template for solving problems that they can apply more generally to their own problems.

Read the Stimulus Sheet aloud to the child, or, if they wish, they can read it to you, and check the child understands the narrative. Summarize the story by saying, 'So when Buzz goes to the shop a boy waits for him outside to take his sweets.' Clarify if the child thinks that is acceptable or not and summarize that it is not okay for someone to take something that doesn't belong to them. This has happened two weeks running – discuss with the child why Buzz did not tell anyone the first time. Help the child to define the problems Buzz is facing and summarize, 'Buzz doesn't know what to do, the boy is bigger than him, he has taken his sweets, and Buzz is scared of the boy. He wants it to stop.' Move on by relating Buzz's experience to one of the child's own experiences, or something experienced by one of their friends or siblings. Encourage the child to tell their story. This might not involve theft, but it may involve other children being spiteful to them, name calling, or bullying. Ask the child what they did and how it ended up.

Move on to helping the child brainstorm possible solutions to Buzz's situation and write these down on the Task Sheet. It doesn't matter whether some seem better than others; the idea is to generate options. These might include: refusing to hand over the sweets, tell the shop keeper, confront the boy, fight the boy, go home and tell his brother or mum and so on. Discuss each option with the child to decide on the best option. This can be achieved using a decisional balance sheet to think about the advantages and disadvantages of each option and recording these in a 'plus' and 'minus' column. When considering dysfunctional options, ensure the disadvantages outweigh the advantages. If the child selects a dysfunctional option to resolve the problem (such as punching the boy or starting a fight), then discuss the potential consequences of that resolution and consider an alternative. It is important to reiterate that physical aggression is never acceptable. Point out to the child that they have brainstormed lots of potential solutions, so if the first choice doesn't work out there are others that can be tried. If the first choice didn't work out, suggest that Buzz thinks about *why* it didn't work out. What happened that he had not anticipated?

When completing the exercise ensure that some generic strategies for resolving problems are included (see Table 11.1), such as asking yourself what the actual problem is (define it), writing out a list of things to do, asking someone for help (specify who), getting information from a book or the Internet, using the decisional balance sheet and remembering that if the first idea doesn't work you should think of the reasons for this. Looking back at the child's own experience, ask them to consider and apply the process to see whether there is something they would have done differently (or the observed person could have done differently). Would they handle the situation differently if it happened again? Invite the child to circle any strategies they produced for Buzz that could help themselves with any future problems.

Give praise for the child's effort in the session. If you choose to set Home Missions based on this worksheet we suggest asking the child to do the following:

1) Decorate the worksheet by colouring in the pictures and thought bubbles, and/or add to them with pictures on the theme of the story. These could be photographs or pictures in magazines or comics.
2) If you have a problem in the week, brainstorm potential solutions and write them down. Make a decisional balance sheet and decide which is the best solution. Circle the one you did and write down how it worked out. Bring it to the next session. Show it to parents/carers and/or teachers if this is appropriate.

If Home Missions are set, remind parents/carers to complete the Home Missions Record Form and to place it in the folder for review at the next session.

Feedback and Rewards

At the end of the session, appropriate rewards identified from the Worksheet 3 Reward Task should be applied, for example, the child could engage in positive self-talk. See Chapter 2 for more information about feedback and rewards.

Working with Parents/Carers

Parents/carers often know when a child has a problem, but if the child doesn't confide in them they feel at a loss as to how to help. Encourage parents/carers to take a pragmatic stance by teaching a problem-solving process at every opportunity so the child develops the necessary skills so that they can translate these to any challenges they grapple with themselves. Parents/carers can start by modelling this when resolving their own problems out loud but, of course, using straightforward problems like having too much to do one day or needing to meet a deadline.

This section presents strategies to support parents/carers to define the child's problems, engage together in a stepped problem-solving process, reduce maladaptive problem-solving strategies, encourage autonomy, address impulsivity and anxiety, and to role-model good problem-solving skills that will reinforce and consolidate the problem-solving process. Usually, adults already have problem-solving skills and apply the process automatically, but it is important to point out the actual stepped process and parents/carers need to be aware of this to communicate it to the child. We also discuss the need for parents/carers to manage their own difficulties and problems, and achieve a balance in their life that will minimize stress in order to be good role-models.

When working with parents/carers, the therapist should introduce suggested techniques and strategies; practise and rehearse them in role-plays during the sessions if appropriate (without the child present). In future sessions, parents/carers should report back to the therapist about how they managed using them at home. It is important to troubleshoot any obstacles and/or difficulties that arise by thinking of ways to adapt the techniques or strategies so they are successful in helping the child.

A key strategy to change behaviour and improve cognitive skills is to find motivators to promote success. Children with ADHD tend to respond better to immediate rewards as they have a difficulty with delayed gratification for longer-term rewards (even if these are bigger and better). Methods to motivate success (including the use of a Star Chart) and other topics that are generic to working with parents/carers are described in Chapter 2. Supplementary information that specifically relates to the delivery of the problem-solving session(s) is outlined in this chapter.

Define the Problem

Parents/carers need to identify what the problem is, bearing in mind that they (and teachers) may have a different perspective to that of the child. This doesn't mean someone is 'right' or 'wrong'. It is important to look beyond the behaviour, as this may be a vehicle to communicate distress. The therapist can demonstrate this to parents/carers with a triangle/iceberg metaphor: the observable problem is the tip and the underlying causes (which might need to be addressed) are the base.

Teach the Problem-Solving Process

Teach parents/carers about the stepped problem-solving process (see Table 11.1). They will probably know this already and do it automatically, but they need to know what you are teaching the child so it can be reinforced at home. If the child has a problem, the parent/carer can then sit down with the child and write out the steps, for example:

> Step 1: What is the problem?
> Step 2: What are the options?
> Step 3: What are the good/bad things about each option?
> Step 4: Try it.
> Step 5: How did it go?

This will help the child to learn the process and support them to apply it. Step 3 can include generating a decisional balance sheet (see the section on Worksheet 20) to help select the best option. It is important that Step 5 is not disregarded as this step involves reflection, after the solution has been implemented, to review its success – considering whether it was the best option and whether anything happened that they did not anticipate (and should next time), and/or obstacles to success. If the first option is unsuccessful, the parent/carer should move to consider other options or go through the process again to think of more options. When a problem turns out well, it is tempting to skip this step, but it is important for the learning curve. It may be that something happened that the child did not anticipate and they had to adapt the resolution in some way.

Stop Maladaptive Strategies

Parents/carers are well placed to notice if their child is using a maladaptive way of managing problems, such as avoidance (ignoring or bottling up problems), rigid responding or blaming others. When these are present, parents/carers must encourage the child to respond differently, for example, by sharing the problem, engaging in the problem-solving process and/or thinking of other ways to resolve the problem. It is important that the child is supported to learn and discover and does not feel criticized or shamed. Praise and rewards should be used when children are able to face their problems and make efforts to find ways to overcome obstacles.

Encourage Autonomy

Parents/carers may notice that in the past they have tended to solve problems for the child. It is a natural instinct to help and support, repair and mend, relieve stress and bring comfort. However, as the child develops, parents/carers must take a step back while the child figures things out for themselves. They must do this or the child will take longer to learn; they must make the problem-solving process autonomous. Talk to parents/carers about their expectations and the factors that might impact on the child's problem-solving efficiency, such as feeling overwhelmed, emotional, tired, impulsive, or problems with specific situations or people. These are the times when the child might need additional support.

Stop and Think

Stop and think is a specific technique that can be taught to the child to interrupt impulsive and automatic responses, and instead promotes a process which guides them to consider alternative outcomes. It can be applied to help the child to slow down and to consider consequences. See parents/carers section in Chapter 6 for further information.

Worries and Anxiety

If the child is very anxious about a problem or the build-up of problems, it will be helpful to include the strategies outlined in Chapter 7.

Role-Model

Remind parents/carers that they can be great role-models for their children by facing rather than ignoring problems. Discuss if there are any areas they would need to work on themselves in order to do this, for example asking for help, repairing relationships or doing household jobs. Facing problems is not the same as making problems, and parents/carers might reflect on how they manage stress, make time for themselves, juggle the demands of parenting and ensure they have quality time with their child. It is important that parents/carers give themselves permission to include time for themselves. It's about getting a good work–leisure and self–other balance.

What Can We Do As Parents/Carers?

Table 11.3 outlines a suggested approach, including a list of strategies that can be implemented at home. To maximize the effect of strategies, it is helpful to discuss them with your child's teacher so they can be implemented at both home and school (wherever possible). Lots of parents/carers and teachers find that using a 'Home School Diary' is an efficient way to share information (see Chapter 2).

We suggest that parents/carers read Chapter 2, which provides important background information about the delivery of the Young–Smith Programme. For younger children, we suggest that parents/carers set aside some time to sit down with the child (around 45–60 minutes) and work through the worksheets recommended for each topic. Guidance on how to do this is found in the 'CBT Interventions' section in each chapter. The worksheets introducing Buzz and his family are outlined in Chapter 3. All the materials (worksheets and Home Missions Record Form) are available to download from the

Table 11.3 Home strategies for problem-solving.

Define the problem
- Think about what is really causing the problem.
- Consider the facts. Do not make assumptions.
- Anger and anxiety may be an outcome of the problem, not the cause.

Teach the problem-solving process
- Sit down with your child and teach them the process in Figure 11.1.
- Write down a summary of the steps (see parent/carer section).
- Take every opportunity to use and reinforce the process.
- Do not skip step 5 as it is important to reflect on obstacles to achievement.
- Apply the process with your child to get past problems and difficulties.

Stop maladaptive strategies
- Watch out for avoidance behaviours.
- Watch out for strategies of bravado and bottling things up.
- Consider what factors influence the child's problem-solving skills, like feeling overly tired and/or emotional.

Encourage autonomy
- Help your child when they need it, but let your child practise themselves first.

Stop and Think
- Teach the Stop and Think process by using the STOP mnemonic (see Chapter 6).
- Identify a signal to trigger the process (both verbal and visual).

Emotional control
- If appropriate, apply strategies for managing anxiety (see Chapter 7).
- If appropriate, apply strategies for managing frustration and anger (see Chapter 8).

Role-model
- Role-model how to face (appropriate) problems by explaining your own problem-solving out loud.
- Ensure you allow yourself a good work–leisure and self–other balance.

companion website, www.wiley.com/go/young/helpingadhd. For older children (i.e., 12 years-plus), you can dispense with the Buzz Worksheets, if necessary, and instead introduce the child directly to the topic and, using the prompts on the Discussion Sheet, apply this to the child's experience and discuss suggested strategies. Set Home Missions and support the child in completing them. Don't forget to give frequent feedback and praise. Make a Star Chart (see Chapter 2), put it in a prominent place and start to use it on a daily basis.

Working with Teachers and Schools

Probably the most common problems that teachers will observe, and be in a position to help with in school, relate to interpersonal relationship problems. It is in the school environment that children must: make and maintain friendships; work collaboratively with others in individual work, group work and in teams; manage relationships with children they may dislike; manage relationships with adults; and respect rules and authority. This involves managing emotions and interpersonal conflict. A common issue in classrooms that teachers should look out for is When children have not understood the task but do not want to ask for help. The child may feel embarrassed and/or fear they will be perceived as stupid. This leaves the child with a dilemma and/or anxiety. It is important that the child is supported to learn and discover, and not to feel criticized or shamed.

In addition, problems may relate to the home environment. A teacher may be perceived by the child to be a valued and trusted confidante, someone to turn to with worries or problems that the child is reluctant to discuss at home. For serious problems this may activate an official process, but for less serious problems teachers can help and support the child by teaching them problem-solving strategies, including how to define problems, engage in a stepped problem-solving process, reduce maladaptive problem-solving strategies, encourage autonomy and address impulsivity and anxiety. Usually, adults already have these skills and apply the process automatically, but it is important to point out the actual stepped process, and they need to be aware of this to communicate it to the child.

Teachers and schools will already have structures in place to support many of the interventions introduced in the Young–Smith Programme. It will be useful to link up parents/carers and teachers to encourage an integrated strategy and share success. It is important to troubleshoot any obstacles and/or difficulties that arise by thinking of ways to adapt the techniques or strategies so they are successful in helping the child. Methods to motivate success and other topics that are generic to working with teachers and schools are described in

Chapter 2. Supplementary information that specifically relates to the delivery of the problem-solving session(s) is outlined in this chapter.

Define the Problem

When a developing problem is observed in class or in the playground, or otherwise suspected, talk to the child about what is going on. Help the child to identify the problem, bearing in mind that the teacher (and parents/carers) may have a different perspective to that of the child; this doesn't mean someone is 'right' or 'wrong'. It is important to look beyond the behaviour, as this may be a vehicle to communicate distress. The therapist can demonstrate this to the teacher with a triangle/iceberg metaphor: the observable problem is the tip and the underlying causes (which might need to be addressed) are the base.

Teach the Problem-Solving Process

Teachers have many ways of helping children in school to solve problems and they should start with considering what usually works well for that particular child. Identify strategies that are helpful in school and consider how the teacher could work with parents/carers to communicate and transfer successful strategies to the home environment. For example, this may include methods to encourage perseverance, and rewards for trying out new methods (even if they don't work out, effort should be rewarded). Introduce the problem-solving steps described in the parent/carer section, especially if these are being used at home. This process aims to help children slow down and consider multiple possibilities for resolving problems.

Stop Maladaptive Strategies

Teachers are well placed to notice if the child is applying maladaptive methods to manage problems, especially those involving interpersonal relationships and conflict resolution. When maladaptive strategies are noted, such as avoidance (ignoring or bottling up problems), rigid responding or blaming others, teachers should introduce the child to alternative methods, for example by sharing the problem, engaging in the problem-solving process and thinking of other ways to resolve the problem. It is important that the child is supported to learn and discover and does not feel criticized or shamed. The therapist should discuss the priorities for the child in school with the teacher and suggest the teacher sets a specific goal (or goals) that might help the child to deal with problems. The teacher should aim to generate a constructive pathway for the child to follow by asking questions such as, 'What do you want?' and 'What steps do you need to take to achieve that that?' Praise and rewards should be given when children face their problems and make the effort to overcome obstacles to efficient resolution.

Encourage Autonomy

Skilled problem-solving does not mean a 'win' or 'lose' dichotomy has to be faced and resolved. There are a range of outcomes that may involve compromise and apology. Teachers are good at honing these skills. Sometimes it is quicker for teachers to intervene with instructions and direction, but this should be discouraged, as for autonomous problem-solving it is better to engage in the stepped process outlined in this programme, as this will teach the child the skills to find the solution themselves. For example, when talking to children who have had an argument or disagreement, the teacher could clarify, 'Chris, you want this and, Sam, you want that. How can you both get a bit of what you want? How can we work this out? You are both feeling upset. How can we fix that?'

Stop and Think

Teachers can help impulsive children to take a step back and consider options rather than rushing straight in with the first idea. The 'STOP and THINK' technique will be especially important if the teacher has noted the development of repeated, unhelpful patterns. See Chapter 6 for further information.

Worries and Anxiety

If the child is very anxious about a problem or the build-up of problems, it will be helpful to include the strategies outlined in Chapter 7.

What Can We Do As Teachers?

Table 11.4 outlines a suggested approach for teachers, including a list of strategies that can be implemented at school. To maximize the effect of strategies, it is helpful to discuss these with the child's parents/carers so that similar or complementary strategies are implemented at home and school (wherever possible). Both teachers and parents/carers find that using a 'Home School Diary' is an efficient way to share information (see Chapter 2).

We suggest that teachers read Chapter 2, which provides important background information about the delivery of the Young–Smith Programme. It is unlikely that teachers will have the time to go through specific Worksheets with children, although if parents/carers are unable to do this it would be helpful to make arrangements with the Special Educational Needs Coordinator. Guidance on how to do this is found in the 'CBT Interventions' section in each chapter. The worksheets introducing Buzz and his family are outlined in

Chapter 3. All the materials (worksheets and Home Missions Record Form) are available to download from the companion website, www.wiley.com/go/young/helpingadhd. For older children (i.e., 12 years-plus), one may dispense with the Buzz worksheets if necessary, and instead introduce the child directly to the topic and, using the prompts on the Discussion Sheet, apply this to the child's experience and discuss suggested strategies. Set Home Missions and support the child in completing them. Don't forget to give frequent feedback and praise. If a Star Chart is used (see Chapter 2) then this could be put in the 'Home School Diary' where parents/carers can also review it on a regular basis.

Table 11.4 School strategies for problem-solving.

Define the problem
- Think about what is really causing the problem.
- Consider the facts. Do not make assumptions.
- Anger and anxiety may be an outcome of the problem, not the cause.

Teach the problem-solving process
- Consider what works well and what works less well for the child.
- Discuss and share strategies with parents/carers.
- Review the process in Table 11.1 and consider how it may be applied in school.
- Take every opportunity to use and reinforce the process.
- Do not skip step 5 as it is important to reflect on obstacles to achievement.

Stop maladaptive strategies
- Watch out for avoidance behaviours.
- Watch out for strategies of bravado and bottling things up.
- Set specific goals that will help the child deal with problems and ask questions that will help the child to generate a constructive pathway to achieve them.
- Consider what factors influence the child's problem-solving skills, like feeling overly tired and/or emotional.

Encourage autonomy
- Help the child when they need it, but let them practise first.

Stop and Think
- Teach the Stop and Think process by using the STOP mnemonic (see Chapter 6).
- Identify a signal to trigger the process (both verbal and visual).

Emotional control
- If appropriate, apply strategies for managing anxiety (see Chapter 7).
- If appropriate, apply strategies for managing frustration and anger (see Chapter 8).

Staff collaboration
- Ensure that all staff know and understand what strategies are being used and why.

References

Delis, D. C., Kaplan, E., & Kramer, J. H. (2001). *Delis–Kaplan Executive Function System (D-KEFS)*. San Antonio, TX: The Psychological Corporation.

Gioia, G. A., Isquith, P. K., Guy, S. C., & Kenworthy, L. (2000). *Behavior Rating Inventory of Executive Function (BRIEF)*. Odessa, FL: Psychological Assessment Resources.

Sexias, M., Weiss, M., & Müller, U. (2012). Systematic review of national and international guidelines on attention deficit hyperactivity disorder. *Journal of Psychopharmacology, 26*(6), 753–765.

12

Mood and Self-Esteem

Self-esteem has been defined as a 'sense of positive self-worth and attribution' (Rosenberg, 1965) and a 'judgemental process in which an individual examines their performance, capacities and attributes and arrives at a decision of their own worthiness' (Coopersmith, 1967). Hence, self-esteem is multi-modal with cognitive (beliefs and attributions about the self), affective (feelings of worth or value) and behavioural (positive control and action) elements. Young children are unlikely and/or unable to reflect on such abstract concepts but instead absorb feedback (both explicit and implicit) from people around them. This may explain why children with ADHD tend to have low self-esteem as, compared with their non-ADHD peers, they are more likely to receive reprimands and negative feedback from parents/carers, teachers and peers, and experience failure. Furthermore, adults with ADHD who reflect back on their life often report a sense of always feeling different from others when growing up – usually in a negative way (Young, Bramham, Gray & Rose 2008).

In understanding the development of the concept of the self and self-esteem we can draw upon Beck et al.'s (1979) cognitive behavioural model of depression. This describes the development of beliefs about the self, the world and others, based on early experience, self-evaluation and messages received from others. These beliefs, in some part, go on to establish the lens through which the world is understood, leading to the development of assumptions. For example, someone with the belief, 'I'm not good enough' is likely to assume that if a situation does not work out well, 'it's because I did something wrong.' This person is likely to experience a plague of thoughts in everyday challenging situations such as, 'I might as well not bother as things never turn out well' or 'I'm useless.' These cognitions lead to avoidance behaviour and a feeling of worthlessness. Hence, the child misses out on opportunities to develop a positive sense of control, mastery and self-efficacy. A vicious cycle is created with the child being unlikely to develop positive self-esteem and instead experiencing disillusionment and disengagement, factors known to increase the risk of conduct

Helping Children with ADHD: A CBT Guide for Practitioners, Parents and Teachers,
First Edition. Susan Young and Jade Smith.
© 2017 John Wiley & Sons Ltd. Published 2017 by John Wiley & Sons Ltd.
Companion website: www.wiley.com/go/young/helpingadhd

and behavioural difficulties. It may also drive young people towards social environments in which it is easier for them to gain an identity and 'taste' success, for example, joining street gangs.

The chapter looks at the relationship between ADHD, mood and low self-esteem, and suggests methods to promote self-esteem across contexts and within relationships using cognitive behavioural strategies. It is important for children to know they are loved and valued, despite their difficulties. Positive parenting is a key part of any support programme. Parents/carers may need to be more explicit about the fact that they like and love their child with ADHD, even though their symptoms may lead them to experience problems from time to time

Presentation

Compared with their peers, children with ADHD are likely to have negative experiences more frequently, in particular feeling singled out and/or perceiving disapproval. This may be especially the case for older children who receive a diagnosis later as, without a clinical framework of understanding, parents/carers and teachers may have interpreted their behaviour as being oppositional, naughty and/or lazy. They may be labelled as 'problem children', and if this is communicated to the children they may also perceive themselves to be 'problem children'.

Behavioural Functioning

Low self-esteem, a lack of positive regard for oneself and poor confidence in one's own abilities are risk factors for developing low mood. When present, this is likely to exacerbate cognitive problems, as mood and attention are closely related. When people are depressed, for example, we know that they have a shorter attention-span and more memory problems. Thoughts about themselves, others, the world and the future tend to have a negative bias. It is as if they are wearing dark glasses – everything seems grey and shaded. Children with ADHD who develop low self-esteem often feel a sense of hopelessness, which means they avoid rather than embrace tasks and activities. They also feel that they don't measure up to the standards of others and often withdraw from social situations. Naturally, children struggle to understand and manage these unpleasant feelings. They may become irritable and stressed. Some children may even become aggressive; this may be directed at themselves as well as others, such as hitting out physically or acting out verbally.

Academic Functioning

A child with low self-esteem presents as hesitant, uncertain and emotional. They may withdraw from school activities, both social and academic. This may especially be the case for work that requires sustained mental effort (e.g., in handwritten tasks), as a child with low self-esteem might go to great lengths to avoid tasks they associate with failure. It may also lead the child to anticipate failure again. The child with low self-esteem needs encouragement to attempt tasks and plenty of praise for his/her efforts. This will foster positive experiences, which in turn will promote the development of self-efficacy and self-confidence.

Interpersonal Functioning

Children who lack confidence may also have peer relationship problems. They may self-isolate and avoid mixing with peers. They may also be vulnerable to being picked on, teased or bullied. Some children develop one best friend and their confidence is tied to doing activities only in their company. Others put on a brave face and mask their feelings with bravado – by playing them down or engaging in outlandish behaviours. Some children may seek to 'fit in' by ingratiating themselves to others; they may be easily led, sexually promiscuous and/ or engage in antisocial behaviours.

Coping

An increased experience of failure will inevitably lead to feelings of poor self-efficacy and low self-esteem. Children with ADHD are less able to cope with these negative emotions because they have poor problem-solving skills (their symptoms cause them to be less able to accurately appraise a problem, generate several solutions, plan, organize and follow through with the best solution). Children may respond with dysfunctional coping strategies of withdrawal and avoidance. Having a low mood or depression leads to a focus on the negative, pessimistic aspects of the future, and misappraisal of the intentions and responses of others. The child may not communicate negative thoughts and feelings but instead suffer in silence because everything seems to be hopeless and they feel helpless. When a child presents in this way, it is important to break through and light the way out of the shade.

Warning signs of more complex and serious self-esteem and mood problems are indicated by self-harming behaviours, persistent withdrawal and avoidance of social activities, expressions of negative thoughts about themselves and/or suicidal ideation. These behaviours may indicate clinical depression, requiring referral for clinical assessment. In cases where there is significant or immediate risk to the child's life they should be taken to hospital emergency services.

Assessment

International guidance on the assessment and treatment of ADHD recommends that a comprehensive assessment procedure is carried out by trained and qualified healthcare practitioners in order to assess ADHD (Sexias,

Weiss & Müller, 2012). This often includes a multi-method assessment, involving psychometric questionnaires, a clinical interview and observation of the child to assess difficulties and behaviour in different contexts and settings. It is preferable to obtain multiple perspectives from different people involved in the child's care (including that of the child if possible), often requiring multi-agency liaison. To develop a care plan with appropriate interventions that are likely to succeed it is important to fully understand the nature and complexity of the child's difficulties across their development, including historic, environmental and psychosocial factors, the child's strengths and weaknesses and the support that they currently receive.

Measures

Probably the most well-known self-esteem rating scale is that developed by Rosenberg (1965). For younger children, the 'How am I doing?' Clinical Outcome Rating Scale (Miller & Duncan, 2000) is recommended. If low self-esteem is suspected to be due to an underlying mood disorder, the assessment should include a comprehensive assessment of mood and depression. There are several measures that assess mood in children, including feelings of worthlessness and depression. Commonly used ones include the Strengths and Difficulties Questionnaire (SDQ; Goodman, 1997) for age two upwards, measuring emotional symptoms, and the Revised Children's Anxiety and Depression Scale (RCADS; Chorpita, Yim, Moffitt, Umemoto & Francis, 2000), which measures symptoms of depression, for age six upwards. These are rated by parents/carers and teachers based on observation and knowledge of the child, and child self-report measures are also available. An adult should provide support to children completing self-report questionnaires: children with ADHD may misread questions, miss out answers, respond impulsively and/or miscommunicate the rating. However, it is essential that responses are not influenced by leading questions. Children who struggle with reading should always have items read out to them. As for many measures, ratings may be subject to bias and must be interpreted cautiously by a trained practitioner.

Clinical Interview

It can be difficult for parents/carers and teachers to resist comparing children to each other as society has 'norms', milestones and ideas about what is typical. Unfortunately, this may mean that the child receives excessive criticism from others for not listening, not following rules, not finishing things and so on. The child with ADHD who is compared with peers may not have their personal skills and strengths acknowledged because, by nature of the disorder, the child suffers impairment or deficits across various domains. In turn, the child may internalize criticism and develop a biased self-perception that they are inadequate, leading them to have low self-esteem and a poor sense of self-worth.

Consider whether the environment and people around the child are adaptive and supportive. You should also carefully assess the perspective of adults around the child by assessing whether they have overly high expectations of the child. Unrealistic expectations of what the child may achieve can lead the child to believe that he/she is not good enough. Furthermore, unrealistic expectations may not only be a feature of parents', carers' and teachers' expectations, they may be present in the child themselves. In addition, note whether negative attitudes are present, either about themselves and/or from parents/carers and teachers. Parents/carers may be feeling particularly stressed by the child's behaviours; they may feel upset about the diagnosis and what this means and unintentionally place blame or burden on the child. It is also helpful to talk to the child's teacher to get a perspective of the child's presentation in class and with peers. Ask teachers and family what is going well and what is going less well at the moment.

Thoughts

It is important to talk to the child and identify any negative or critical thoughts they have about themselves and their future, such as devaluing themselves, a sense of hopelessness or worthlessness and/or generalized negativity, for example, 'Nothing will ever go right' or 'No one will ever like me.' Thoughts that are overly self-critical and negative are indicators of a potential mood problem and/or low self-esteem. It may not be easy for a child to communicate thoughts in this way and the therapist may need to apply the three-word technique described in the creative methods section later in this chapter. If a child presents with thoughts of harm to themselves we advise seeking professional advice.

Feelings and Physiology

Aside from negative cognitions there are physical indicators of depression, including an increase in emotional lability (greater irritability, more temperamental), becoming easily distressed and tearful, a change in sleeping pattern (sleeping in the daytime, having difficulty getting off to sleep, early waking), becoming withdrawn, lack of motivation, low energy, lethargy, fatigue and concentration problems. These are all problems that become more marked than the child's typical presentation; in other words there appears to be a worsening of symptoms. Children may report having less energy, feeling heavy, slow thinking, having headaches, a loss of appetite and/or sleep problems.

Younger children can be supported to communicate their feelings using a face chart or the bag of feelings technique described in the creative methods section. Older children may be able to link their feelings to specific events, interpersonal relationship problems, worries and anxiety.

Behaviours

The most common behavioural presentations are withdrawal, avoidance, irritability and/or lethargy. Children may increasingly lack enjoyment in things that they used to enjoy and withdraw from favoured activities. It is important to determine the onset of this presentation, and consider what makes it better/easier and what makes it harder/worse. Some irritable or oppositional behaviour may indicate that demands have been put on the child that are too high; the stress of this leading the child to act out. Check these things out by asking, 'So when X happens and you feel Y, what do you do then?' or 'If something is very hard and you think "I don't know if I can do this", then what happens?' 'Do you do something that helps?' Using specific examples that the child has given will make it easier.

Consider the interpersonal styles of family members and teachers, their availability and the level of support provided. All these factors impact on relationship warmth and satisfaction. Disruption to relationships can lead to the child feeling rejected, isolated and/or confused. It may not be clear exactly which factors have contributed to a relationship breakdown, especially when a downward and vicious cycle has developed. We suggest that the therapist identifies areas of rigidity that will indicate when parties are 'stuck', as this will provide a point for intervention (e.g., through negotiation and compromise).

It is very important to determine the onset of depressive symptoms, as the therapist must differentiate between the 'usual' presentation and the presentation exacerbated by depressive symptoms. If cognitive and behavioural patterns have qualitatively and substantially changed in the recent past, this may be due to a depressive disorder. Behaviours such as withdrawing, crying, giving up on things more often and not enjoying the things they used to should be taken seriously. Children who have withdrawn from activities or relationships are likely to then receive less positive reinforcement, and this can decrease mood. Avoidance or withdrawal from situations may help manage feelings in the short term, but over time this does not improve the situation because the child does not learn to share feelings and identify solutions.

Creative Methods

Some children (especially younger children) will have difficulty identifying and/or communicating their thoughts and feelings. There are several techniques the therapist can use to assist the process. For feelings, you can ask the child to draw a picture of themselves indicating how they feel. Alternatively, you can present the child with a face chart of 'How I feel' and ask them to indicate their emotion, and then move on to try to garner the thoughts that are associated with that feeling. The 'anxiety bag' technique described in the creative methods section of Chapter 7 is another technique that can be adapted to identify feelings associated with low mood and poor self-esteem.

For thoughts, use the three-word technique. This method prompts a three-word cue to elicit negative thoughts and beliefs such as, 'Can you tell me three words that best describe you?' To gain insight into how the child believes they are perceived by others say, 'Tell me in three words what kids in your class [your teachers/siblings/best friend/parents/carers] most often say [or think] about you.'

To identify the strength of the child's thoughts and feelings, use the analogy of a 'feeling thermometer', with ratings of 1–10 that correspond with very weak to very strong feelings. A 'thought thermometer' can be similarly used with ratings of 1–10 that correspond with not believing in the thought at all, to very strongly believing the thought.

CBT Interventions for Mood and Self-Esteem

If the therapist is treating younger children and/or the worksheets are being used as a basis for treatment, the first session should always commence with Worksheets 1, 2 and 3 to introduce the child to Buzz and his family (Worksheet 1), introduce positive self-talk (Worksheet 2) and identify a reward system (Worksheet 3). The reward and self-talk strategies are applied in the session, at home and/or at school. See Chapter 3 for a suggested outline of how to plan and conduct the introductory session. All the worksheets are available on the companion website, www.wiley.com/go/young/helpingadhd.

The aims of the interventions and worksheets in the mood and self-esteem session(s) are to introduce children to positive thinking styles in relation to positive self-esteem and to help children to continue to realize their positive qualities and feel good about themselves. The therapist will achieve this by setting an agenda, reviewing Home Missions completed between sessions, working through new worksheets (or just the strategies for older children) and setting new Home Missions. If required, a mid-session break can be offered halfway through the session; this may be particularly important for younger children. Chapter 2 provides generic information on the structure and content of sessions (irrespective of topic); supplementary information is included within this chapter that specifically relates to the delivery of the mood and self-esteem session(s).

Agenda

At the beginning of the session, show the child the written agenda (see Figure 12.1) that you have prepared prior to the session and go through it, verbally linking the themes and Worksheets that you will introduce during the session. For the mood and self-esteem module, introduce Worksheets 21 and 22 by saying:

> Buzz is feeling very proud after he writes a story and comes second in a competition. We can talk more about the things that you enjoy and try hard at. After that, we will have a short break and you can colour in the Worksheet using these crayons. Then we will hear about how Buzz turns a bad day into a good day.

Agenda

Folder Review

Buzz Writes a Story [Worksheet 21]

Break

Buzz has a Bad Day [Worksheet 22]

Home Missions

Figure 12.1 Example agenda for mood and self-esteem session(s).

Folder Review

When reviewing the folder with the child, aside from checking whether the Home Missions are completed, take the opportunity to revise important information and/or concepts, as this will support the child to consolidate learning points and/or newly acquired skills. Ensure that you make time to look at the illustrations, colourings, paintings, magazine cuttings and/or photographs that the child has added to the folder. Discuss them and try to relate these to discussions about Buzz and his family and/or topics or strategies that have been covered. Aside from acting as a revision prompt, this will also act as a reward system for the child. Praise should be given verbally, but you can also reward by adding stickers, handwritten notes or smiley faces. If Home Missions were set then you should review the Home Missions Record Form for comments and feedback from parents/carers and discuss this with the child. See Chapter 2 for more information about the folder review and Home Missions.

Worksheet 21 aims to help children acknowledge the positive qualities, skills and talents that they have as a person. It is important to recognize that all people have strengths and weaknesses, and this is introduced in the exercise through Buzz being good at writing stories but having difficulty settling to complete tasks, even those he enjoys. From this platform, the child applies the experience of Buzz and relates this to their own strengths and difficulties.

> **Worksheet 21 Buzz Writes a Story**
>
> **Worksheet Description**
>
> Buzz often daydreams about adventures and he likes to write stories about them. Buzz is good at writing stories, but he struggles to sit still and listen when his teacher reads out stories. Sometimes he gets very fidgety when he has to write long stories at school. Buzz's teacher knows he likes stories and suggests he enters a story competition. Buzz writes a story about when Wilma was a puppy and wriggled through a hole in the garden fence and got lost in the woods. He writes a little bit every day. Buzz is thrilled when his story comes second in the competition! He has a certificate that the teacher puts on the wall for everyone to see. Buzz feels very proud.
>
> To download this worksheet, please visit the companion website
>
> **Worksheet Prompts**
>
> What do you think Buzz is good at? What is he not so good at?
> Why did Buzz write a little bit of the story every day?
> What does proud mean? Why was Buzz feeling proud?
> Buzz's story was about Wilma getting lost. If you had to do this, what would you write about?
> Buzz is good at writing stories. Write a list of some of the things that you are good at. It doesn't matter how big or small they are.

Additionally, the exercise aims to build resilience through the message that it is important to stick with things even when they are difficult and that achievement may be associated with reward.

Read the Stimulus Sheet aloud to the child, or, if they wish, they can read it with you. Check that the child was listening and has understood. Discuss what Buzz is good at (e.g., thinking up adventures, writing stories, taking advice from the teacher, finding ways to help him finish difficult tasks). Discuss what Buzz finds more difficult (e.g., sitting still, finishing tasks, listening). Ask the child to consider why Buzz writes a bit of the story each day. There are many possible answers; for example, it's a helpful way to do a big task, he can focus on smaller steps or it's less daunting. Summarize the child's ideas by saying, 'That's right; Buzz might have found it easier to do a little bit as he didn't get fidgety and not finish the task.'

Move on to ask the child what they think 'proud' means. After exploring this, summarize the child's answer, 'So, proud is when you feel really pleased and happy with something you have done or tried.' Help the child to think about why Buzz was feeling proud. Be sure to include that Buzz was proud of his own achievement, but also proud about the feedback of others (i.e., the judges of the competition who put him in second place and his teacher who put the certificate on the wall where everyone in class will see it). Comment that, 'Buzz was feeling proud because he wrote a story and got a certificate, even though he didn't find it easy. Buzz worked out the best way *for him* to do the task and he came second in the competition. Other people could see that Buzz had tried hard.'

The child is then given an opportunity to show their imaginative and creative side by telling the therapist a story about one of their own adventures. If the child doesn't seem to know what to say, you can reflect, 'It can be difficult to make up a story on the spot, but there isn't a right or wrong answer. You can make it about anything you want and give it a go.' If necessary, prompt the child to think of a story about something that happened at school, on holiday or on their birthday. Next, ask the child to write a list of things they are good at. The aim is to help them identify and be able to share positive things about themselves. Remember to be curious and interested in what they have to tell you. Talk about why they believe they are good at these things. Do they work hard to be good at it? Do they practice? You might ask the child what other people have said to them, or done, to indicate the child is good at the activity/task. Don't just focus on tangible achievements but include intangible things, such as being a good friend, talking to new people or helping out at home. Highlight some of the skills you have noticed in sessions, 'I noticed that you are really good at sharing your ideas with me, you are also good at colouring and decorating the worksheets.'

Give praise for the child's effort in the session. If you choose to set Home Missions based on this worksheet we suggest asking the child to do the following:

1) Decorate the worksheet by colouring in the picture and stars, and/or add to them with pictures on the theme of the story. These could be photographs or pictures in magazines or comics.
2) During the week, add more things that you are good at to the Task Sheet.
3) Ask your parents/carers and/or teachers to write a list of things you are good at.
4) Write your own adventure story and bring it to the next session!

If Home Missions are set, remind parents/carers to complete the Home Missions Record Form and to place it in the folder for review at the next session.

Mid-session Break

This should be provided at an appropriate point in the session as outlined in Chapter 2.

Worksheet 22 Buzz has a Bad Day

Worksheet Description

Sometimes Buzz feels that everything goes wrong. Today he feels upset; he tells his Mum that he gets told off more at school than anyone else, even though he tries really hard. Buzz's Mum says that these are 'enemy thoughts' and they won't help to make him feel better. She tells him to fight them with 'friendly thoughts'. Buzz's Mum reminds him of the time he came second in a story competition and the teacher put his certificate on the wall. Buzz's Mum tells him how much she loves him and how proud she felt. She tells him these are 'friendly thoughts' and asks him to think of some more. Buzz does that and thinks of Wilma who wags her tail and always looks happy to see him. He also thinks about the weekend when his Mum is taking him and his best friend bowling.

To download this worksheet, please visit the companion website

Worksheet Prompts

In the picture you can see Buzz's enemy thoughts. Together, let's add some friendly thoughts. Colour the enemy thoughts red and the friendly thoughts green.
Do you ever have a bad day? What helps you feel better?
Let's write your name in the centre of this page and put some friendly thoughts around you that you can use to help you feel better next time you have a bad day.

Worksheet 22 is a self-esteem exercise that introduces children to positive thinking styles that counteract negative thoughts and maintain a positive mood. Children will discuss Buzz's thoughts and feelings that sometimes make him feel bad about himself and may contribute to his low self-esteem. Children are directed to identify negative thinking as 'enemy thoughts' that need to be fought with 'friendly thoughts'; the latter being a strategy of applying positive self-statements to motivate a positive thinking style. The exercise asks them to colour 'enemy thoughts' red and 'friendly thoughts' green – consistent with stop/go visual cues. From this basis, the therapist then talks to the child about the child's own thoughts and feelings about themselves and the child generates a list of 'friendly thoughts' that may be helpful.

Read the Stimulus Sheet aloud to the child. or, if they wish, they can read it with you. Check that the child has understood the story and that they have understood the concept of 'enemy thoughts' and 'friendly thoughts'.

You can ask them 'What is the difference?' 'How do "friendly thoughts" make you feel?' 'How do "enemy thoughts" make you feel?' Help the child to think of some friendly thoughts to add to the thought bubbles around Buzz. The examples in the worksheet can be used, but the child might also draw on other things they have learned about Buzz in the course of the sessions. Ask the child to colour the 'enemy thoughts' in red and the 'friendly thoughts' in green. If this is too time-consuming, the child could just draw around the thought bubbles in these colours. Make the red–green association with traffic lights by saying, 'This is like traffic lights – red to stop the enemy thoughts and green to start the friendly thoughts.'

Move on to asking the child if they can think about a time when they've had a bad day and/or things didn't go so well. Ask them to tell you what happened. Try to get as much detail as possible, including whether any 'enemy thoughts' were present and what these were. Then ascertain what, if anything, they did to make them feel better (i.e. talk to someone, had a rest, played sport). Did they think of any 'friendly thoughts'? What helps them feel better on days when things aren't going so well? You can prompt the child by asking, 'What do you look forward to?' 'Do you have a hobby?' 'Do you do an activity?' 'Sometimes people choose to play with toys, watch something or talk to someone, do you do these things?' Move on to asking who the child can talk to about how they are feeling. Be interested and curious about who these people are and what they say that helps. Do they solve the problem? Do they listen? Do they do anything in particular, like give hugs or make the child laugh or feel safe?

It is unlikely the child will knowingly use the 'enemy–friendly' thoughts strategy. Ask the child to come up with their own 'friendly thoughts'. On the Task Sheet, ask the child to write their name in the middle and put some friendly thoughts in the thought bubbles. The statements might be specific, such as 'I got 10/10 for spellings' or general, such as 'I am kind'. These are statements that might start with, 'I am good at ...', 'I try to be ...', 'I can do ...' or 'People say that I...'.

Give the child praise for their effort in the session. If you choose to set Home Missions based on this worksheet we suggest asking the child to do the following:

1) Decorate the Worksheet by colouring in the picture and smiley faces, and/or add to them with pictures on the theme of the story. These could be photographs or pictures in magazines or comics.
2) Share the Task Sheet with your parents/carers and ask them to add some more with you. This might mean that you need to start a new sheet!
3) Put a photograph of yourself under your name on the Task Sheet or draw a picture of yourself.
4) Pin up the Task Sheet in your bedroom and next time you have a bad day, read it to help you.

If Home Missions are set, remind parents/carers to complete the Home Missions Record Form and to place it in the folder for review at the next session.

Feedback and Rewards

At the end of the session, appropriate rewards identified from the Worksheet 3 Reward Task should be applied (e.g., the child should engage in positive self-talk). See Chapter 2 for more information about feedback and rewards.

Working with Parents/Carers

In this section we discuss strategies that parents/carers can apply to support their child to develop positive thoughts and feelings about themselves. It is important that parents/carers have realistic expectations of what their child can achieve, or else they will set the child up for failure. We present cognitive and behavioural techniques to support the child when they feel low in mood and/or a sense of helplessness. Early intervention of this nature will likely prevent the child from slipping into depression. We also present strategies to avoid negative cycles of interaction between the parent/carer and child, together with positive steps to raise self-esteem.

When working with parents/carers, the therapist should introduce suggested techniques and strategies; practise and rehearse them in role-plays during the sessions if appropriate (without the child present). In future sessions, parents/carers should report back to the therapist about how they managed with the strategies at home. It is important to troubleshoot any obstacles and/or difficulties that arise by thinking of ways to adapt the techniques or strategies so they are successful in helping the child.

A key strategy to change behaviour and improve cognitive skills is to find motivators to promote success. Children with ADHD tend to respond better to immediate rewards as they have a difficulty with delayed gratification for longer-term rewards (even if these are bigger and better). Methods to motivate success (including the use of a Star Chart) and other topics that are generic to working with parents/carers are described in Chapter 2. Supplementary information that specifically relates to the delivery of the mood and self-esteem session(s) is outlined in this chapter.

Realistic Expectations

It is important for parents/carers to have realistic expectations of their child's abilities, skills and behaviour. This may be situation-specific, for example, a tired child is more likely to be inattentive and restless and unable to do something that they can manage when they feel fresher. Talk to parents/carers about the factors that may influence their child's cognitive ability, engagement and behaviour, such as tiredness, hunger, time of day, enjoyment of an activity, who else is present and so on. Ask:

> 'Has your child been able to manage that in the past?' 'How much support did they need'? 'At what point did they get stuck?' 'What helped to overcome that?' 'What's your understanding of what affects your child's ability to do X at that time or in that situation?' 'In what way do you think your child's feelings or mood impact on what they are doing?'

Engaging in this process will help parents/carers to step back, take time to reflect and reconsider their expectations. This will help them to identify when to support the child, what they can do, how to address feelings of failure and low mood and/or how to prevent a negative cycle developing between them.

Watch Out for Mood Dips

Direct parents/carers to note (and record if necessary) the child's mood and, in particular, to watch out for mood dips that may last for several days. At such times, note if the child seems lethargic, withdrawn, poorly motivated and/or lacks interest in activities they usually enjoy. Counter this with positive self-talk (friendly thoughts), breathing and relaxation exercises and/or physical exercise such as swimming or team sports as well as time to have fun!. A typical breathing and relaxation exercise is included in the psychoeducational booklet 'So I have ADHD', which can be downloaded from the Psychology Services Website (www.psychology-services.uk.com/resources). If the child is upset about a problem, encourage the use of problem-solving strategies to address it. Parents/carers should practise the techniques with their child to help the child gain control of their mood. Remind parents/carers that the more children practise these techniques, the more natural they will become.

Help the Child to Learn and Succeed

Parents/carers can help their child to learn and succeed in many ways. This requires supporting the child to cope better in an environment and/or changing the environment in order to maximize the support and opportunity to learn. There are many strategies in this book that can be applied; the ones that might be particularly helpful to review are in Chapters 4, 5 and 6, which focus on the three core symptoms.

Avoid Negative Feedback

Encourage parents/carers to think about how they refer to their child and to talk about the child's strengths and difficulties. If this is negative, and 'problem talk' outweighs positive communication about the child's skills and strengths, this should be addressed. Similarly, if emphasis is placed on success to the detriment of effort, this should also be rebalanced. These messages influence how the child thinks about themselves and what they value. If the child perceives that they are viewed as a problem, they are more likely to think of themselves in this way. Remind parents/carers that their child and their child's behaviour are not always one and the same. Parents/carers should take care to ensure that negative discussions about the child are not overheard.

Praise the Child's Efforts

Remind parents/carers that one of the greatest things they can do for their child is to notice, comment on and praise when they see their child making an effort, doing what they need to, managing their feelings and/or showing positive qualities. Encourage parents/carers to give praise immediately following the desired behaviour as this maximizes its impact and effectiveness. Also, encourage parents/carers to be 'descriptive' as this provides explicit feedback and makes it easier for the child to associate rewards with specific behaviours, for example, 'You waited patiently in the shop, well done.' Parents/carers can also encourage the child to praise themselves: the child could say a positive statement in their mind or out loud. Equally, it is important that praise does not lose its value by being offered too generously or inappropriately; it is important to get the balance right.

Foster a Positive Environment

Children thrive when they have warm, accepting and supportive people around them to help them make sense of life and to validate their experience and feelings. Discuss with parents/carers the need to maximize a positive environment around their child. It is not uncommon for parents/carers to feel overwhelmed and stressed at times. Encourage them to take time out for themselves and, if necessary, work on their own problems and feelings and/or receive emotional or practical support from others. The aim is to maximize the amount of positive and rewarding time they spend together as a family.

Out-of-School Clubs

Parents/carers should encourage the child to engage in out of school clubs in order to broaden the child's interests and maximize the opportunity to develop social skills and develop different social networks.

What Can We Do As Parents/Carers?

Table 12.1 outlines a suggested approach, including a list of strategies that can be implemented at home. To maximize the effect of strategies, it is helpful to discuss them with your child's teacher so they can be implemented at both

home and school (wherever possible). Lots of parents/carers and teachers find that using a 'Home School Diary' is an efficient way to share information (see Chapter 2).

We suggest that parents/carers read Chapter 2, which provides important background information about the delivery of the Young–Smith Programme.

Table 12.1 Home strategies for mood and self-esteem.

Realistic expectations
- Take time to consider whether your expectations of your child are realistic.
- Ask yourself if there are specific times when your child struggles more (e.g., when tired, specific times of day or when the child is with specific people).
- Work out when, and how, it is best to intervene.

Watch out for mood dips
- If low mood persists, make a record of your child's activities and behaviours.
- Use a 'thought thermometer' or 'feeling thermometer' to get your child to gauge how they are feeling.
- Prompt your child to use positive self-talk (friendly thoughts).
- Engage the child in physical activities.
- Consult your doctor if you are concerned about your child seeming withdrawn, tearful and/or expressing worthlessness or intent to self-harm.
- Introduce your child to breathing and relaxation exercises and practise them.

Help the child to succeed and learn
- Revise strategies from the relevant chapters of this book, especially the core symptom Chapters 4, 5 and 6.

Avoid negative feedback
- Don't let your child overhear negative discussions about them.
- Feedback should be constructive.
- Balance constructive feedback with positive feedback.
- Remember – your child is not the problem; your child has a problem they are coping with.

Praise your child's efforts
- Praise effort as well as achievement.
- Give immediate praise – say it when you see it.
- Notice your child's accomplishments, however small.
- Be precise and descriptive with praise – be specific about what the praise is for.
- Set yourself a target – make a point of praising your child three times each day.

Foster a positive environment
- Take time out for yourself.
- Have fun together.

Out of school clubs
- Encourage your child to join clubs to maximize skills and social networks.

For younger children, we suggest that parents/carers set aside some time to sit down with the child (around 45–60 minutes) and work through the Worksheets recommended for each topic. Guidance on how to do this is found in the 'CBT Interventions' section in each chapter. The worksheets introducing Buzz and his family are outlined in Chapter 3. All the materials (worksheets and the Home Missions Record Form) are available to download from the companion website, www.wiley.com/go/young/helpingadhd. For older children (i.e., 12 years-plus), you can dispense with the Buzz Worksheets if necessary and instead introduce the child directly to the topic, and, using the discussion prompts on the Worksheets, apply this to the child's experience and discuss suggested strategies. Set Home Missions and support the child to complete them. Don't forget to give frequent feedback and praise. Make a Star Chart (see Chapter 2), put it in a prominent place and start to use it on a daily basis.

Working with Teachers and Schools

Receiving frequent negative feedback about your behaviour and academic efforts can be upsetting, and will lead some children to become low in mood and develop low self-esteem. This section presents strategies that teachers can apply to promote resilience and coping, and to support the child to develop positive self-esteem. If teachers observe a dissonance between parents/carers' expectations and the child's ability, and/or negative cycles of interaction, this needs to be addressed. We present cognitive and behavioural techniques to support the child when they feel low in mood and/or a sense of helplessness, and to raise self-esteem. Early intervention of this nature will likely prevent the child from slipping into depression.

At school, children must master, learn and develop skills. For children with ADHD, the best approach to success is when the academic curriculum is carefully balanced with breaks, variation in teaching aids and fun activities. We therefore suggest that teachers foster a balance between academic activities and extra-curricular pursuits, and, when appropriate, employ the services of educational psychologists and/or Special Educational Needs Coordinators to provide support or guidance. This is especially important if the child is presenting with the severe symptoms of depression and low self-esteem described in the introduction.

Teachers and schools will already have structures in place to support many of the interventions introduced in the Young–Smith Programme. It will be useful to link up parents/carers and teachers to encourage an integrated strategy and share success. It is important to troubleshoot any obstacles and/or difficulties that arise by thinking of ways to adapt the techniques or strategies so they are successful in helping the child. Methods to motivate success and other topics that are generic to working with teachers and schools are described in

Chapter 2. Supplementary information that specifically relates to the delivery of the mood and self-esteem session(s) is outlined in this chapter.

Realistic Expectations

It will be useful to refer to the 'realistic expectations' Expectations sub-section in the parents/carers section, as the same techniques described there may also be applied when working with teachers. Some children may require referral to an educational psychologist and/or a Special Educational Needs Coordinator for assessment and guidance on the child's cognitive deficits and/or behaviours. This may require adaptation of teaching styles and/or the curriculum. Furthermore, teachers may need to help parents/carers to realign their academic expectations.

Watch out for Mood Dips

Children who strive to attain goals that they cannot obtain are likely to become disheartened. If they feel that they are failing, letting people down and/or are not good enough, this may lead to low mood and the risk that it will spiral into depression. As is the case for parents/carers, teachers should also note (and record if necessary) the child's mood and, in particular, watch out for mood dips that may last for several days. If a change in behaviour is noticed at school, with the child presenting as more lethargic, withdrawn, poorly motivated and/or lacking interest in activities they usually enjoy, teachers should contact the parents/carers to determine whether the child's presentation is the same at home. Helpful strategies incluse prompting the child to apply positive self-talk (friendly thoughts) and to engage in physical activity.

Note Negative Interactions

Teachers should watch out for negative interactions between parents/carers or teachers and the child and the use of negative generalized statements about the child, such as, 'He/she always does X' or 'He/she never manages X'. Discuss with teachers how they might address this when talking with or writing to parents/carers, and point out the deleterious effect negative generalized statements may be having on the child's self-esteem at home or school. You can rehearse this together. It is important that teachers are sensitive to the situational context and avoid judgemental or blaming language, for example:

> You told me that [child] is always rude and impatient. It seems that he doesn't feel very good about himself because he sees that his friends are able to wait when they need to. I noticed that in class [child] has been trying really hard to wait for his turn to answer questions. Even though it's something he finds difficult, we should let him know that we have noticed and praise him for making the effort.'

Help the Child to Learn and Succeed

Teachers can help the child to cope better in the school environment by making small changes that will maximize the opportunity to learn. There are many strategies that can be applied; those that might be particularly helpful to review are in Chapters 4, 5 and 6, which focus on the three core symptoms.

Praise the Child's Efforts

Praise and rewards are classroom techniques that are often given for tangible output. To ensure that the child with ADHD also receives praise and rewards, teachers should ensure they praise intangible observations, such as when they noticed that the child has engaged in a planning process or engaged in a consequential thinking process. Teachers can also encourage the child to praise themselves: the child could say a positive statement in their mind or out loud – this will also motivate the child to stay on task.

Extra-curricular Activities

There are often many extra-curricular activities available to the child in school, and teachers have the opportunity to suggest those that may help the child with the development and rehearsal of new skills. For example, joining a chess club is likely to help the child develop skills in concentration, planning and strategic thinking; joining the football or netball club will help improve team skills; joining the debating club with help with listening and turn-taking skills. Such activities also provide the opportunity for the child to work on social skills in different settings. This may be an important factor for maintaining a positive sense of self in relation to others. A child may struggle with academic subjects but be the captain of the netball team, for example. Discuss with teachers how they can help the child to feel valued by others, for example, by reminding the child of their positive qualities, prompting the child's use of social cues and mediating interpersonal conflict to ensure positive outcomes.

What Can We Do As Teachers?

Table 12.2 outlines a suggested approach for teachers, including a list of strategies that can be implemented at school. To maximize the effect of strategies, it is helpful to discuss them with the child's parent/carers so that similar or complementary strategies areimplemented at home and school (wherever possible). Both teachers and parents/carers find that using a 'Home School Diary' is an efficient way to share information (see Chapter 2).

We suggest that teachers read Chapter 2, which provides important background information about the delivery of the Young–Smith Programme.

It is unlikely that teachers will have the time to go through specific worksheets with children, although if parents/carers are unable to do this it would be helpful to make arrangements with the Special Educational Needs Coordinator. Guidance on how to do this is found in the 'CBT Interventions' section in each chapter. The Worksheets introducing Buzz and his family are outlined in Chapter 3. All the materials (worksheets and the Home Missions Record Form) are available to download from the companion

Table 12.2 School strategies for mood and self-esteem.

Realistic expectations
- Take time to consider whether your expectations of the child are realistic.
- Ask yourself if there are specific times when the child struggles more (e.g., when tired, specific times of day, or when the child is with specific people).
- Work out when, and how, it is best to intervene.
- Obtain advice and guidance from educational specialists when required.

Watch out for mood dips
- If low mood persists, make a record of the child's activities and behaviours.
- Talk to the child and parents/carers about the child's mood and feelings.
- Use a 'thought thermometer' or 'feeling thermometer' to get the child to gauge how they are feeling.
- Prompt the child to use positive self-talk (see Chapter 3).
- Call a joint parent/carer and teacher meeting to discuss concerns if the child presents as withdrawn, tearful and/or expresses worthlessness or intent to self-harm.

Note negative interactions
- Watch out for negative interactions between the child and parents/carers.
- Watch out for parents/carers using negative generalized statements about the child.
- Talk to the parents/carers about their interactions in a non-judgemental or blaming way.

Help the child to succeed and learn
- Revise strategies from the relevant chapters of this book, especially the core symptom chapters (4, 5 and 6).

Praise the child's efforts
- Praise effort as well as achievement.
- Give immediate praise – say it when you see it.
- Notice the child's accomplishments, however small.
- Be precise and descriptive with praise – be specific about what the praise is for.
- Set yourself a target – make a point of praising the child three times each day.

Extra-curricular activities
- Encourage the child to join and engage in appropriate extra-curricular activities that will maximize the child's skills and expand the child's social networks.

Staff collaboration
- Ensure that all staff know and understand what strategies are being used and why.

website, www.wiley.com/go/young/helpingadhd. For older children (i.e., 12 years-plus), one can dispense with the Buzz worksheets if necessary and instead introduce the child directly to the topic, and, using the discussion prompts on the worksheets, apply this to the child's experience and discuss suggested strategies. Set Home Missions and support the child to complete them. Don't forget to give frequent feedback and praise. If a Star Chart is used (see Chapter 2) then this could be put in the 'Home School Diary' where parents/carers can also review it on a regular basis.

References

Beck, A. T., Rush, A. J., Shaw, B. F., & Emery, G. (1979). *Cognitive therapy of depression*. New York: Guilford Press.

Chorpita, B. F., Yim, L., Moffitt, C., Umemoto L. A., & Francis, S. E. (2000). Assessment of symptoms of DSM-IV anxiety and depression in children: A Revised Child Anxiety and Depression Scale. *Behaviour Research and Therapy, 38*(8), 835–855.

Coopersmith, S. (1967). *The antecedents of self-esteem*. San Francisco: W. H. Freeman.

Goodman, R. (1997). The strengths and difficulties questionnaire: A research note. *Journal of Child Psychology and Psychiatry and Allied Disciplines, 38*(5), 581–586.

Miller, S. D., & Duncan, B. L. (2000). *The Outcome Rating Scale*. Chicago, IL: Authors.

Rosenberg, M. (1965). *Society and the adolescent self-image*. Princeton, NJ: Princeton University Press.

Sexias, M., Weiss, M., & Müller, U. (2012). Systematic review of national and international guidelines on attention deficit hyperactivity disorder. *Journal of Psychopharmacology, 26*(6), 753–765.

Young, S., Bramham, J., Gray, K., & Rose, E. (2008). The experience of receiving a diagnosis and treatment of ADHD in adulthood. A qualitative study of clinically referred patients using Interpretative Phenomenological Analysis. *Journal of Attention Disorders, 11*(4), 493–504.

Index

Page references to Figures or Tables will be followed by the letters 'f' or 't' in italics as appropriate

a

ABC charts *see* Behaviour Diary
abdominal breathing 91, 95
    see also breathing/relaxation techniques
academic functioning
    anxiety 124
    attention problems 47–48
    frustration and anger 149–150
    goal setting/planning ahead
        206–207
    hyperactivity 76–77
    impulsivity 100–101
    mood and self-esteem 248–249
    problem-solving 226–227
    social skills/relationships 181–182
Achenbach System of Empirically Based
    Assessment (ASEBA), Child
    Behaviour Checklist (CBC) 152
ADHD *see* attention deficit hyperactivity
    disorder (ADHD)
'ADHD Do's, Don'ts and Rewards: A Guide
    for Parents and Carers' 25, 27
'ADHD? Information for Parents, Carers
    and Teachers' (psychoeducational
    booklet) 24
alarm prompts 217, 221
anger *see* frustration and anger
anxiety 121–146

academic functioning 124
assessment 125–129
and attention 49
avoidance behaviours 121, 123, 125,
    127, 128, 134, 138, 143
behavioural functioning 123–124
CBT formulation of 122*f*
CBT interventions 129–135
    agenda, showing to child 130
    feedback and rewards 135
    folder review 130–135
coping strategies, dysfunctional 125
delayed gratification for longer-term
    rewards, difficulty with 136
'fight or flight' reactions 121, 123,
    125, 141
hyperactivity 79
interpersonal functioning 124–125
management of
    breathing/relaxation 138, 143
    facing (graded hierarchy) 137, 142
    home strategies 140*t*
    problem-solving 138, 143, 240, 244
    realistic expectations 137, 142
    restlessness 137–138, 143
    role models, parents/carers
        acting as 139
    self-talk 138–139, 143

Helping Children with ADHD: A CBT Guide for Practitioners, Parents and Teachers,
First Edition. Susan Young and Jade Smith.
© 2017 John Wiley & Sons Ltd. Published 2017 by John Wiley & Sons Ltd.
Companion website: www.wiley.com/go/young/helpingadhd

anxiety (cont'd)
  older children, adapting Young–Smith Programme for   128, 129, 132, 139, 145
  presentation of symptoms   121–125
  recommended actions for parents and carers   139–140
  recommended actions for teachers and schools   144–145
  restlessness in   123, 137–138, 143
  social   185
  waiting, problems with   127
  withdrawal behaviours   123
  working with parents and carers   136–139
  working with teachers and schools   140–143
  younger children, adapting Young–Smith Programme for   127, 128, 129, 132, 139, 142
'anxiety bag' technique   129, 252–253
assertiveness   196–197, 200
assessment
  anxiety   125–129
  attention difficulties   49–54
  frustration and anger   151–156
  goal setting/planning ahead   207–210
  hyperactivity   78–82
  impulsivity   102–105
  measures see assessment measures
  mood and self-esteem   249–253
  multi-method
    anxiety   125
    attention difficulties   49–50
    frustration and anger   151
    goal setting/planning ahead   207
    hyperactivity   78
    impulsivity   102
    mood and self-esteem   250
    problem-solving   228
    social skills/relationships   183
  problem-solving   228–231
  social skills/relationships   183–187
assessment measures
  anxiety   126
  attention difficulties   50–51
  frustration and anger   151–152
  goal setting/planning ahead   208
  hyperactivity   78
  impulsivity   102–103
  mood and self-esteem   250
  problem-solving   228–229
  social skills/relationships   184–185
attention deficit hyperactivity disorder (ADHD)
  across the lifespan   2, 4
  avoidance of term, in Young–Smith Programme   8–9, 15
  coexisting conditions   1, 2, 121, 181
  cognitive behavioural therapy see cognitive behavioural therapy (CBT)
  defined   1
  discrepancy between potential and performance   48
  dynamic nature   5
  early intervention, need for   4, 5, 6, 259, 263
  families of children with   3
  heritability   1
  prevalence   1
  resilience, promoting   4–5
  and schools   3–4
  with special educational needs   47
  triggers for problems, in children with   2, 152, 166–167, 173
attention difficulties   2, 45–73
  academic functioning   47–48
  anxiety   49
  assessment   49–54
  Behaviour Diary   53–54, 62
  behavioural functioning   47
  CBT interventions   54–61
    agenda, showing to child   54
    feedback and rewards   61
    folder review   55–61
  coping strategies, dysfunctional   49
  definition of attention   45
  delayed gratification for longer-term rewards, difficulty with   61
  distraction   47, 48, 52, 63

DSM-5 diagnostic criteria for ADHD
    symptoms 45, 46t
  and hyperactivity 84
  interpersonal functioning 48
  management of
    activity breaks 71
    asking for help/clarification 68
    chunking of information 62, 67
    environment, changing 63, 69
    fiddle toys 71
    goals, steps and check-points
      64–65, 70
    name of child, using 62, 67–68
    praise 64, 69
    self-talk 65, 70
    summarizing/concept
      checking 62–63, 68
    'time out' space 30, 69
    verbal prompts 68
    visual cues and prompts 63–64, 69
  older children, adapting Young–Smith
    Programme for 65, 71
  presentation of symptoms 46–49
  recommended actions for parents and
    carers 65, 66t
  recommended actions for teachers and
    schools 71–72
  types of attention 45, 46t
  working with parents and carers 61–65
  working with teachers and
    schools 66–71
  younger children, adapting Young–Smith
    Programme for 51, 54, 62, 65,
    67, 70
attention-control processes 45
auditory attention 46t
Autism Spectrum Condition 181
autonomy, encouraging 240, 244
avoidance behaviours
  anxiety 121, 123, 125, 127, 128, 134,
    138, 143
  hyperactivity 77, 80
  mood and self-esteem 247, 249, 252
  problem-solving 228, 230, 231,
    233–234, 239, 243
  social skills/relationships 195

b
Baddeley, A. D. 45
Beck, A. T. 247
bedtime routines 77, 81, 91
Behaviour Diary
  attention difficulties 53–54, 62
  frustration and anger 155–156, 167
  hyperactivity 81–82, 89, 93
  impulsivity 105, 112
  problem-solving 231
  social skills/relationships 185, 187, 194
Behaviour Impact Scale, hyperactivity 80t
behavioural assessment
  anxiety 128–129
  attention difficulties 52
  frustration and anger 154
  goal setting/planning ahead 210
  hyperactivity 80–81
  impulsivity 104
  mood and self-esteem 252
  problem-solving 231
  social skills/relationships 186
Behavioural Assessment of Dysexecutive
    Syndrome in Children (BADS-C)
  attention difficulties 50–51
  goal setting/planning ahead 208
  impulsivity 103
behavioural functioning
  anxiety 123–124
  attention problems 47
  frustration and anger 148–149
  goal setting/planning ahead 206
  hyperactivity 76
  impulsivity 100
  mood and self-esteem 248
  problem-solving 226
  social skills/relationships 181
behavioural management strategies 25
beliefs and feelings, hyperactivity
    92, 96
'black and white' thinking 6
body sensations, anger 168
boredom, low tolerance for 32, 114, 149
breaks, Young–Smith Programme 19–20
  anxiety 133
  attention difficulties 71

breaks, Young–Smith Programme (cont'd)
   check-points, use of   19
   frustration and anger   161
   hyperactivity   86, 88, 90, 95
   impulsivity   109
   mood and self-esteem   253, 256
   problem-solving   235
   social skills/relationships   191
breathing/relaxation techniques   20
   see also stress management; visualization techniques
   anxiety   135, 138, 143
   frustration and anger   170, 175
   hyperactivity   88, 90–91, 94, 95
Brief Rating Inventory of Executive Functioning (BRIEF)
   attention difficulties   50
   goal setting/planning ahead   208
   impulsivity   103
   problem-solving   228
bullying   181, 182
   addressing   200

C

calendars/diaries   218, 221
   see also Behaviour Diary
catastrophic thinking   6
check-points, use of   19
   attention difficulties   64–65, 70
Child Behaviour Checklist (CBC), Achenbach System of Empirically Based Assessment (ASEBA)   152
clinical interviews
   anxiety   126–127
   attention difficulties   50, 51–52
   frustration and anger   152–153
   goal setting/planning ahead   208–209
   hyperactivity   78–79
   impulsivity   103
   mood and self-esteem   250–251
   problem-solving   229–230
   social skills/relationships   185
Clinical Outcome Rating Scale   250
coaching techniques   25
coexisting conditions   1, 2, 121, 181

cognitive behavioural therapy (CBT)   5–7
   see also folder reviews; worksheets; Young–Smith Programme
   aims   5–6
   attention difficulties   54–61
   cycle   5f, 6
   format of modules in Young–Smith Programme   13
   frustration and anger   156–164
   goal setting/planning ahead   210–216
   hyperactivity   82–88
   impulsivity   106–111
   mood and self-esteem   253–259
   problem-solving   231–237
   social skills/relationships   187–193
   'thinking errors'   6, 40, 41f
   treatment targets   6, 14
collaboration   24
compensatory strategies   2, 49, 108, 125, 148
   social skills/relationships   179, 181, 183
Conners' Continuous Performance Test, attention difficulties   51
Conners' Rating Scales
   attention difficulties   50
   frustration and anger   152
   goal setting/planning ahead   208
   hyperactivity   78
   impulsivity   102
coping strategies, dysfunctional
   anxiety   125
   attention problems   49
   frustration and anger   150–151
   goal setting/planning ahead   207
   hyperactivity   77
   impulsivity   101–102
   mood and self-esteem   249
   problem-solving   228
   social skills/relationships   183
creative methods, use in assessment
   anxiety   129
   frustration and anger   154
   mood and self-esteem   252–253
   social skills/relationships   186

d

daydreaming 47
delayed gratification for longer-term rewards, difficulty with
  see also under rewards
  anxiety 136
  attention difficulties 61
  frustration and anger 166
  goal setting/planning ahead 205, 206, 209, 217
  hyperactivity 89
  impulsivity 112, 114, 117, 118
  mood and self-esteem 259
  problem-solving 238
  social skills/relationships 194
Delis–Kaplan Executive Function System (DKEFS)
  goal setting/planning ahead 208
  impulsivity 103
  problem-solving 228
delivery of Young–Smith Programme 11, 12, 13, 17, 35
  see also Young–Smith Programme
  anxiety 129, 136, 139, 142, 145
  attention difficulties 54, 62, 65, 67, 71
  frustration and anger 157, 166, 170, 173, 177
  goal setting/planning ahead 211, 217, 220, 221, 223
  hyperactivity 83, 89, 92, 94, 97
  impulsivity 106, 112, 115, 117, 120
  'mix and match' approach 11, 17
  mood and self-esteem 253, 259, 262, 264, 265
  problem-solving 232, 238, 241, 243, 244
  social skills/relationships 188, 194, 198, 199, 201
  style of delivery 14–15
Developmental NEuroPSYchological Assessment (NEPSY-II) 50
Diagnostic and Statistical Manual 5 (DSM-5), diagnostic criteria for ADHD symptoms
  attention difficulties 45, 46t
  hyperactivity 75, 76t
  impulsivity 100

diaphragmatic breathing 91, 95
  see also breathing/relaxation techniques
dietary factors, in hyperactivity 75, 80, 82
Discussion Sheet 17, 38
  frustration and anger 162
  hyperactivity 85
distraction 47, 48, 52, 63, 182
divided attention 45, 46t
dopamine 1, 99
double-checking, encouraging in impulsivity 115, 118
'Draw a World' task 185

e

emotional regulation 101, 148
'enemy thoughts' (thinking errors) 6, 40, 41f
  mood and self-esteem 257, 258
environment
  changing, with attention difficulties 63, 69
  positive, fostering of 261
escalation, avoiding 167–168, 174
exercise 19–20, 89, 94
expectations see realistic expectations
extra-curricular activities 265

f

family dynamics 3, 150, 179, 252
  see also parents and carers, recommended actions for; parents and carers, working with; siblings
fatigue, hyperactivity 79
feedback and rewards 20–21, 31, 43
  see also praise and rewards
  anxiety 135
  attention difficulties 61
  frustration and anger 164, 171
  goal setting/planning ahead 216
  hyperactivity 88
  importance 20
  impulsivity 111
  mood and self-esteem 259
  negative feedback, avoiding 260–261
  problem-solving 237
  social skills/relationships 193

feelings and physiology, assessing
  anxiety 127–128
  attention difficulties 52
  frustration and anger 153–154
  goal setting/planning ahead 210
  hyperactivity 79–80
  impulsivity 103–104
  mood and self-esteem 251
  problem-solving 231
  social skills/relationships 186
fiddle toys 71
folder reviews
  see also worksheets
  anxiety 130–135
  attention difficulties 55–61
  frustration and anger 157–164
  goal setting/planning ahead 211–216
  hyperactivity 83–88
  impulsivity 107–111
  mood and self-esteem 254–259
  problem-solving 233–237
  social skills/relationships 188–193
friendships 192–193
  see also social skills/relationships
frustration and anger 147–177
  academic functioning 149–150
  assessment 151–156
  Behaviour Diary 155–156, 167
  behavioural functioning 148–149
  CBT interventions 156–164
    agenda, showing to child 157
    feedback and rewards 164
    folder review 157–164
  confrontation 167, 168
  coping strategies,
    dysfunctional 150–151
  delayed gratification for longer-term
    rewards, difficulty with 166
  expression of 101–102
  injury to others 148, 154
  interpersonal functioning 150
  management of
    body sensations and anger 168
    boundaries, setting and consistently
      applying 166
    breathing/relaxation techniques
      170, 175
  escalation, avoiding 167–168, 174
  home strategies 171*t*
  identifying triggers 166–167, 173
  negative thinking, addressing
    169, 174
  peer role models 175
  problem-solving 169, 175
  self-talk 169, 175
  teacher control 175
  visualization techniques 169–170
  warning signals, identifying
    167, 174
  and ODD 149
  older children, adapting Young–Smith
    Programme for 153, 157, 170, 177
  physical aggression, build up to
    161–162
  presentation of symptoms 148–151
  property damage 148, 154
  recommended actions for parents and
    carers 170–171
  recommended actions for teachers and
    schools 175, 177
  'red zone,' approaching 165, 167
  violent behaviours 148, 154
  withdrawal behaviours 168
  working with parents and
    carers 164–170
  working with teachers and
    schools 172–175
  younger children, adapting Young–Smith
    Programme for 153, 156, 157, 159,
    166, 170

g

games 91
gender factors in ADHD 1
genetic factors in ADHD 1
gifted children with ADHD 2
goal setting/planning ahead 205–223
  academic functioning 206–207
  assessment 207–210
  behavioural functioning 206
  CBT interventions 210–216
    agenda, showing to child 211
    feedback and rewards 216
    folder review 211–216

coping strategies, dysfunctional   207
delayed gratification for longer-term rewards, difficulty with   205, 206, 209, 217
executive functions   205
interpersonal functioning   207
long- and short-term goals   205
management of
  alarm prompts   217, 221
  calendars/diaries   218, 221
  lists   218, 222
  planning process, teaching   217, 221
  rewards and self-praise   219, 222
  routines   218
  verbal prompts   217, 221
  visual symbols   218, 221
older children, adapting Young–Smith Programme for   209, 211, 220, 223
presentation of symptoms   205–207
recommended actions for parents and carers   219–220
recommended actions for teachers and schools   222–223
waiting, problems with   205
working with parents and carers   216–219
working with teachers and schools   220–222
younger children, adapting Young–Smith Programme for   210, 211, 215, 220, 221
graded practice technique   114

h

Halperin, J. M.   5
help or clarification, asking for   68
Home Missions, setting   12, 16, 21–23, 36, 38, 43
  aims   21
  anxiety   129, 130, 133, 135, 140
  attention difficulties   55, 57–58, 59, 61
  frustration and anger   157, 158, 160, 163–164, 171
  goal setting/planning ahead   210–211, 212, 216

  hyperactivity   83, 84, 85–86, 88, 92
  impulsivity   106, 107, 109, 115
  mood and self-esteem   253, 258–259, 267
  problem-solving   233, 235, 237
  social skills/relationships   168, 189, 191, 193, 198
Home Missions Record Forms   22f
  anxiety   130, 133, 135
  attention difficulties   55, 57–58, 65
  frustration and anger   158, 160, 164, 177
  goal setting/planning ahead   212, 220, 223
  hyperactivity   84, 86, 92, 97
  impulsivity   107, 109, 115, 120
  mood and self-esteem   254, 259, 263, 266
  problem-solving   233, 235, 237, 241, 245
  social skills/relationships   189, 193, 198, 201
Home School Diary   30–31, 33
  anxiety   139, 141, 145
  frustration and anger   170
  goal setting/planning ahead   218, 220, 221
  hyperactivity   92, 96
  impulsivity   115, 120
  mood and self-esteem   265
  problem-solving   245
  social skills/relationships   201
home strategies
  see also parents and carers, working with; school strategies
  anxiety   140t
  attention difficulties   66t
  frustration and anger   171t
  goal setting/planning ahead   219t
  hyperactivity   93
  impulsivity   116t
  mood and self-esteem   262t
  problem-solving   241t
  social skills/relationships   197
house rules   26
hyperactivity   75–98
  academic functioning   76–77
  assessment   78–82

hyperactivity (cont'd)
   and attention difficulties 84
   avoidance behaviours 77, 80
   Behaviour Diary 81–82, 89
   behavioural functioning 76
   CBT interventions 82–88
      agenda, showing to child 83
      feedback and rewards 88
      folder review 83–88
   coping strategies, dysfunctional 77
   delayed gratification for longer-term rewards, difficulty with 89
   dietary factors 75, 80, 82
   DSM-5 diagnostic criteria for ADHD symptoms 75, 76t
   interpersonal functioning 77
   management of
      beliefs and feelings 92, 96
      calm breathing 90–91, 95
      games 91
      physical activity 89, 94
      positive requests and reinforcement 90, 95
      responses of others 95–96
      self-talk 91, 96
      signs and places 92, 96
      sleeping routines 91
      wiggle space 90, 94
   older children, adapting Young–Smith Programme for 83, 92, 97
   physical 76
   presentation of symptoms 75–77
   recommended actions for parents and carers 92
   recommended actions for teachers and schools 96–98
   record example 79t
   sleep problems 77
   waiting, problems with 82
   working with parents and carers 88–92
   working with teachers and schools 93–96
   younger children, adapting Young–Smith Programme for 82, 83, 92

i

impulsivity 99–120
   academic functioning 100–101
   assessment 102–105
   Behaviour Diary 105, 112
   behavioural functioning 100
   CBT interventions 106–111
      agenda, showing to child 106–107
      feedback and rewards 111
      folder review 107–111
   classification of responses 99
   coping strategies, dysfunctional 101–102
   delayed gratification for longer-term rewards, difficulty with 112, 114, 117, 118
   DSM-5 diagnostic criteria for ADHD symptoms 100
   and executive functioning 99
   interpersonal functioning 101
   management of
      alternatives and distractions 114, 118
      answering questions/taking turns 118
      double-checking, encouraging 115, 118
      graded practice technique 114
      home strategies 116t
      planning ahead 117
      risk management 117
      risks 113
      small steps, working through 115, 118
      Stop and Think technique 113–114, 118
      stopping, encouraging 103, 108
   older children, adapting Young–Smith Programme for 106, 115, 120
   planning ahead 112–113
   presentation of symptoms 100–102
   recommended actions for parents and carers 115
   recommended actions for teachers and schools 119–120
   thought-to-action process 99

waiting, problems with   100, 109, 111, 112, 114, 117, 118
working with parents and carers   112–115
working with teachers and schools   116–118
younger children, adapting Young–Smith Programme for   106, 115
inattention *see* attention difficulties   2
Individualized Educational Programmes   8, 13
information, chunking of   62, 67
interpersonal functioning
  anxiety   124–125
  attention problems   48
  frustration and anger   150
  goal setting/planning ahead   207
  hyperactivity   77
  impulsivity   101
  mood and self-esteem   249
  problem-solving   227
  social skills/relationships   182–183, 196, 200

l

language capabilities   15
learning, enabling, to enhance mood and self-esteem   260, 265
lists, making   218, 222
maladaptive strategies, stopping   239, 243

m

medications, hyperactivity   80
messages, internalizing   4
mood and self-esteem   247–267
  academic functioning   248–249
  'anxiety bag' technique   252–253
  assessment   249–253
  avoidance behaviours   247, 249, 252
  behavioural functioning   248
  CBT interventions   253–259
    agenda, showing to child   253–254
    feedback and rewards   259
    folder review   254–259

  coping strategies, dysfunctional   249
  delayed gratification for longer-term rewards, difficulty with   259
  depressive symptoms   251, 252
  feeling proud   255–256
  interpersonal functioning   249
  management of
    extra-curricular activities   265
    helping child learn/succeed   260, 265
    mood dips, watching out for   260, 264
    negative feedback, avoiding   260–261
    negative interactions, noting   264
    out-of-school clubs   261
    positive environment, fostering   261
    praise   261, 265
    realistic expectations   259–260, 264
  older children, adapting Young–Smith Programme for   248, 253, 263, 267
  presentation of symptoms   248–249
  recommended actions for parents and carers   261–263
  recommended actions for teachers and schools   265–267
  working with parents and carers   259–261
  working with teachers and schools   263–265
  younger children, adapting Young–Smith Programme for   250, 251, 252, 253, 263

n

name of child, using   62, 67–68
negative social interaction cycle   180*f*
negative thinking, addressing   169, 174
non-verbal behaviour, processing   182–183, 190
Norman, D. A.   45

o

observation
  attention difficulties   50, 52
  impulsivity   103

older children, adapting Young–Smith Programme for
see also younger children, adapting Young–Smith Programme for
anxiety   128, 129, 132, 139, 145
attention difficulties   65, 71
CBT interventions   16, 37, 39, 54
delivery style of programme   14
frustration and anger   153, 157, 170, 177
goal setting/planning ahead   209, 211, 220, 223
hyperactivity   83, 92, 97
impulsivity   106, 115, 120
mood and self-esteem   248, 253, 263, 267
problem-solving   229, 232, 242, 245
social skills/relationships   183, 188, 198, 201
time management skills   16
Oppositional Defiance Disorder (ODD)   149
out-of-school clubs   261

p

Parent Stress Index   80
parents and carers, recommended actions for
anxiety   139–140
attention difficulties   65, 66t
frustration and anger   170–171
goal setting/planning ahead   219–220
hyperactivity   92
impulsivity   115
mood and self-esteem   261–263
problem-solving   240–242
social skills/relationships   197–198
parents and carers, working with   25–29, 44
see also home strategies
anxiety   136–139
attention difficulties   61–65
frustration and anger   164–170
goal setting/planning ahead   216–219
house rules   26
hyperactivity   88–92

impulsivity   112–115
joint working with parents, carers and teachers   24–25
mood and self-esteem   259–261
problem-solving   238–240
realistic expectations   26
rewards, praise and motivators   26–27, 31
social skills/relationships   193–197
Star Chart *see* Star Chart
strategy monitoring   28–29
peer role models   175
physical activity   19–20, 89, 94
planning ahead, impulsivity   117
planning process, teaching   217, 221
praise   27
see also feedback and rewards
anxiety management   133, 137
attention difficulties, coping with   64, 69
frustration and anger management   171
hyperactivity management   90, 95
impulsivity management   108
mood and self-esteem, enhancing   256, 261, 265
and motivators   26–27, 31
problem-solving   237
and rewards   26–27
self-praise, in goal-setting and planning   219, 222
social skills/relationships   196, 199
problem-solving   138, 143, 175, 225–246
academic functioning   226–227
assessment   228–231
avoidance behaviours   228, 230, 231, 233–234, 239, 243
Behaviour Diary   231
behavioural functioning   226
brainstorming of solutions   236
CBT interventions   231–237
agenda, showing to child   232
feedback and rewards   237
folder review   233–237
cognitive development   225
coping strategies, dysfunctional   228

delayed gratification for longer-term rewards, difficulty with 238
frustration and anger 169, 175
interpersonal functioning 227
maladaptive strategies 233–234
 stopping 239, 243
management of
 autonomy, encouraging 240, 244
 defining the problem 238–239, 243
 maladaptive strategies, stopping 239, 243
 role models 240
 Stop and Think technique 240, 244
 teaching the problem-solving process 238–239, 243
 worries and anxiety 240, 244
necessity for skills in 225
older children, adapting Young–Smith Programme for 229, 232, 242, 245
presentation of symptoms 226–228
problem-solving process 227t 238–239, 243
recommended actions for parents and carers 240–242
recommended actions for teachers and schools 244–245
traffic light system of problem severity 230f
working with parents and carers 238–240
working with teachers and schools 242–244
younger children, adapting Young–Smith Programme for 229, 230, 231, 232, 241
psychoeducation 15–16
psychometric questionnaires 50, 78

r

realistic expectations
 in anxiety 136, 137, 142
 in enhancement of mood and self-esteem 259–260, 264
 hyperactivity 88
 parents and carers, working with 26
 teachers and schools, working with 31

resilience, promoting 4–5
resources, Young–Smith Programme 14, 32–34
restlessness 2, 19
 in anxiety 123, 137–138, 143
 in hyperactivity 76, 84
Revised Children's Anxiety and Depression Scale (RCADS) 126, 184, 250
rewards
 see also delayed gratification for longer-term rewards, difficulty with; feedback and rewards; praise
 examples 26–27
 immediate, responding to 26
  anxiety 136, 141
  attention difficulties 61
  frustration and anger 166
  goal setting/planning ahead 205, 217
  hyperactivity 89
  impulsivity 112
  mood and self-esteem 259
  problem-solving 238
  social skills/relationships 194
risk management, impulsivity 113, 117
role models
 anxiety management 139
 peer role models, in anger management 175
 problem-solving 240
 social skills/relationships 194–195, 199
role-play/rehearsal strategies 195, 199
Rosenberg, M. 250
routines 32, 218
 bedtime 77, 81, 91

s

school strategies
 see also home strategies; teachers and schools, recommended actions for
 anxiety 144t
 attention difficulties 72t
 frustration and anger 176t
 goal setting/planning ahead 222t
 hyperactivity 97It

school strategies (cont'd)
    impulsivity 119t
    mood and self-esteem, enhancing 266t
    problem-solving 245t
    social skills/relationships 202t
schools
    additional support 4
    classroom environment 3
    example of self-fulfilling prophecy 7f
    frustration and anger 149
    school environment and ADHD 3–4
    strategies see school strategies
    transition to secondary school 2
secondary school, transition to 2
selective attention 45, 46t
self-esteem
    see also mood and self-esteem
    defined 247
    low 5, 247, 248, 249
    multi-modal 247
self-praise 219, 222
    see also praise
self-regulation issues 147
self-talk
    anxiety 138–139, 143
    attention difficulties 65, 70
    frustration and anger 169, 175
    hyperactivity 91, 96
    positive 6–7
serotonin 1, 99
sexual promiscuity 183
Shallice, T. 45
siblings 3, 77
sleep issues, hyperactivity 77, 91
sleeping animal game 91
'So I have ADHD' (psychoeducational booklet) 138, 170, 260
social anxiety 185
social skills/relationships 179–203
    academic functioning 181–182
    in adolescence 179
    assessment 183–187
    avoidance behaviours 195
    Behaviour Diary 185, 187, 194
    behavioural functioning 181

bullying 181, 182
    addressing 200
    CBT interventions 187–193
        agenda, showing to child 188
        feedback and rewards 193
        folder review 188–193
    coping strategies, dysfunctional 183
    delayed gratification for longer-term rewards, difficulty with 194
    and impulsivity 101
    interpersonal functioning 182–183
    management of
        assertiveness 196–197, 200
        bullying, addressing 200
        interpersonal conflict 196, 200
        new social situations 200–201
        prompts 199
        role models 194–195, 199
        role-play/rehearsal strategies 195, 199
        stress management 196, 200
    negative social interaction cycle 180f
    non-verbal behaviour, processing 182–183, 190
    noticing positive social skills 196, 199
    older children, adapting Young–Smith Programme for 183, 188, 198, 201
    opportunities to practise 195
    praise, giving 196, 199
    presentation of symptoms 180–183
    questionnaire 184t
    recommended actions for parents and carers 197–198
    recommended actions for teachers and schools 201
    school strategies 202t
    waiting, problems with 190
    working with parents and carers 193–197
    working with teachers and schools 198–201
younger children, adapting Young–Smith Programme for 180, 183, 187, 188, 198

Sonuga-Barke, E. J. S.   5
Special Educational Needs
    Coordinators   8, 13
  anxiety   145
  attention difficulties   71
  frustration and anger   177
  goal setting/planning ahead   223
  hyperactivity   97
  impulsivity   120
  mood and self-esteem   263, 266
  problem-solving   244
  social skills/relationships   198, 201
Spence Children's Anxiety Scale   126
Star Chart   27–28
  anxiety   137, 140, 145
  attention difficulties   65
  frustration and anger   166, 171
  goal setting/planning ahead   217
  hyperactivity   92, 98
  impulsivity   113, 120
  mood and self-esteem   259, 267
  problem-solving   245
  social skills/relationships   201
Stimulus Sheet   17, 38, 42
  anxiety   131, 134
  attention difficulties   56, 58, 60
  goal setting/planning ahead   215
  hyperactivity   85, 87
  impulsivity   108
  mood and self-esteem   255, 257
  problem-solving   234, 236
  social skills/relationships
    190, 192
Stop and Think technique
  impulsivity   113–114, 118
  problem-solving   240, 244
Strategy Evaluation Record   28
strategy monitoring   28–29
Strengths and Difficulties Questionnaire
    (SDQ)
  anxiety   126
  attention difficulties   50
  frustration and anger   151
  hyperactivity   78
  impulsivity   102
  mood and self-esteem   250
  social skills/relationships   184

stress management   196, 200
summarizing/concept checking
    62–63, 68
sustained attention   45, 46*t*

t
Task Sheet   17, 43
  attention difficulties   59
  frustration and anger   160
  goal setting/planning ahead   215
  hyperactivity   87
  mood and self-esteem   258
  problem-solving   234
  social skills/relationships   190–191
teachers and schools, recommended actions
    for
  see also school strategies
  anxiety   144–145
  attention difficulties   71–72
  frustration and anger   175, 177
  goal setting/planning ahead
    222–223
  hyperactivity   96–98
  impulsivity   119–120
  mood and self-esteem   265–267
  problem-solving   244–245
  social skills/relationships   201
teachers and schools, working
    with   29–32, 44
  anxiety   140–143
  attention difficulties   66–71
  frustration and anger   172–175
  goal setting/planning ahead   220–222
  hyperactivity   93–96
  impulsivity   116–118
  joint working with parents, carers and
    teachers   24–25
  mood and self-esteem   263–265
  problem-solving   242–244
  social skills/relationships   198–201
termination of treatment, preparation
    for   24
Test of Everyday Attention for Children
    (TEA-Ch)
  attention difficulties   50, 51
  impulsivity   103

'thinking errors'   6, 40, 41f
    mood and self-esteem   257, 258
thought patterns, assessing
    see also negative thinking, addressing
    anxiety   127
    attention difficulties   51–52
    exercise grid of enemy and friendly
        thoughts   40, 41t
    frustration and anger   153
    goal setting/planning ahead
        209–210
    hyperactivity   79
    impulsivity   103
    mood and self-esteem   251
    problem-solving   231
    social skills/relationships   185
'time out' space   30, 69
time perception problems   206
triggers for problems, in children with
        ADHD   2, 152
    frustration and anger   166–167, 173

V

verbal prompts
    attention difficulties   68
    goal setting/planning ahead
        217, 221
visual attention   46t
visual cues and prompts
    attention difficulties   63–64, 69
    goal setting/planning ahead   218, 221
visual symbols   218
visualization techniques   169–170

W

waiting, problems with
    anxiety   127
    goal setting/planning ahead   205
    hyperactivity   82
    impulsivity   100, 109, 111, 112, 114,
        117, 118
    social skills/relationships   190
warning signals, identifying   167, 174
wiggle space   90, 94
withdrawal behaviours   123, 168
worksheets   16–17, 18–19t   33
    see also cognitive behavioural therapy
        (CBT); folder reviews; Young–Smith
        Programme
    adjustment of   15
    anxiety   131–135
    attention difficulties   55–60
    Buzz and family narrative for younger
        children   12, 13, 14
    Worksheet 1 (Buzz and His
        Family)   20–21, 36, 37–39, 82, 106,
        129, 156, 187, 210, 231, 253
    Worksheet 2 (Buzz and Self-talk)   36,
        39–42, 82, 106, 129, 156, 187, 210,
        231, 253
    Worksheet 3 (Buzz enters a
        Competition)   36, 42–43, 82, 106,
        129, 135, 156, 187, 210, 216, 231,
        232, 237, 253
    Worksheet 4 (Spot the
        Difference)   54, 55–57
    Worksheet 5 (Buzz Gets his Cycling
        Badge)   20, 54, 57–59
    Worksheet 6 (Buzz does his
        Homework)   54, 60
    Worksheet 7 (Buzz at School)
        83, 84–86
    Worksheet 8 (Buzz at Bedtime)
        83, 86–88
    Worksheet 9 (Buzz goes to
        Hospital)   106, 107–109
    Worksheet 10 (Buzz at the Theme
        Park)   106, 110–111
    Worksheet 11 (Buzz goes
        Camping)   130, 131–133
    Worksheet 12 (Buzz and School
        Play)   130, 133–135
    Worksheet 13 (Buzz reads a
        Book)   157, 158–161
    Worksheet 14 (Buzz makes a Birthday
        Present)   157, 161–164
    Worksheet 15 (Buzz goes to the
        Movies)   188, 189–191, 195
    Worksheet 16 (Buzz goes to the
        Park)   188, 191–192
    Worksheet 17 (Buzz goes to the
        Circus)   211, 212–214

Worksheet 18 (Buzz and his Birthday Party) 211, 214–215
Worksheet 19 (Buzz makes a Castle) 233–235
Worksheet 20 (Buzz and the New Boy) 235–237
Worksheet 21 (Buzz Writes a Story) 254–256
Worksheet 22 (Buzz has a Bad Day) 254, 257–259
Discussion Sheet *see* Discussion Sheet
goal setting/planning ahead 212–216
impulsivity 107–111
introducing in sessions 17
'mixing and matching' 11, 17
mood and self-esteem 255–259
problem-solving 233–237
social skills/relationships 189–193
Stimulus Sheet *see* Stimulus Sheet
Task Sheet *see* Task Sheet

y

younger children, adapting Young–Smith Programme for 14, 17, 19, 23, 35
see also older children, adapting Young–Smith Programme for; *under* worksheets
anxiety 127, 128, 129, 132, 139, 142
attention difficulties 51, 54, 62, 65, 67, 70
frustration and anger 153, 156, 157, 159, 166, 170
goal setting/planning ahead 210, 211, 215, 220, 221
hyperactivity 82, 83, 92
impulsivity 106, 115
mood and self-esteem 250, 251, 252, 253, 263
problem-solving 229, 230, 231, 232, 241
social skills/relationships 180, 183, 187, 188, 198
Young–Smith Programme 11–34
see also assessment; breaks, Young–Smith Programme; cognitive behavioural therapy (CBT); folder review; older children, adapting Young–Smith Programme for; worksheets; younger children, adapting Young–Smith Programme for
agenda, showing to child 16, 35–36
anxiety 130
attention difficulties 54
frustration and anger 157
goal setting/planning ahead 211
hyperactivity 83
impulsivity 106–107
mood and self-esteem 253–254
problem-solving 232
social skills/relationships 188
attention difficulties 45–73
avoidance of term 'ADHD' 8–9, 15
as a cognitive behavioural intervention 5
content 11–12
delivery of *see* delivery of Young–Smith Programme
delivery style 14–15
feedback and rewards *see* feedback and rewards
flexibility 7, 17
folder, introducing 36–44
frustration and anger 147–177
functional problems, focus on 8
Home Missions *see* Home Missions, setting
hyperactivity 75–98
impulsivity 99–120
joint working with parents, carers and teachers 24–25
modules 11–12
format 13–14
narrative used in CBT exercises throughout 35–44
agenda, showing to child 35–36
exercise grid of enemy and friendly thoughts 40, 41*t*
folder, introducing 36–44
worksheets 37–40
overview 7–9
parents and carers, working with 25–29, 44

Young–Smith Programme (*cont'd*)
   house rules 26
   realistic expectations 26
   rewards, praise and motivators
      26–27, 31
   Star Chart *see* Star Chart
   strategy monitoring 28–29
  psychoeducation 15–16
  resources 14, 32–34

routine and novel occupations 32
social skills/relationships 179–203
suitable for children without
   ADHD 7
teachers, working with 44
teachers and schools, working
   with 29–32
termination of treatment, preparation
   for 24

Printed and bound by CPI Group (UK) Ltd, Croydon, CR0 4YY